UNIVERSITY OF NORTH CAROLINA AT CHAPEL HILL
DEPARTMENT OF ROMANCE LANGUAGES

NORTH CAROLINA STUDIES
IN THE ROMANCE LANGUAGES AND LITERATURES

Founder: URBAN TIGNER HOLMES
Editor: CAROL L. SHERMAN

Distributed by:

UNIVERSITY OF NORTH CAROLINA PRESS

CHAPEL HILL
North Carolina 27515-2288
U.S.A.

NORTH CAROLINA STUDIES IN THE
ROMANCE LANGUAGES AND LITERATURES
Number 279

THE INVENTION OF THE EYEWITNESS
WITNESSING AND TESTIMONY
IN EARLY MODERN FRANCE

THE INVENTION OF THE EYEWITNESS

WITNESSING AND TESTIMONY IN EARLY MODERN FRANCE

BY
ANDREA FRISCH

CHAPEL HILL

NORTH CAROLINA STUDIES IN THE ROMANCE
LANGUAGES AND LITERATURES
U.N.C. DEPARTMENT OF ROMANCE LANGUAGES

2004

Library of Congress Cataloging-in-Publication Data

Frisch, Andrea
　　The invention of the eyewitness: witnessing and testimony in Early Modern France / Andrea Frisch.
　　p. cm. – (North Carolina Studies in the Romance Languages and Literatures; no. 279).
　　Includes bibliographical references.
　　ISBN 0-8078-9283-1
　　1. Witnesses–France–History. 2. Eyewitness identification–France–History. 3. Witnesses–Europe–History. 4. Eyewitness identification–Europe–History. 5. Evidence–History. I. Title. II. Series.

KJV3952.F75 2004
347.44'066'09–dc22   2004049278

Cover design: Heidi Perov

© 2004. Department of Romance Languages. The University of North Carolina at Chapel Hill.

ISBN 0-8078-9283-1

DEPÓSITO LEGAL: V. 3.017 - 2004

ARTES GRÁFICAS SOLER, S. L. - LA OLIVERETA, 28 - 46018 VALENCIA

TABLE OF CONTENTS

	Page
ACKNOWLEDGEMENTS	9
INTRODUCTION: THE TESTIMONY OF HISTORY	11
CHAPTER ONE: THE WITNESS AND THE JUDGE	21
CHAPTER TWO: ETHOS	41
CHAPTER THREE: EXPERIENCE	76
CHAPTER FOUR: THE FIRST PERSON	117
CHAPTER FIVE: PRESENCE	141
EPILOGUE: A RETURN TO DIALOGUE	181
BIBLIOGRAPHY	188

ACKNOWLEDGEMENTS

I am grateful for the intellectual, moral and emotional support of a number of colleagues and friends, and to the financial support of a number of institutions. Some of the ideas in this book date back to my days in graduate school at Berkeley, where I first became interested in the early modern period in Tim Hampton's seminars. Tim has continued to be a steady source of good counsel, gracious professional support, and wonderful scholarship on the Renaissance. Many fellow students from Berkeley – Jann Purdy, Andy Cowell, Sarah Pelmas and Dave Code, especially – made my experience there (and beyond) an especially enriching one.

I was lucky enough to have Chris Braider as my boss at my first job. The example of Chris's erudition, warmth and humanity allowed me to begin to think of what I did as a vocation, and helped me grow as a person. Chris has also been an unfailing source of professional support and encouragement, as well as a wellspring of ideas. At USC, I enjoyed the good fellowship and critical acumen of the Law and Humanities Reading Group, whose members – especially Nomi Stolzenberg and Clyde Spillenger – gave early versions of some of the book's chapters an engaged and thoughtful evaluation. I thank Ariela Gross, the group's fearless leader, for inviting me to share my work.

Somewhere along the line, I met George Hoffmann, an exemplary colleague whose enthusiastic support of my work has made a significant difference at crucial points during the composition of this book. George also put me in contact with André Tournon, who kindly read and commented on parts of the manuscript. I have frequently crossed paths with Tom Conley. Tom's energy and enthusiasm are infectious; I have moreover benefited enormously, in ways both material and intangible, from his genuine interest in the scholarship of his younger colleagues. Roland Greene gave generously of his time and imagination at the proposal-writing stage, and, as I recall, came up with the book's title. More recently, I have had the pleasure of sharing my ideas with Tim Reiss, whose attentive reading of the manuscript has made this book a better one, and whose continuing interest in my work has given me a welcome sense of belonging to an intellectual community.

I gratefully acknowledge financial support for this book from the University of Colorado-Boulder; the Newberry Library; and the University of Southern California. I thank Carol Sherman at the University of Carolina Press for welcoming the book into the NCSRLL series, and Frank Dominguez for seeing it through to publication.

Small parts of chapter two appeared in "*Quod vidimus testamur*: Testimony, Narrative Agency and the World in Pantagruel's Mouth" (reprinted from *French Forum* volume 24, number 3 [September 1999] by permission of the University of Nebraska Press. Copyright © 1999 by French Forum Publishers, Inc.). Part of chapter five appeared as "In a Sacramental Mode: Jean de Léry's Calvinist Ethnography" (© 2002 by The Regents of the University of California. Reprinted from *Representations* 77 by permission of the University of California Press). Parts of chapter one and of the epilogue appeared in "The Ethics of Testimony: A Genealogical Perspective" (reprinted from *Discourse: Journal for Theoretical Studies in Media and Culture* 25:1&2 [Winter 2004] 36-54 with permission of the Wayne State University Press). I thank all of these journals for permission to republish the material in its revised form. Unless otherwise credited, all translations are my own.

Finally, I thank Mathias and Julia Frisch. Ich habe Euch so sehr lieb.

I dedicate this book to the memory of my father.

Introduction

THE TESTIMONY OF HISTORY

In Anglo-American legal circles, there is a growing sense that eyewitness testimony is unreliable; or at least, not as reliable as had previously been thought. Rob Warden, executive director of the Center on Wrongful Convictions at Northwestern University's School of Law, asserts that "erroneous eyewitness testimony – whether offered in good faith or perjured – no doubt is the single greatest cause of wrongful convictions in the U.S. criminal justice system." As Warden reports, The Center on Wrongful Convictions analyzed the cases of eighty-six defendants who had been sentenced to death but legally exonerated since the U.S. Supreme Court's 1972 decision in Furman v. Georgia restored capital punishment. The analysis shows that of the eighty-six, eyewitness testimony played a role in the convictions of forty-six; that eyewitness testimony was the *only* evidence against thirty-three defendants; and that only one eyewitness testified in thirty-two of the forty-six cases in which eyewitness testimony played a role. The news is not so much that eyewitnesses lie – although they obviously do sometimes – but rather because, it turns out, eyewitnesses regularly make honest mistakes.

The potential accuracy of eyewitness testimony is compromised by several factors. Perhaps the most widely acknowledged are the limitations of human sense perception and the complexity of the process of memory, which are the subjects of the majority of scientific psychological studies of eyewitness testimony (see Loftus). It has also been shown that the nature of the questions asked of a witness and the identity and behavior of the people who ask those questions (what a recent article in the *Pennsylvania Law Weekly* termed "deposition dynamics") also impinge upon testimony given in good faith (Suplee and Donaldson). When one takes account of the multiple influences that shape eyewitness testimony – the impact of many of which can be measured with technology no more advanced than paper and pen – the common-sense belief that such testimony is one of the better sources of accurate information begins to look less obviously sensible. If we are to come to terms with eyewitness testimony, with its potential and its limitations, we must take account of its status as an act of human communication in an institutional, social and historical context.

The testimonial situation always implicates more than just a witness's knowledge by bringing into play the complex rhetorical, social and ethical dimensions of human dialogue. In recognizing this, we are in fact rediscovering aspects of testimony that have at other times and in other places been granted a much greater prominence. The idea that what is at issue in testimony is first and foremost a witness's knowledge is, in historical terms, a relatively recent one. *The Invention of the Eyewitness* argues that several historical, political, social and technological factors contributed to the slow, unsystematic emergence of the modern notion of eyewitness testimony as a monologic discourse of first-person experiential knowledge. I seek here to trace the complex processes by which the epistemic eyewitness (what I also refer to as the "modern witness") gained priority over the ethical eyewitness. The figure of the modern eyewitness, I argue, arrives at the intersection of an outmoded feudal ethics and an embryonic nation-state in the age of print, and the firsthand account of America was one of the privileged loci of its development and diffusion (as distinct from its creator).

The invention of the eyewitness did not occur at one revolutionary moment; neither was it driven by any single event or circumstance. As any student of classical rhetoric knows, "invention" does not refer to an inspired act of creation *ex nihilo*, but to the labor of finding the appropriate material to serve a specific end with respect to a specific audience. The process of inventing the modern eyewitness thus involved searching for the best ways in which to establish the credibility of testimony given particular cultural constraints. Those constraints, in their pre- and early modern manifestations, are the primary subject of this study.

The broadly-focused investigation of the genealogy of testimony in early modern Europe undertaken in this book suggests that the expectation that eyewitnesses provide quasi-objective information – that is, that their statements are privileged sources of an epistemic truth independent of any particular social context – is in fact neither a philosophical necessity nor a historical constant. In medieval jurisprudence, *scientia* or knowledge was the province of the judge, and not the witness. Moreover, neither medieval folklaw nor the early inquisition assumed that testimony was essentially or even primarily a discourse of first-person experience; rather, as a participant in a dialogic exchange, the witness functioned as a *second* person whose ethical relations with his juridical interlocutors determined the credibility of his testimony.[1]

This does not mean that medieval law had no concern for "facts," or that the act of seeing for oneself enjoyed no particular epistemological prestige in the Middle Ages. On the contrary: Philippe de Beaumanoir's thirteenth-century manual of customary law states that the witness who "wants to say 'I know it for certain' cannot say this unless he also states 'I was present and I saw it'" ("qui veut dire: «Je le sai de certain», il ne le peut dire s'il ne dit: «J'i fui presens et le vi»").[2] Though they granted the epistemological potential of firsthand experience, however, medieval and early modern jurists approached the testimony of eyewitnesses primarily in terms of the social context in which it was delivered. In the chapters that follow, then, I set the writings that most consistently raised, confronted, and discussed issues of what made a testimonial account believable – firsthand accounts of travel – into the context of the literary, legal, religious and technological influences that shaped the rhetoric of witnessing in the early modern period.

The fundamental thesis of this study is that the figure of the eyewitness is a historical construct rather than a philosophical abstraction. The majority of contemporary humanistic discussions of testimony, by contrast, elevate the modern eyewitness – in other words, the first-person, epistemic eyewitness – to the status of a universal principle, testimony's *sine qua non*. As chapter one con-

---

[1] The term "inquisitional procedure" here designates lay legal proceedings that attempt to reconstruct the facts of a case via an inquest, in contrast to the oaths and ordeals of folklaw. It does not refer to the Catholic church's pursuit of heretics under the auspices of canon law.

[2] *Coutumes de Beauvaisis*, section 1234. I will give references to Beaumanoir according to section number, not page number, since several printed editions of his customal exist.

tends, some of the most influential approaches to testimony in the humanities are predicated on the conceptual abstraction of the eyewitness as a quasi-Cartesian first person, an abstraction that simply ignores the web of social relationships in which witnesses and testimony have historically been implicated. This chapter argues that much current scholarship on testimony assigns to the witness functions that both folklaw and early inquisitional procedure reserved for either the accused or the judge. Rather than simply deconstruct this modern point of view, however, I suggest that we need to have a better understanding of its origins if we hope to articulate alternatives to it.

Accordingly, subsequent chapters offer a chronological account of the evolution of the discourse of testimony in medieval and early modern Europe, focused primarily on France. While the writings of Herodotus might seem to be an obvious point of departure for a study that revolves around the figure of the eyewitness in firsthand accounts of travel, the "father of history" had a much greater influence on learned writing in Latin in early modern Europe than he did on the vernacular material I study here. From the Merovingian era up through at least the fifteenth century, the discourse of testimony is primarily a juridical discourse; to speak of witnesses in this context is therefore necessarily to speak of juridical witnesses. Paul Guilhiermoz emphasizes the broad familiarity with judicial procedure that the French population had in the feudal era:

> la procédure . . . n'était pas alors . . . un jargon et un grimoire ignorés du public, et dont la connaissance et l'application appartînt uniquement à une catégorie particulière de personnes, juges ou hommes de loi de profession; à cette époque [13e siècle], au contraire, d'une part, tout le monde pouvait être appelé à user personnellement de la procédure, puisque la représentation en justice commençait à peine à s'ébaucher, et, d'autre part, les fonctions judiciaires se trouvaient être exercées par un très grand nombre de personnes, pour aucune desquelles elle n'était une profession, mais simplement une des conséquences multiples de leur situation féodale, municipale, administrative ou politique. La procédure, dont la connaissance était ainsi répandue dans la nation toute entière, se trouvait tenir par suite une place considérable dans la vie publique (50)

> [juridical] procedure . . . was not at the time . . . a specialized jargon with which the general public was unfamiliar, nor did knowledge

and practice of it belong exclusively to a particular category of persons, judges or professional lawyers. On the contrary: at the time [13th century], anyone could find it necessary to personally participate in legal proceedings, since the practice of obtaining legal representation was itself just beginning; moreover, judicial duties were carried out by a large number of persons for whom the practice of law was not a profession, but simply one of the many consequences of their feudal, municipal, administrative or political situation. Legal procedure, familiar throughout France, thus had a considerable place in public life

Rather than a specialized institutional domain, then, legal discourse is a central part of feudal society, and its presuppositions are widely diffused. Chapter two thus establishes a juridical framework as a point of departure for a discussion of the figure of the eyewitness in the travel writings of Marco Polo and John Mandeville, and the novels of François Rabelais. After establishing the extent to which the "ethical" witnessing characteristic of medieval European folk-law (and parodied by Rabelais) persisted in both juridical theory and practice after the introduction of the so-called rational procedures of the inquisition, I read Polo and Mandeville's travel testimonies in terms of the ethical paradigm. Whereas Mandeville's textual persona goes to great lengths to incarnate the *ethos* of his Christian audience, Polo emphasizes his close ties to the Mongol emperor and his fluency in Asian languages, qualities that would enhance his status as an epistemic witness but that threaten his ethical authority before a medieval Christian audience. This ethical contrast, I argue, offers a powerful explanation for the initial skepticism with which Polo's account was met, as well as for the early success of Mandeville's book.

While ethical criteria dominate the evaluation of testimony in the late Middle Ages, Rabelais's novels register an increasingly explicit tension between ethical and epistemic eyewitnesses in the sixteenth century. My analysis of the figure of the eyewitness narrator in *Pantagruel* at the end of chapter two sets the stage for chapter three's account of the long decline of ethical witnessing and the emergence of a new focus on epistemic witnessing in the law courts over the course of the fourteenth and fifteenth centuries. I do not claim here that ethical considerations simply disappear during this period; rather, I show how epistemic criteria for the evaluation of testimony emerge as the largely unintended by-product of the impracticability of the ethical model in an increasingly depersonalized system of justice.

In part because of the persistence of feudal values, juridical conceptions of the witness continue to dominate the discourse of testimony on into the sixteenth century, and play a significant role in shaping the figure of the eyewitness in travel writing about the New World. Moreover, the first French eyewitness account of a voyage to America, Paulmier de Gonneville's 1505 *Relation authentique*, is a juridical deposition. Like Gonneville's *Relation*, the majority of eyewitness accounts of the New World composed within the first quarter century after Christopher Columbus's initial landfall on Hispaniola took the form of official reports (the case, for example, with the writings of Columbus, Amerigo Vespucci, Hernán Cortés and Jacques Cartier) and thus had more in common with a legal document than with a work of historiography in the humanist vein. Thus, chapter three first maps the trajectory of the ethical witness in legal theory and practice from about 1450-1600 before tracing a roughly parallel path through sixteenth-century French accounts of the New World, from Gonneville's *Relation* to Jean de Léry's 1580 *Histoire d'un voyage en la terre de Bresil*, via Michel de Montaigne's 1580 essay "Des cannibales." In light of the legal background, the self-conscious promotion of firsthand experience for which Léry's account is known – and which is entirely absent from Gonneville's *Relation* – appears to be pushed from behind by the slow disintegration of ethical witnessing in the courts of law rather than pulled ahead by the *telos* of a modern scientific worldview.

In her recent book on seventeenth-century English epistemology, *A Culture of Fact*, Barbara Shapiro persuasively argues that "Legal modes of establishing appropriate belief played a larger role in the development of [English] truth-establishing practices than has hitherto been recognized" (33). One might say that I am making a similar argument regarding the broader diffusion of juridical conceptions of witnessing and testimony in France in the period from about 1300-1600. However, whereas Shapiro goes on to claim that "the criteria of [Royal Society] credibility . . . were substantially the same as those of the courtroom" (118), I do not wish to argue that the figure of the eyewitness historian was "substantially the same" as the witness one encounters in juridical theory and practice. I see juridical norms as impinging upon, rather then wholly determining, conceptions of testimony in extra-legal discourses. Travel accounts had and have their own peculiar constraints, and these constraints often led eyewitness historians to depart significantly from their juridical models. Indeed, the very attempt to superimpose legal protocols onto travel writing necessarily deformed those protocols. Moreover, legal approaches to the question of the witness become less central in the age of print.

Thus, though chapter four pursues the account of the evolution of juridical testimony, it is focused primarily on the technological medium of the witness deposition (by which I mean its material support). Here, I argue that writing provides a necessary (though not sufficient) impetus for the invention of the first-person eyewitness. When a physically absent witness addresses an anonymous audience, pre-modern ethical modes of testimony reach the limits of their efficacy, and the model of the witness as a second person is fundamentally transformed. No longer a matter of "being here" to bear ethical witness among familiars, witnessing becomes associated with the notion of "being there," alone, to have an epistemic experience of something alien or unprecedented. Though I argue that the discourses of witnessing and testimony are significantly influenced by the expansion of writing in juridical procedure, I do not espouse a McLuhanesque technological determinism; nor do I adopt Walter Ong's model of a thoroughgoing cultural divide between oral and literate societies, not because I don't find it theoretically compelling, but rather because the discourses I study here, like most verbal productions, consist of a complex hybrid of oral and literate practices.[3] It is ultimately the very tension *between* the conditions of oral exchange, on the one hand, and those of written communication, on the other, that gives rise to the use of the first-person singular in eyewitness histories.

Of course, French eyewitness historians were not the only Europeans printing firsthand accounts of the New World in the sixteenth century. Nevertheless, the situation of the French witness differed in several important ways from those of his English and

---

[3] Michael Clanchy's study of the gradual spread of literacy in late medieval England, as well as Richard Firth Green's recent exploration of the shift from (oral) "ethical truth" to (written) "objective truth" in Ricardian England, provide a more nuanced examination of these issues, but neither addresses the context of France; nor do they take up the question of print.

Spanish counterparts, and these differences will condition the emergence of a specifically French first person, as well as a peculiarly French rhetoric of eyewitness testimony, that will be enormously influential in the modern period. It was singularly difficult to adapt the pre-modern rhetoric of *ethos* to the printed page in sixteenth-century France. Due to the French crown's failure to provide sustained support for imperial projects, French eyewitness historians could not presume to speak with the authority of an institution, as did Spaniards or English colonists; nor did they have an obvious (much less a clearly-defined) addressee for their writings. Rather than produce an "imagined community" in sixteenth-century France, the printed travel account redefines the act of witnessing in terms that reinforce the dissolution of community and make of testimony the discourse of the solitary (as opposed to the representative) first person. As I argue in chapter five, this is in part due to the fact that French New World testimony is more explicitly caught up in the upheavals of the Reformation than are Spanish or English accounts.

Since some of the fundamental theological conflicts between French Catholics and Protestants turned on questions of witnessing and testimony, the sixteenth-century French context engenders a body of theological reflections on the question of testimony unparalleled in Europe in this period. Chapter five demonstrates the impact on the Huguenot Jean de Léry's *Histoire* of Jean Calvin's views on martyrological testimony, and more extensively, of Calvin's eucharistic theology, which Léry discusses in his account of Brazil. Calvin elaborates a theory of explicitly testimonial mediation between the human and the divine to explain the sacrament of the Eucharist, a theory that Léry will adapt in his attempt to serve as an ethnographic witness of the New World in the Old. The Calvinist witness is a particular individual who presumes to testify to an absolute truth that is valid outside the parameters of any given community; thus, Calvin's theology contributes to the emergence of a rhetoric of eyewitness testimony as certain knowledge, or *science*.

Though when I follow Jean de Léry into the battles sometimes known as the French "Wars of Religion," the premises of my argument depend more on the particular circumstances of sixteenth-century France, this is not meant to suggest that I believe that the influence of the developments I trace here is restricted to France. Quite the contrary: Léry's *Histoire*, which Claude Lévi-Strauss famously dubbed "le breviaire de l'ethnologue" (*Tristes tropiques* 89), is widely acknowledged as an important, indeed a founding instance of ethnographic witnessing. However, by providing Léry's eyewitness with a rich historical context, one can shed light on the stakes and implications of his act of witnessing – stakes and implications that have heretofore gone unrecognized, and that continue to bubble under the surface of the discourse of testimony in the West.

CHAPTER ONE

THE WITNESS AND THE JUDGE

IN most current humanistic scholarship on the question of testimony, the witness is cast as a first-person observer who has some privileged empirical knowledge upon which he subsequently reports. C.A.J. Coady, the author of a recent philosophical study of testimony, writes that "testimony . . . is the evidence given by persons. . . . The persons in question are referred to as 'witnesses' but a visual analogy is not essential (obviously a blind man can be a perfectly good witness for some purposes and indeed, in some circumstances, e.g. the dark, he may be an even better witness than someone who is sighted)" (27). The implicit assumption here is that a person becomes a witness – and thus eligible to give testimonial evidence – the moment he gains knowledge of an event or circumstance through firsthand experience (be it visual or not).

Some of the earliest and most often-cited examples of this type of what I shall call "epistemic" witnessing in the European tradition come from eyewitness travel literature. Early modern eyewitness accounts of the Americas in particular are frequently put forth as proof of the new epistemological prestige of firsthand experience in the sixteenth century. Most students of New World testimony assume, with Anthony Pagden, that eyewitness narratives of the New World shifted the criteria of testimonial authority away from the citation of third parties and toward the assertion of the presence of an "'I' who has seen what no other being has seen" (39).[1] However,

---

[1] For statements of this view, see for example the essays collected in *New World Encounters*, edited by S. Greenblatt (Berkeley and Los Angeles: U of California P, 1992); as well as Mary C. Fuller's *Voyages in Print*, a thoughtful exploration of "the

given this well-established view, it is hard to know what to make of passages like the following, from the polemical eyewitness historian Bartolomé de Las Casas's *Historia de las Indias*. Las Casas composed and revised his history over a period of several years, from 1527 until the 1560's.[2] Arguing for his friend Columbus's priority as the first European in the Gulf of Paria, he uses the term *"testigo"* in ways utterly unaccounted for by Coady's definition or Pagden's characterization: "Y esta postrera está probada . . . que [Colón] haya sido el primero que descubrió a Paria . . . y este tiene probado el Almirante D. Diego, su hijo, con sesenta testigos de oídas y con veinte y cinco de vistas . . . . Probó, asimismo, que por haber el dicho [Colón] descubierto estas Indias e islas . . . primero que otro alguno, se atrevieron a ir a descubrir los otros que después dél fueron descubridores . . . . Esto prueba con diéz y seis testigos de oídas y con cuarenta y uno que lo creen y con veinte que lo saben y con trece que afirman que descubrió primero que otro alguno, y por aquello lo creen" (I:560; "And the latter is proved . . . that {Columbus} was the first to discover Paria . . . and his son the Admiral Don Diego has proved this with sixty earwitnesses and twenty-five eyewitnesses. . . . He proved, likewise, that since {Columbus} discovered these Indies and islands . . . before anyone else, others who discovered lands were inspired to go on voyages of discovery. . . . This he proves with sixteen earwitnesses and with forty-one who believe it and with twenty who know it and with thirteen who affirm that he was the very first to discover these lands, and for this reason they believe it"). Given Las Casas's own forceful assertions of his eyewitness status elsewhere in his writings, and given the nature of the point under dispute, it seems rather remarkable that the eyewitness enjoys no special prestige here, but instead rubs elbows with everyone from earwitnesses to what we might call true believers (the forty-one witnesses whose only qualification is that they believe the

---

ways in which the failure of [Elizabethan English] voyages and colonies was recuperated by rhetoric" (12); Anthony Pagden's *European Encounters with the New World: from Renaissance to Romanticism*; and Mary Louise Pratt's *Imperial Eyes*, which focuses on the "scientific gaze" as the ordering principle in eighteenth-century travel narratives. Though Anthony Grafton's *New Worlds, Ancient Texts* emphasizes the debt eyewitness travel accounts owed to traditional patterns of thought in the context of the history of ideas, it does not examine the figure of the witness per se; see chapter four *infra*.

[2] The *Historia* was not printed until 1875. For a discussion of the composition and diffusion of the work, see Lewis Hanke's "Las Casas historiador."

proposition Las Casas is trying to prove). What's more, he cites Diego's earwitnesses first, perhaps owing to the fact that there was apparently such a great number of them; the attention to quantity betrays a distinct lack of concern to establish narrowly epistemic criteria for what makes someone an acceptable witness. Most striking, perhaps, is the fact that Las Casas (and Diego) allow for a separate category of witnesses who "know" that Columbus was the first European to reach the New World, thus implying that knowing something is *not* a necessary prerequisite to testifying about it.

The assumption that testimony is primarily a first-person discourse about experiential knowledge of past events clearly cannot serve as the point of departure for an analysis of the witnesses put forth in the *Historia*. The fact that Las Casas puts his eyewitnesses on par with witnesses who simply attest to a belief indicates that eyewitnessing, regardless of the prestige it may have enjoyed in the law courts as a way of knowing, was not synonymous with testimony, much less with credible testimony. The citation of witnesses who simply "affirm" something suggests that the status of a witness's knowledge, however it was obtained, was clearly not the determining factor in the evaluation of his testimony.

This is not to claim that the question of what a witness knew was irrelevant in Las Casas's time; rather, I seek here to illuminate the existence – and indeed, the centrality – of other, non-epistemic criteria for the evaluation of testimony at the dawn of the modern age. That the early modern travel narrative has functioned as a *locus classicus* of a specifically modern, epistemic paradigm of testimony in the majority of critical accounts that deal with it is at least in part due to the fact that such accounts tend to read modern presuppositions about testimony back into the material. However, the narrow terms of the modern, epistemic paradigm simply do not account for the range of discourses that form and inform early modern testimony. The eyewitness constituted but one subtype of witness among many in sixteenth-century Europe, and as such, was subject to the norms governing early modern witnessing and testimony quite broadly construed. These norms extend well beyond the primarily epistemological assumptions about testimony that are usually associated with writing about the New World, and that inform most humanistic discussion of testimony today. In order to make sense of Las Casas's case on behalf of Columbus, then, we need to look backwards in time rather than forwards.

A Merovingian adultery case sheds considerable light on the presuppositions that guided the evaluation of testimony in the medieval period, and that continue to shape conceptions of the witness in Las Casas's time. As the seventeenth-century jurist Jean Danty sums up the legal proceedings, "Fredegonde accusée d'adultere par Chilperic son mari, fit jurer 3 Evesques & 300 Seigneurs de sa Cour, qu'ils croyoient que l'enfant né d'elle, estoit légitime" (35; "Accused of adultery by her husband Chilperic, Fredegonde had three bishops and three hundred lords of her court swear that they believed the child born of her was legitimate"). Even if we imagine that they were, like Coady's blind man, good witnesses "in the dark," Fredegonde's three bishops and three hundred lords clearly did not vouch for the legitimacy of her child based on firsthand knowledge of the circumstances of the baby's conception. Nor did Fredegonde choose these particular witnesses because all three hundred and three of them "knew" the biological status of the child with what we might call Cartesian certitude.

What Danty describes here is the medieval juridical procedure known as compurgation or oath-helping. Compurgatory testimony was not evaluated in terms of empirical knowledge of an event or circumstance on the part of witnesses, but rather first and foremost in terms of the witnesses' imbrication in an ethical community. François Olivier-Martin explains that according to the procedure of the *serment purgatoire* (also known as the *justification canonique* due to its origins in canon law) "l'accusé doit produire devant le juge un certain nombre de co-jureurs . . . qui se porteront avec lui garants de son innocence. . . . Les co-jureurs ne peuvent être sure, matériellement, de l'innocence de l'accusé; mais ils ont confiance en sa parole; ils le savent trop loyal pour les mettre dans un mauvais cas; ils sont, en somme, des témoins de moralité" (58-9; "the accused must present before the judge a certain number of co-swearers . . . who will offer themselves with him as guarantors of his innocence. . . . The co-swearers cannot be materially certain of the innocence of the accused; but they have faith in his word; they know he is too loyal to put them in the position of supporting a bad case; they are, in sum, witnesses to his moral integrity"). Compurgatory witnesses in effect swear an oath of solidarity with a *person*; they do not offer evidence about an experience or an event. The belief indexed by the compurgatory oath is thus predicated on an ethical relationship, and not on an epistemic commitment to a proposition about what may have occurred at some time in the past. The testimony that Las Casas presents on behalf of Columbus is clearly informed by this mode of bearing witness: Diego Colón's witnesses, like Fredegonde's, do not testify so much about their knowledge of the fact on which their testimony bears as to their solidarity with the person or persons it implicates.

The testimony in Fredegonde's case vividly highlights the distinction between the purgatory oath and the modern notion of evidence. Chilperic's accusation of adultery implies an account of Fredegonde's child's origins to which the oaths sworn on behalf of the child's legitimacy do not offer an epistemic alternative, but an alternative of another order altogether. The question of what the witnesses know about the baby's conception, and how they know it, is simply irrelevant here. This point is made all the more clear when we recall that a child's legitimacy is in itself ultimately an attribute bestowed upon him by the community. I hasten to add, however, that compurgation was used to decide cases of all types; it had no privileged link to matters in which social consensus might be viewed as unavoidably paramount. Moreover, unlike modern "character witnessing," to which it bears an undeniable resemblance, compurgatory testimony was often the sole evidence upon which juridical verdicts were based in medieval folklaw.

By testifying to the child's legitimacy, Fredegonde's co-swearers have in fact *established* it – though in a performative and not an epistemic sense. There is never any talk in accounts of this case about what the bishops and lords "really" believed, since the test of "real" belief in this context was, precisely, the willingness to swear a compurgatory oath in the context of a juridical procedure. Moreover, the belief attested by the bishops and lords here, like the belief attested by most of the witnesses Las Casas describes, was not evaluated in epistemic terms – one did not seek to learn what they "really knew" about the point of contention – but rather in ethical terms: one sought to determine whether they were willing to give their word in solidarity with another person. As long as a witness had previously been deemed fit to testify – a process about which I will have more to say later – his oath did not raise questions about what he knew, but instead sealed his ethical commitment to one of the parties in a legal conflict.

The case of Chilperic v. Fredegonde, along with the passage from Las Casas, certainly do not show that Coady is "wrong" about testimony; they show, rather, that his presupposition that testimony is primarily a discourse of knowledge is inapplicable to the historical context of premodern Europe.[3] Yet Coady's "epistemic" view of testimony is one that has been essentialized in much current scholarship. Though humanistic studies of testimony in the twentieth century consistently ran up against the limitations of the epistemic model, very few students of testimony have been able to imagine witnessing in non-epistemic terms.[4]

The dominance of what I'm calling the epistemic paradigm of testimony is most striking in poststructuralist work – not, of course, because the testimony-as-knowledge model of the witness is taken there to be unproblematic, but rather because it is necessarily posited there in order that its underlying tensions may be exhibited. Deconstruction in particular, as Jacques Derrida has always acknowledged, is parasitical upon the classical ontology it complicates; not surprisingly, then, Derrida's own influential writings about testimony ultimately repose upon a modification of the proposition *cogito ergo sum*. In two recent essays, Derrida's insistence on considering both the witness and his testimony in terms of the first person and of transcendental knowledge yields an approach to testimony that ultimately fails to account for the kinds of witnessing performed by Fredegonde's oath-helpers or the crowd of *testigos* described by Las Casas.

In *Demeure: Fiction and Testimony*, a reading of Maurice Blanchot's *The Instant of My Death* (a first-person narrator's account of a young man's experience of near execution at the hand of the Nazis, whose title marks it as autobiographical), Derrida announces that "in essence a testimony is always autobiographical: it tells, in the first person, the sharable and unsharable secret of what happened to me, to me, to me alone, the absolute secret of what I was in a position to live, see, hear, touch, sense, feel" (43). Like Pag-

---

[3] To be fair, I should point out here that Coady provides a brief sketch of the ways in which the domain of testimony has historically been perceived in his first chapter; nonetheless, chapter two establishes a rather more universal point of departure: its title is "What is Testimony?"

[4] The bulk of work on the topic, of course, comes from Holocaust studies. While some recent scholarship in that field has attempted to get beyond a model of witnessing predicated first and foremost on epistemic criteria (see my concluding chapter), the discussion is still largely dominated by the attempt to grapple with the problem of how "knowledge" of this "event" is possible.

den's "I who has seen what no other being has seen," Derrida's witness is defined *a priori* as an isolated individual. The emphasis on first-person experience as the "essence" of testimony is reiterated throughout this essay and in a recent reading of Paul Celan's "Aschenglorie," in which Derrida explains that nobody can substitute for the witness "because he is . . . the only one to know what he has seen, lived, felt" (*Self* 199). By construing testimony in terms of experience, Derrida predicates the ontology of the witness on an act of cognition directed toward an event. It is by virtue of experientially knowing event X that I can become a witness to X; similarly, testimony about event X presupposes a certain kind of experiential knowledge about prior event X.

The predication of witnessing and testimony on the epistemic experience of a prior event necessarily introduces a temporal gap between the moment of witnessing and the moment of bearing witness. For Derrida, this unavoidable gap introduces a fundamental ontological divide within testimony: "to testify is always *on the one hand* to do it *at present*. . . . If that to which I testify is divisible, if the moment in which I testify is divisible, if my attestation is divisible, at that moment it is no longer reliable, it no longer has the value of truth, reliability or veracity that it claims absolutely. Consequently, for testimony there *must* be the instant. And yet, *on the other hand*, this condition of possibility is destroyed by the testimony itself. . . . The moment one is a witness and the moment one attests, *bears witness*, the instant one gives testimony, there must also be a temporal sequence. . . . Consequently, the instant is . . . divided, destroyed by what it nonetheless makes possible – testimony" (*Demeure* 32-3; emphases in original). Derrida will of course go on to complicate the notion of testimony that he has thus defined; it turns out that it is "pure testimony as impossible testimony" (100), for reasons that anyone familiar with deconstruction will be readily able to supply.

Yet it is not clear that "undivided" testimony is impossible. The swearing of a purgatory oath or the undergoing of an ordeal – the two primary means of producing juridical verdicts in medieval folk-law – occur exclusively in the present. There is no temporal or ontological distinction between the moment in which Fredegonde's lords and bishops are witnesses and the moment in which they bear witness, since their testimony is not predicated on some prior epistemic experience. For the compurgator, or the witness who publicly testifies to a belief, the moment of bearing witness is all there is; there is no separate (and certainly no *prior*) moment of experiential witnessing on which his testimony is predicated.

Because of the simultaneity in folklaw testimony of the two moments Derrida designates as "[being] a witness" and "bearing witness," the problematic of the "instant" does not quite apply there. Though testimonial acts in medieval folklaw usually had some linguistic component, they did not involve any linguistic reconstruction of facts. Whereas modern French dictionaries define the witness as someone who has seen or heard something and who can subsequently certify it, the majority of the 145 subentries under the main entry *Tesmoing* in Robert Estienne's 1549 *Dictionnaire Français-Latin* indicate that even as late as the mid-sixteenth century, the principal meaning of the term is simply "a deponent, or one that gives in evidence" (611-13).[5] As Estienne's lexicon suggests, the witness was historically considered primarily from the perspective of the moment in which he testifies, and not in relation to the moment in which he has some experience to which his testimony is supposed to refer.

Because of its status as an act in the present, medieval compurgatory testimony is best approached as a performative utterance. Derrida acknowledges the performative dimension of testimony in a short passage on the martyr in *Demeure*: "The essence of testimony cannot necessarily be reduced to ... knowledge; it is first a present act. When he testifies the martyr does not tell a story, he offers himself. He testifies to his faith by offering himself or offering his life or his body, and this act of testimony is not only an engagement, but his passion does not refer to anything other than its present moment" (38). The testimony of the martyr, however, like the testimony of the compurgator, does not quite fit into the problematic of the instant that Derrida elaborates. It is instructive in this regard to go back to one of Derrida's best-known discussions of the performative. In "Signature Event Context" ("*sec*"), Derrida questions J.L. Austin's distinction between constative and performative utterances on the grounds that performative communication, like constative utterances, constitutes "the communication of an intentional

---

[5] For the modern definition, see e.g. the Larousse *Dictionnaire de la langue française/lexis*: "personne qui a vu ou entendu quelquechose et peut le certifier" (1854).

meaning" (322) – which, in the case of Fredegonde's witnesses, would presumably be the intent to express juridical solidarity with another person by means of an oath. By pointing out the necessarily formulaic nature of performative utterances like oaths (though the oath is not one of his examples), Derrida emphasizes the fundamental citationality of the performative: rather than a singular event whose force or meaning derives primarily from the particular intentions of a given speaker, the felicitous performative speech act owes its success at least partly to the fact that, as an instance of formulaic speech, it can and indeed must continue to perform outside of any particular context. In other words, the effect of the oath of Fredegonde's co-swearers depends not only on the intentions of the witnesses (not to mention their physical presence), but also on the fact that the oath they utter conforms to an iterable pattern which remains intelligible in the absence of those intentions (and of those witnesses).

All of this makes perfect sense. From the perspective of premodern testimony, however, there is a crucial element missing from Derrida's discussion of the performative: the addressee. The question of the addressee brings to the fore the ways in which the system of interpretation Derrida takes as his point of departure in that essay and elsewhere is problematic for thinking about premodern testimony, and thus more historically specific than Derrida himself seems to allow. Derrida proposes that writing (and by extension, all communication) "must . . . remain legible despite the absolute disappearance of every determined addressee in general for it to function as writing, that is, for it to remain legible. It must be repeatable – iterable – in the absolute absence of the addressee or of the empirically determinable set of addressees" (*sec* 315). Whereas autobiographical assertions of the type Derrida considers as the quintessence of testimony in his essays on Blanchot and Celan can indeed be approached in the terms he derives from his reconsideration of what he calls a "properly philosophical" hermeneutics – one that imagines communication in terms of a first-person subject who intends to express something to a (potentially absent) audience – the pre- and early modern ethical testimony we have been considering possesses a very different structure.

Most forms of folklaw testimony were, precisely, *not* repeatable in the sense of being citable. In his essay on Austin, Derrida asks, "what would a mark be that one could not cite?" (321). The testimonial performance of the folklaw witness (the dueler, certainly, but also the compurgator) cannot be cited without destroying its status *as* testimony. Moreover, as I discuss at more length in chapter five, early written records of inquisitional testimony were not considered to be testimony in another form; they were, rather, considered purely as memory aids. They did not count as testimony per se; thus, the inquisitional witness was frequently required to reiterate his testimony orally even when written records of it existed. Similarly, a witness's signature on a contract did not initially stand in for him in his absence; as a record of his presence at some prior moment, it actually required his reappearance (and his renewed attestation) in order to function as testimony. As Beaumanoir indicates, this system ran up against the problem of mortality: witnesses inevitably died, and the testimonial potential of their signature died with them. In an important sense, then, such signatures were tethered to a source, and ceased to function as signatures in the absence of that source.

One of the fundamental distinctions in medieval law is that between the witness and the document. The initial resistance to construing a written document as a form of testimony is intimately related to the specifically *dialogic* framework in which witness depositions were always inserted – and, one might argue, in which all testimony is always situated. One cannot testify in the theoretical or empirical absence of an addressee; it is always necessary to testify *to* another. The potential absence that Derrida posits as a necessary precondition for communication is precisely what pre- and early modern testimony absolutely and explicitly excludes. In the folklaw context, there is no such thing as bearing witness *tout court*; rather, one always bears witness *to* someone. It is utterly impossible to imagine a judicial ordeal without an audience, much less a duel with only one participant. If we think of testimony as the proverbial tree falling in the forest, both pre- and early modern juridical theory and practice insist that it simply makes no sound unless someone hears it.

The necessity of an audience for testimony goes beyond the realm of the particular conventions that make performative speech acts felicitous. The acts and utterances of an individual in isolation would not be unfelicitous testimony; rather, they would never have been thought of in terms of testimony in the first place. Unlike a strictly autobiographical utterance, testimony in general requires others in order to come into being as testimony. Legal discourse in general makes this structural feature of testimony explicit: the witness is never the sole author of his testimony; on the contrary, he usually has several co-authors, foremost among them the plaintiff and the accused, who define the parameters of the matter under dispute, and, in the case of inquisitional procedure, the court, which formulates and articulates the questions put to witnesses.

The very fact that a true performative must occur in the presence of at least one witness perhaps constitutes the fundamental distinction between it and what Austin called the "non-serious" performative in *How to Do Things with Words*. Granted, this is not the grammatical or semantic criterion Austin was after, but this highlights the degree to which both Austin's investigations and Derrida's critique bracket intersubjectivity (as distinct from conventionality) in their discussions of the performative, as if other people could simply be factored out of acts of human communication. Perhaps the best linguistic model for the testimonial performative is Mikhail Bakhtin's dialogism.[6] Testimony is first and foremost a *response*; it is divided insofar as it is necessarily *shared* with other people. By this I mean not only that the witness always testifies *to* someone, and thus necessarily has an addressee, but also that the addressee of a testimony takes a necessary part in its very construction.

In pre-modern inquisitorial procedure, as in contemporary Continental and Anglo-American legal procedure, the intersubjective dimension of testimony takes on an explicitly dialogic form. One testifies because one is called to do so. Jean Imbert's 1563 *Practique judiciaire* specifies that witnesses can be fined or imprisoned if they do not respond to this call ("Il sera . . . ordonné . . . à la peine de certaine somme de deniers . . . [que les témoins viennent] deposer a un certain jour: auquel s'ilz ne viennent . . . ilz seront contrainctz par saisie de leurs biens, & emprisonnement de leurs personnes"; 178). Thus, the witness is constituted as a witness in response to an institutional call that constrains him to give testimony. Moreover, once he does appear before the law, the witness is not called upon simply to "tell his story," in the lyric mode of autobiography. Rather, his testimony consists of his responses to specific

---

[6] The most comprehensive presentation of Bakhtin's linguistic theories in English can be found in *Speech Genres and Other Late Essays*.

questions put to him by a functionary of the court. As Imbert remarks, witness depositions on matters other than those addressed in the "articles" – that is, the official set of questions produced by the court to adjudicate a given legal dispute – are not valid testimony ("La deposition d'un tesmoing ne vaut en ce qu'il depose oultre les choses articulées"; 378). The interrogatory addressee of a testimony is thus also one of its co-authors, and not merely the eventual recipient of a discourse whose structure has been determined without regard to him. The ontological status of testimony *qua* testimony is in this context not determined (or determinable) as a purely linguistic structure, but is rather only consolidated at the moment the testimony is *received*. Consequently, testimony cannot be reduced to a monologic "concept" whose "essence" is inherently divided against itself.

As an institutional construct, the medieval witness is taken to have neither a subjective nor an objective perspective, but an *intersubjective* point of view. The overtly dialogic and intersubjective character of medieval testimony always implies relations among persons, and never an individual subject in isolation. Since medieval juridical testimony is inherently dialogic, not lyric, it demands a model other than that of the isolated, individual first person that serves as the point of departure for most contemporary discussions of witnessing and testimony. The medieval witness neither gave an autobiographical account of his own experiences in potential isolation from other persons, as might the accused; nor was he in the position to synthesize all of the evidence in a case in order to reach a verdict, as was the judge. He gave testimony that necessarily bore on another party (no one was considered a "witness" on his own behalf), *in the presence of that party*.

Even after the introduction of inquisitional procedure, in which witness testimony was sometimes given to a judicial functionary in the absence of the parties in question, the testimonial utterance *par excellence* – the oath – was uttered in the presence of all concerned. In other words, it was not enough for the witness to be present to take the oath as a first person; rather, it was necessary that he take the oath in the presence of the parties on which his testimony bore. Thus, his status as a witness was established on the basis of an act that had itself to be witnessed by others, not simply performed. In the eyes of the participants in folklaw proceedings, then – the primary context in which the pre-modern witness as such existed – I believe it is most accurate to speak of the witness as a *second* person (as the term "second" in a duel suggests).

To discuss the witness in terms of the second person is not to argue that the medieval era, or medieval law, had no concept of the first person. It means, rather, that the *witness* was not conceived of as a first person. In the institutional context of juridical practice, the witness is a species distinct from the accused, the judge or the plaintiff. The vast majority of literary and cultural studies of witnessing approach the topic from the standpoint of the first person in part because they ultimately focus on the figure of the plaintiff (Holocaust studies) or that of the accused (studies of confession-cum-autobiography). Broader studies of evidence, on the other hand (e.g. Shapiro) often conflate the perspective of the witness with that of the judge, which is inevitably identified as that of a third person. In any case, existing scholarship seems to offer us only two ways in which to think about witnessing, in terms of either the first or the third person. The second person is never entertained as a legitimate category of analysis, and as a result, the juridical category of the witness is never studied on its own terms.[7]

In justifying his characterization of the witness as a first person in the essay on Celan, Derrida cites Emile Benveniste's *Vocabulaire des institutions européennes* for the Latin etymology of the term "witness" (*testis*); he approaches the Greek term *marturion* (and its relatives) by way of Appian of Alexandria. His discussion of this family of terms in German (*Zeuge, bezeugen*, etc.) invokes Celan himself, as well as Heidegger, Kant and Hegel. The privileged reference points here thus come from the philosophical canon, which notoriously omits precisely the extended historical period under consideration here, and which imagines itself to be situated beyond the confines of historical practice and institutional constraints. The existence of forms of testimony in which the moment of "being a witness" and that of "bearing witness" are indistinguishable suggests that the ontological divide Derrida detects within testimony

---

[7] A partial exception is Peter Brooks's recent *Troubling Confessions*, one of the few humanistic studies that appreciates the inescapably dialogic nature of the utterances generated by a legal proceeding. Brooks's attention to dialogue is no doubt the product of his engagement with actual juridical practice, as opposed to the more or less exclusively theoretical texts that inform studies like Shapiro's.

derives from the philosophical presuppositions that he assumes. This may explain why neither folklaw testimony nor early inquisitional testimony can be properly understood in terms of the first person that Derrida adopts.

In both medieval folklaw and early modern inquisitional procedure, the accusations of the plaintiff and the confession or denial of the accused were not classified under the rubric of testimony. Moreover, the repeated citation in the Middle Ages and Renaissance of the Old Testament Book of Deuteronomy's prohibition on the testimony of a lone witness, together with its Roman analogue ("*testis unus, testis nullus*"), highlights the fact that for the period in question here, witnesses necessarily came at the minimum in pairs, if not in even larger groups such as those called upon to testify to the legitimacy of Fredegonde's offspring or Columbus's navigational achievements. Thus, when we consider testimony in the pre- and early modern periods, we should not imagine the witness as an isolated individual, much less as a first person.

Indeed, the figure of the modern epistemic witness has more in common with the medieval judge than with the medieval witness. The distinction between the juridical verdict reached via testimony, on the one hand, and that based on the judge's own perceptions, on the other, is a central one throughout the Middle Ages, and on into the sixteenth century and beyond. In his seventeenth-century commentary on the 1566 ordinance of Moulins, Jean Danty borrows from Bartolus and Baldus to distinguish three kinds of juridical fact: *faits notoires*, "that is to say evident, that have no need of proof"; *faits incertains*, "where proof is necessary, as are all things that depend on human whim or on chance"; and *fait impertinens*, "superfluous and immaterial to the case" (8). Each type of *fait* is associated with specific forms of proof and produces verdicts of different degrees of certitude. Testimony only comes meaningfully into play when the facts are uncertain, and when no confession has been obtained from the accused. Baldus says that the *probatio plena*, arrived at by a series of proof calculations that assign standard values to various pieces of evidence (including witness testimony), is inferior to the proof provided by the *fait notoire* because the former is not established on the basis of the direct sense perception of the judge, and is thus "speculative et augmentative" in nature. It does not establish "perfecta scientia," but a "probabilis certitudo" that produces a "plena fides, plena credulitas" on the part of the judge (see Lévy 67). The realm of *scientia* and that of a *probabilis certitudo* are utterly distinct for the jurists: unlike the *fait notoire* or a confession, the *probatio plena* admits to counter-proof and to appeal.

If we return to Derrida's essays, we may note that in contrast to Baldus and Danty, he proposes that testimony "claims absolutely" the "value of truth." Taking his presuppositions from the phenomenological tradition with which he is in dialogue, he proposes that the individual experiences of the witness stake a claim to transcendental validity as universal judgments. This becomes more apparent when Derrida specifies that the witness implicitly claims that the experiences he has had as a first person could have, would have been had by any person: "In saying, I swear to tell the truth, where I have been the only one to see or hear and where I am the only one who can attest to it, this is true to the extent that anyone who *in my place*, at that instant, would have seen or heard or touched the same thing and could repeat exemplarily, universally, the truth of my testimony. . . . The singular must be universalizable; this is the testimonial condition" (*Demeure* 40-41; emphasis in original). Whereas Derrida implies that the position of the judge and that of the witness must be interchangeable ("the singular must be universalizable"), as we have seen, the medieval glossaters work from the assumption that they are fundamentally distinct. The kind of testimonial "truth" Derrida refers to is consequently not at all the same thing as the medieval glossaters' "full proof." The truth that is the horizon of testimony as Derrida describes it is in fact the very *perfecta scientia* that the medieval jurists reserved for cases in which witness testimony is not involved.

The premise that the witness should fulfill the function of the judge is not peculiar to deconstruction; moreover, the merging of these two positions has important consequences for the way we think about the nature of the testimony witnesses can or should provide. Like Derrida, Jean-François Lyotard is preoccupied with the (im)possibility of knowing and representing phenomena conceived as pure singularities. In *Le Différend*, this problem is conceived in juridical terms: "As distinguished from a litigation, a differend would be a case of conflict, between [at least] two parties, that cannot be equitably resolved for lack of a rule of judgment applicable to both arguments' (xi). As Lyotard's definition indicates, he is concerned primarily with the philosophical question of *judgment* – indeed, of synthetic judgments. Consequently, when the question of testimony appears in his discussion of the differend, it is addressed in terms of definitive transcendental judgments, and not in terms of the provisional *credulitas* that is the explicit domain of all forms of testimony in medieval jurisprudential theory.

Attempting to demonstrate the logical impossibility of testifying to the existence of the gas chambers at Auschwitz, Lyotard proposes that those who survived them cannot claim to be witnesses, since – as Lyotard imagines the revisionists stipulating, but effectively stipulates himself – "either you were not there, and you cannot bear witness; or else you were there, you could not therefore have seen everything, and you cannot bear witness about everything" (102). The unstated presuppositions here are that to be a witness one must have "been there" – that is, one must have had a firsthand experience of some event; and that testimony requires that one "bear witness about everything." Contrary to what Lyotard's struggle with the differend implies, however, pre-modern juridical practices suggest that the position of the witness needn't be construed in terms of that of the judge; in other words, testimony does not have to be the equivalent of the Hegelian *Resultat* that Lyotard shuns. In the juridical context, testimony has not historically been regarded as having the potential to produce an unassailable verdict, much less certain knowledge. *Perfecta scientia* was reserved for the subject-as-judge, since the judge was the only one capable of establishing a "scientific" verdict based on a *fait notoire*. The only other unappealable verdict resulted from the confession of the subject-as-accused. When we consider the question of the verdict where witnesses are involved, we are in the realm of probability, faith and belief. Thus, the *object* of testimony – that which is attested – is not considered in terms of the absolute and the singular, but rather in terms of the provisional and the unstable.[8]

This is in one sense exactly where Derrida ends up. In a

---

[8] There exists a powerful symbiosis between analyses of testimony that enlist (if only to problematize) the notions of the singular and the absolute, on the one hand, and a particular conception of the Holocaust, on the other. Both Derrida and Lyo-tard implicitly position the Holocaust in absolute terms, as opposed to historical, partial and contingent ones, and then go on to observe how reliable testimony becomes impossible under such circumstances. See the Epilogue *infra*.

phrase that he will reiterate in both *Demeure* and the essay on Celan, he maintains that "there is no testimony that does not at least structurally imply in itself the possibility of fiction, simulacra, dissimulation, lie, and perjury – that is to say, the possibility of literature. . . . If this possibility that it seems to prohibit were effectively excluded, if testimony thereby became proof, information, certainty, or archive, it would lose its function as testimony. In order to remain testimony, it must therefore allow itself to be haunted" (*Demeure* 29-30). And yet, only a testimony that has a transcendental *scientia* as its horizon (a philosophical testimony, perhaps) could be "haunted" in the way that Derrida describes here. Since *scientia* was never considered a potential product of medieval testimony, it was effectively the possibility of testimony's ever becoming "proof, information, certainty or archive" that was always already excluded in medieval law. It makes no sense, for example, in the context in which Fredegonde's child's legitimacy was established, to consider testimony in terms of (mis)information or (un)certainty. The testimony of her witnesses is not haunted by fiction, but simply *is* fiction, in the sense of overtly constructed and made. It thus has no stable identity or definition; rather, it is a provisional structure that is formed, reformed and deformed depending on its context. Strictly speaking, then, testimony understood in this way cannot be deconstructed, because it has no definitive structure.

My aim here is not simply to juxtapose two distinct discourses of testimony and show that they are different, indeed incommensurable. The rest of this book studies the institutional, technological and political conditions that played a critical role in the formation of the very model of the witness that serves as the object of Derrida's deconstruction. By making of the ontological question of testimony first and foremost a problem of individual epistemic experience, Derrida omits precisely that ethical, intersubjective foundation that has historically distinguished testimony from other, primarily epistemic discourses (those which, in medieval terminology, could produce *scientia*). This is not to suggest that the ethical dimension of testimony is lost on Derrida, or on the many other students of testimony who share his presuppositions (if not his conclusions). Rather, it is to point out that in Derrida's discussions of testimony (and in contemporary discussions of the witness more generally), ethics remains secondary to epistemology.[9] For Derrida, the ethical dimension of testimony seems to derive from testimony's limitations as an epistemic discourse (which in turn derive from its ontological dividedness against itself, as is the case with all concepts under the regime of a Derridean "hauntology").

Medieval testimony, by contrast, was an ethical discourse through and through. Rather than presupposing rational actors whose aim is to construct a Habermasian "public sphere," medieval folklaw procedure required parties who had established ethical relations with one another.[10] In order to be eligible to give testimony, a folklaw witness had to be recognized as a legitimate deponent in the eyes of his community. This legitimacy was not based on a witness's epistemic capacities, but rather on his socio-ethical status. As a consequence, the "verdicts" reached via testimony were not considered synonymous with objective knowledge about the facts under dispute. As Richard Firth Green has recently emphasized, medieval folklaw was oriented toward settling disputes, a goal whose achievement does not necessarily require the enlistment of some notion of objective truth. Medieval forms of juridical "proof" were designed to establish what Green terms an "ethical truth" based in social consensus, and not some approximation of the "facts." Testimony, then, like the other proofs, was meant to allow for the *founding* of a state of affairs, not a satisfactory *representation* of some current of previous set of circumstances. Nonetheless, the verdicts yielded by testimony were always subject to revision if a new ethical consensus was reached.

Ethical consensus was in fact what ordeals, the most notorious of early medieval forms of juridical proof in criminal matters, were meant to establish. The duel was by far the most commonly used form of the *ordalie* in the Middle Ages. The judgment rendered by the ordeal of the duel was interpreted in broadly ethical rather than epistemic terms: rather than imply any account of an accused person's behavior in the matter in question, the results of the ordeal

---

[9] In *Politics of Friendship*, Derrida explicitly distinguishes between what he calls the "philosophical" question, "what is friendship?" and the "ethical" question, "Who is my friend?" In the essays under consideration here, Derrida never asks the "ethical" question of the witness, only the philosophical question "What is testimony?" (cf. Coady).

[10] Habermas notes the differences between the feudal and the modern "public" in the first chapter of *The Structural Transformation of the Public Sphere*.

yielded an overarching ethical judgment about his cosmic status as innocent or guilty. Those who had lost a duel were not simply punished for an act; they lost their social, and thus juridical, status forever and were no longer allowed to serve as witnesses (Lévy 33). The ordeal was thus first and foremost a test (in the sense of *une épreuve*) of character, and only secondarily a form of epistemic evidence.

Similarly, the explicit premise of the compurgatory oath is that testimony must be taken on faith or not at all. Thus, in the medieval period, perjury has no special relationship to "fiction"; it is instead, quite simply, bad faith. A false witness was one who swore an oath he was ultimately unwilling or unable to defend, and not a witness who had not "told the truth." Defending one's good faith did not entail demonstrating the truth of some proposition about a prior event; it required a fight for one's life. In the tenth century, the duel rose to the top of the hierarchy of proofs as the means to "fausser les serments" – in other words, to test the juridical legitimacy of an oath (Lévy 17). Defending one's oath thus demanded an ethico-ontologic rather than an ethico-epistemic commitment on the part of the witness.

Due to the distinct presuppositions that underlie premodern and modern conceptions of witnessing, the role played by death in premodern testimony is exactly the inverse of the one Derrida and Lyotard ascribe to it. For them, testimony becomes increasingly impossible the closer one moves toward death. Death – construed as an *experience* (indeed, it is meant to stand in for experience *tout court*) – on the one hand, and testimony, on the other, are according to this way of thinking incommensurable, because it is logically impossible to experience death (either one's own or another's) completely and thus to report on it. In medieval law, by contrast, the witness was never asked to *recount* his death; he was, rather, required to risk actually dying. Without the threat of death, there could be no testimony; customary law makes this clear by allowing only those persons eligible to engage in a duel to serve as witnesses. Here, then, the very existence of the witness *qua* witness is predicated on his mortality. Far from being a merely theoretical boundary, however, the death of the witness was an empirical eventuality in the context of a juridical dispute. The testimony of the folklaw witness was predicated on his potential death, a death that nobody else could die for him. Rather than representing the most intensely private, personal and autobiographical moment of one's existence, the moment of death here represents the moment that makes ethical relations with other human beings possible: a witness's death is his alone, but his capacity to die is also precisely what links him to a broader community of mortals. Death for the premodern witness is an act performed before others, and not an experience had by an isolated self. Though the witness cannot logically experience his own death as an act, that is how it functions for the community in whose eyes he is a witness. In any case, as we saw in the case of Fredegonde v. Chilperic, the witness's experiences are not the crux of his testimony; his public acts are. Thus though we may speculate that the pre-modern witness taken *as an individual* may very well have experienced his death as the "unexperienced experience" Derrida describes, we must bear in mind that in the pre-modern context, the individual, autobiographical "I" is not the subject of testimony: the *intersubjective I* is.

CHAPTER TWO

ETHOS

IN his collection of *Navigazioni e viaggi*, published over the course of the 1550's, Giovanni Battista Ramusio remarks that, upon finally returning to Venice from the land of the Tartars, Marco Polo, his father and his uncle met with a reception similar to the one that greeted Odysseus: "questi tre gentiluomini, dapoi tanti anni ch'eran stati lontani dalla patria, non furno riconosciuti da alcuno de' loro parenti" (3:29; "these three gentlemen, after so many years away from their homeland, were not recognized by any of their relatives"). Ramusio goes on to explain that the Polo family did not recognize their kin because the returning travelers appeared to be more Tartar than Venetian. "Si trovavan questi gentiluomini, per la lunghezza e sconci del viaggio, e per le molte fatiche e travagli dell' animo, tutti tramutati nella effigie, che rappresentavano un non se che del tartaro nel volto e nel parlare, avendosi quasi dimenticata la lingua veneziana. Li vestimenti loro erano tristi e fatti di panni grossi, al modo de' Tartari" (3:29; "On account of the length and misadventures of their voyage, and due to the hardships they endured, these gentlemen were completely transformed physically, and exhibited a Tartar *je ne sais quoi* in their countenance and speech, having all but forgotten the Venetian tongue. Their clothes were drab and made of rough cloth, in the Tartar style"). Ramusio tells this story in order to bolster his sixteenth-century readers' confidence in Polo's narrative. For the Renaissance historian, the Polos' assimilation of Tartar culture only reinforces the authenticity of Marco Polo's account of his twenty-six years in Asia. He blames scribal error for Polo's reputation as a liar, and believes that his "corrected" version of the text will prove more compelling.[1] The ethical transformation of the erstwhile Venetians, we are made to understand, is proof of the depth of Polo's experience in the Mongol empire.

Polo's medieval readers were, by contrast, notoriously skeptical of his account.[2] An early 14th-century copy of the *Imago mundi seu Chronica* by Jacopo d'Acqui provides a particularly instructive sample of reactions to Polo's book. It is to Acqui that we owe the oft-quoted story that a dying Marco Polo insisted to his friends that he had not told the half of what he had seen on his travels. As Acqui tells it, Polo's implicit endorsement of his book is his direct response to the skepticism of his friends: "Et quia ibi . . . quasi incredibilia reperiuntur, rogatus fuit ab amicis in morte quod librum suum corrigeret" (Benedetto CXCIV; "And since they found [Polo's account] fairly incredible, his friends begged him on his deathbed to amend his book"). One could argue that the fact that Acqui tells this anecdote implies that Acqui himself wished to reinforce belief in Polo's book: after all, it depicts the Christian traveller on his deathbed refusing to disavow what it contains. But the force of this refusal depends upon the existence of a tradition of reception that does not find the text entirely credible.

Though there exist no documents to prove conclusively whether Ramusio's reconstruction of the Polos' return to Venice is anything but imaginative, the scenario he imagines is extremely suggestive. While Polo's account itself indicates that it was far from unthinkable in the medieval era to base a wide-ranging geographi-

---

[1] Ramusio laments that Marco Polo's book, "per causa de infinite scorrezioni ed errori, è stato molto decine d'anni riputato favola, e che i nomi delle città e provincie fussero tutte fizioni e imaginazioni sanza fondamento alcuno, e per dir meglio sogni" (22). Ramusio's version of Polo is *sui generis*, not conforming closely enough to any of the known manuscript versions for its provenance to be identified. It contains extensive prefatory material authored by Ramusio, including the description of the Polos' homecoming that I cite here. In addition to modernizing Polo's place-names, Ramusio's version also offers accounts of particular experiences that are absent from all other known manuscripts. This of course reinforces the sense that the link between experience and credibility was becoming increasingly strong by the mid-sixteenth century.

[2] Though John Larner has recently tried to revise the notion that Polo's account met with incredulity on the part of his contemporaries, the paucity of available evidence leads him to spend a fair amount of time extrapolating from the silences of Marco's medieval contemporaries scenarios that would allow for the possibility that they did not necessarily find his account incredible.

cal account on firsthand experience, its fate indicates that the authority of the resulting testimony did not ultimately derive from that experience. In what follows, I look to the criteria for evaluating witnesses given in medieval juridical literature in order to contextualize the medieval reception of the travel accounts of Marco Polo and John Mandeville.[3] As John Critchley notes in his recent study of Polo's book, "it is notorious that in the hundred years following his return home Marco Polo's effect on the state of European knowledge of the world was minimal" whereas Mandeville's *Travels* "was the most famous travel book of the later middle ages" (132; 136-7). Ramusio's sixteenth-century edition was the first to present Polo as a geographical authority, at the very moment when Mandeville's fortunes began to wane; after receiving a half-hearted endorsement in early editions of the *Navigazioni*, Mandeville eventually disappeared from the collection altogether. The two accounts thus seem to counterbalance one another in the popular imagination; where one looks credible, the other doesn't, and vice-versa. And yet, they both present themselves as firsthand, eyewitness accounts. We cannot therefore simply appeal to some general "principle of the eyewitness" in order to explain what it is that determines fluctuating estimations of their credibility in pre- and early modern Europe.[4] Rather, we need to understand what allowed medieval readers to distinguish *among* eyewitness testimonies.

THE MEDIEVAL INQUEST

Most legal histories argue that the introduction of the inquest into medieval lay courts inaugurated a rational search for truth (e.g. Olivier-Martin; Esmein; Langbein, *Prosecuting*). Such studies tend to focus on signs of "progress," however, and not on the persistence

---

[3] For ease of exposition, I will refer to both accounts as "books," even though both originally circulated in multiple and varied manuscript versions. I will also periodically refer to Mandeville and Polo in ways that imply that they were the "authors" of those "books." This is not to ignore the complexities of medieval manuscript production in general, or those of the compositional situation of these two travel accounts in particular, but simply to avoid excessively cumbersome formulations. The issue of composition is treated in depth with respect to Mandeville in Iain Higgins's *Writing East*.

[4] The quoted phrase is Stephen Greenblatt's in reference to Mandeville (*Marvelous Possessions* 28).

of old ways of thinking. While it is undeniable that the inquest's preference for confession and its new focus on referential (as distinct from ethically performative) witness testimony indicates a theoretical commitment to epistemic evidence, one should not underestimate the degree to which old procedures, old forms of proof, and with them old conceptions of witnessing persisted well beyond the end of the thirteenth century. Juridical practice, both within and without the inquisitional setting, continued to encompass and indeed privilege the folklaw notion of ethical truth as late as the sixteenth century. This does not mean that medieval juridical testimony had no epistemic basis; on the contrary, eyewitnesses were held to be in the best position to know about the facts of a case. However, the protocols of the medieval inquisition were such that a witness's social status retained priority over his potential knowledge in determining his juridical legitimacy and thus, his credibility. In both England and France, as late as the fifteenth century, a witness's social standing and his perceived character (the classic grounds of credibility in oral societies) remained the primary grounds on which a juridical witness would establish the credibility of his testimony, and the *only* grounds on which his testimony could be legally contested.

Manuals of customary law from the thirteenth and fourteenth centuries give us some insight into the impact of the advent of inquisitional procedure on witnesses and witness testimony. Of the surviving documents, the jurist and poet Philippe de Beaumanoir's late thirteenth-century *Coutumes des Beauvaisis*, written just after Louis IX's introduction of inquisitional procedure in French royal courts in 1258, offers the most extensive account of a medieval lay court's approach to the inquest. (The few other available sources from the period, such as Jean Boutillier's *Somme rurale* and the *Grant coustumier de Normandie*, tend to corroborate the elements I emphasize in Beaumanoir.) Beaumanoir's detailed description of inquisitional procedure allows us to evaluate the role played by a witness's *ethos* on the one hand, and by his firsthand experience, on the other, in establishing the credibility of juridical witnesses in the early inquest.

In general, the testimony of witnesses was preferred to the evidence of documents in folklaw procedure – hardly surprising in an era of restricted literacy. Moreover, as we have seen, folklaw testimony demanded that the witness perform an act of faith; the witness's willingness to perform this act appears to have satisfied the ethical imperative of pre-inquisitional justice. Such an engagement could not be demanded of a document, which consequently could not possibly participate in the establishment of consensus toward which folklaw verdicts aimed. The persistence of folklaw attitudes toward testimonial proof after the ordinance of 1258 is also attributable to the fact that the limited jurisdiction of the French king left the folklaw in place in much of France. Louis's ordinance orders the use of the inquest exclusively for territories administered by the King ("la domaine du Roi, et non dans la terre de ses barons"; Isambert I:284). As Beaumanoir explains, feudal courts have the option to choose to maintain previous customary law ("tout cil qui ont justice en le conté poent maintenir lor cort, s'il lor plest, selonc l'ancienne coustume") – which gives just one day for the plaintiff to make his case, and which featured the duel as the preferred method of settling disputes quickly (100). Aldhémar Esmein notes that the inquest was thus much more common in royal courts than in feudal jurisdictions, where the old forms prevailed ("l'enquête ne faisait point les mêmes progrès dans les justices des seigneurs que dans les justices royales; on suivait ordinairement dans les cours féodales l'ancienne forme de procéder"; *Histoire* 28). Paul Guilhiermoz reports, moreover, that despite the fact that the inquest was official "French" procedure from St. Louis on, it was regularly avoided ("on cherchait le plus possible de s'en passer"; *Enquêtes* 7). He cites legislation from the mid-1300's through to the mid-1400's that encourages magistrates to reach a decision *without* undertaking an inquest.

Despite the royal introduction of inquisitional procedure, then, the old forms of proof, especially the duel, persisted in large parts of the kingdom of France. Jean-Philippe Lévy notes that the duel had become "la preuve primordiale" in the 10th century, and that ordeals would only disappear from French customary law in the late 14th century (149), while François Olivier-Martin maintains that the recourse to ordeals, especially the duel, persisted well into the Middle Ages ("on retrouvera les ordalies, et notamment le duel judiciaire, en plein moyen âge"; 59). Indeed, while it certainly notes the Saint-King's limitations on the judicial duel, Beaumanoir's customal devotes three full chapters to the conditions for and rituals surrounding the *gages à bataille*, since the aristocracy in a number of regions retained the privilege of refusing the inquest in favor of the duel. In 1306, Philippe le Bel reestablished the use of the duel in criminal cases involving capital punishment where witness testimony was inconclusive. One can only suppose that inquisitional witness testimony was perceived to be inadequate in a significant number of cases, enough to provoke Philippe's reinstatement of the duel. In any case, both royal legislation and the customals indicate the frequent use of the judicial duel well after the official introduction of the inquisitorial model.

In addition to the duel, the purgatory oath – a version of which also existed in canon law – continued to be employed after the introduction of the inquisition, most often in criminal cases where witnesses and documents established insufficient proof (that is, only a *preuve semipleine*). Thus, juridical procedures associated with the folklaw commitment to ethical truth continued to be performed even as the inquisitional search for factual truth had begun. As a consequence, folklaw assumptions about witnesses and testimony were carried over into early inquisitional procedure. Whereas the inquest supposedly focused on the facts of a case, Beaumanoir intimates that thirteenth-century inquisitional witness testimony was not evaluated primarily on the basis of its content. He explains the appropriate outcome in cases deemed undecidable: one decides in favor of the accused if nobody has won on the basis of the number of witnesses, or the bad reputation of the witnesses, or the statements of the witnesses ("nombre de tesmoins, ne par disfame de tesmoins, ne par les dis des tesmoins"; 1205). The actual substance of witness testimony – "le dis des tesmoins" – is but one criterion here, coming in third place behind the sheer number of witnesses presented by each party, on the one hand, and the potentially bad reputation of the witnesses themselves, on the other. Moreover, Louis IX's 1258 ordinance allows a party to call as many witnesses as he can find; thus, early inquisitional procedure itself encouraged thinking about witnesses in terms of sheer quantity, not epistemological capacity. According to Paul Guilhiermoz, it is only in the fourteenth century that a limit of ten witnesses per article is instituted. Guilhiermoz cites a 1262 case in which a party presented over forty witnesses for one article: the adverse party complained, but the court accepted the testimony of all forty (79). The crowds Diego Colón cited to defend his father's claims to have been the first European to reach the New World clearly would have been at home here.

Renommée

Partly as a result of the influence of folklaw attitudes on inquisitional procedure, the perceived reliability of witness testimony in thirteenth- and fourteenth-century France depended heavily on the concept of *renommée* or personal reputation – what Aristotle called a witness's *ethos*. The juridical force of a deposition reposed entirely on a preliminary judgment about a potential witness's reputation and social standing. Once that preliminary judgment had been made, early inquisitional protocol appears to have left little institutional or indeed conceptual room for the contestation of witness testimony. In other words, because they severely restricted who was eligible to testify at the outset of an inquest, thirteenth- and fourteenth-century French lay courts do not appear to have found it necessary to allow for objections to the testimony given by lawful witnesses.

The enduring influence of *renommée* in the assessment of witnesses after the official turn away from folklaw can be readily observed in Beaumanoir's step-by-step description of an inquest. At the outset of the inquest, the disputing parties and their witnesses, whose names had already been made public, were brought together in open court, at which time a disputing party could move to disqualify ("debouter") the witnesses who had been brought to testify against him. The acceptable reasons for disqualifying inquisitional witnesses given by Beaumanoir closely replicate the restrictions he gives elsewhere in his customal regarding who may participate in the duel. This is not surprising, since, as Beaumanoir notes, agreeing to testify could put a witness himself at risk of being challenged to a duel, such that potential witnesses are advised to consider the possible consequences before they agree to depose ("Et por ce se doit bien çascuns se garder comment on entre en tesmongnage en cas ou gage poent queir"; 399). Women, minors, and the mentally incompetent are excluded from giving testimony in the lay inquest, just as they are ineligible to duel. Moreover, the rules regarding the relative social status of potential adversaries in a judicial duel are transposed onto the inquest: in general, only those of the same social class are allowed to testify either on behalf of or against one another. Thus, even when the purported object of juridical procedure was some reconstruction of the facts of a case, a witness was initially accepted or rejected according to criteria related primarily to his social standing. It was only after a witness's status had been determined in this manner that his knowledge could come into play.

If a witness was not disqualified during the initial confrontation of the parties, Beaumanoir indicates that he would then take the testimonial oath in open court and proceed to give his testimony. The jurist reports that after taking the oath, the witness would respond to the questions put to him in secret by an *auditeur*, who would record this deposition in writing and deliver it, sealed, to the judge. Once witnesses had deposed under oath, according to Beaumanoir, the dispute was to be settled on the basis of their sworn statements ("doit estre la querele determinee selonc la deposicion de leur tesmoignage"; 106). Because the witness had successfully passed the initial test of *renommée* and had taken the testimonial oath, his deposition acquired the status of reliable evidence. There was no means to contest a testimony that had been legally deposed; the only opportunity to challenge a witness came during the initial confrontation of the parties that preceded the inquest proper.

Beaumanoir describes some exceptions to the procedure I have just outlined, however. These exceptions, far from constituting a departure from traditional modes of juridical deliberation, reveal the degree to which the medieval inquisition depended on the folk-law principle of ethical recognition to function satisfactorily. In his chapter detailing the circumstances that would either allow or require a duel, as opposed to an inquest, Beaumanoir mentions the case of a dispute between strangers. Because one cannot evaluate their *renommée*, there is no choice regarding which procedure to follow: their case must be settled with a duel ("Et s'ils sont estrange, que l'en ne puist savoir leur renomee, li gage font a recevoir"; 1815). Since there is no way of passing judgment on the reputation of the parties in question, there is no way to establish their capacity to give in testimony; hence, one must take recourse to the duel.

This suggests that the smooth functioning of the inquisitional procedure Beaumanoir describes elsewhere in his customal depends upon its deployment in a relatively circumscribed community. If the parties in the dispute are unknown to the community called upon to adjudicate between them, the inquest as it was then undertaken was inadequate to the task, since it depended on the capacity of parties to make ethical evaluations both of one another and of any witnesses. Early inquisitional procedure thus ultimately proved heavily indebted to folklaw, precisely because it continued to admit witnesses according to the "irrational" criterion of *renommée*. Once a witness had been deemed legitimate, rational means of evaluation were applied to his testimony. However, since it was necessary to lodge objections against a witness *before* that witness's account of the matter in question would even be deposed as testimony, the epistemic basis of his testimony was to play no role in the court's initial determination of his eligibility to testify. Beaumanoir corroborates this view in a striking way when he notes that while the underage are ineligible to be witnesses, they can testify about events that happened in their youth after they come of age (1198). The witness is not the youth who obtained firsthand knowledge about something, but the adult who is admitted as a deponent. Ultimately, then, both the juridical legitimacy and the credibility of the witness rested on ethical criteria applied to him at the time he testified.

MANDEVILLE'S CHRISTIAN ETHOS

Mary B. Campbell writes in her study of the "witness and the other world" that "Neither power nor talent gives a travel writer his or her authority, which comes only and crucially from experience" (3). However, John Mandeville's *Travels*, one of the best known and most widely read medieval travel narratives, belies this principle. Mandeville's book puts the authority of experience into question not because its author apparently didn't actually see most of what he wrote about, but because the rhetoric of eyewitness testimony in Mandeville's book does not consist in the reiterated staging of firsthand experience. Following juridical protocols, Mandeville foregrounds his ethical status even though he purports to be speaking from firsthand experience. His status as a reliable witness is consolidated through his concerted efforts to stage himself as a Christian knight, and thus as a prominent member of the very community he addresses in the *Travels*.[5] From the standpoint of the jurist, whether

---

[5] As Iain Higgins notes in his recent book about Mandeville, "[Mandeville's] *Book* is the work of someone whose authority comes not simply from his own experiences, but also from his membership in a privileged stratum of the larger Christian

Mandeville's purported experiences offered new information or whether they mainly recycled pre-conceived notions about the East mattered less for the credibility of his testimony than did his ethical orientation as a witness. Thus, I wish here to set aside the question of whether Mandeville "really saw" everything the text implies he has seen; rather, what shall interest me are the ways in which Mandeville attempts to establish the reliability of his testimony. Although Mandeville's account supposedly *records* firsthand experiences, it does not draw its *authority* from those experiences.

In most versions of the manuscript, Mandeville's book begins by announcing a series of seemingly non-negotiable presuppositions: "Since it is so that the land beyond the sea, that is to say the land of repromission, that men call the Holy Land, among all other lands is the most worthy land and sovereign of all other, and is blessed and sacred and hallowed of the blood of our Lord Jesu Christ . . ." (1; "Comme il soit ainsi que la terre doultre mer, cest assavoir la terre sainte, la terre de promission, entre toutes autres soit la plus excellente et la plus digne et dame et souveraine de toutes autres terres; et soit benoite, saintefiee et consacree du precieux corps et du precieux sanc nostre seigneur Ihesu Crist. . . ."; 229).[6] Mandeville's "since" (*"comme"* in the French) positions what follows it as a series of premises that his audience will accept without argument – as, indeed, we may suppose his original public did. The passage thus not only sheds light on the eyewitness narrator's ethical stance; it also locates the narrator as a member of the same community as his listeners and readers, a community that shares the fundamental presuppositions Mandeville lays out here. Moreover, a little further on, we learn that this member of the Christian community is not merely one among many; he is in fact exemplary: "[I tell my story] specially for them that will and are in purpose to visit the holy city of Jerusalem and the holy places that are there about; and I shall tell the way that they shall hold thither, for I have many times passed and ridden it in good company of lords" (3; "Je parleray . . . especialement pour ceuls qui volente ont de visiter la cite de Ieru-

---

community" (54). Despite his sensitivity to the complexity of the figure of Mandeville, Higgins ultimately grants to experience a much larger role in authorizing Mandeville's account than I believe is justified, given how seldom first-person experiences are recounted there.

[6] I cite from Malcolm Letts's edition of the Egerton text and give his Paris text in parentheses.

salem et les sains lieux qui entour sont; et leur deviseray et demonsterray quel chemin ilz pourroient tenir, car jen ay par maint passe et chevauchie avecques bonne compagnie, Dieu grace"; 231). Mandeville invites his readers to follow in his footsteps. Whether they will be willing to do so depends less on the fact that Mandeville casts his account of the East as an experience than on the potential affinity his audience feels for his ethical stance. Mandeville exploits his readers' willingness to identify with him via a shared *ethos*, staking his credibility on the degree to which his readers feel that they resemble him. Thus, at the same time that Mandeville distinguishes himself as someone who has traveled east at a time when very few of his readers were doing so, he reinforces a sense of community with those same readers by representing his achievement as one that they have both the desire and the potential to realize themselves. Consequently, Mandeville's staging of himself as an eyewitness never produces an ethical divide between the eyewitness and his audience, and the community referred to by his frequent second-person address ("you" or "vous") tends to be both generally identifiable and reliably stable.

This analysis is borne out by the fact that Mandeville rarely appears as an experiencing subject in the narrative of the East proper. Although he casts the mantle of experience over his account as a whole, he actually presents very little of his material in the form of experiences related in the first person. The few specific experiences Mandeville does recount only serve to reinforce the integrity of his *ethos*, and not to set him apart from his audience. In Egypt, for example, he forgoes "a great prince's daughter and ... many great lordships" because he refuses to abjure his Christian faith (25). The members of his Christian audience – according to their own ideals – would certainly have behaved in the same way. Rather than a moment in which novel experiences as such come to the fore, then, his episode in effect allows Mandeville to stage the *ethos* he shares with his public in the form of a concrete act.

There are very few instances where Mandeville is represented as having any sort of exchange with the East. One is to be found in the Cotton, Bodleian and Egerton manuscripts, where we learn about a waterless sea teeming with fish, and that "I John Mandeville ate of them" (190). However, the explicit claim that Mandeville has eaten of these fish is absent from other manuscripts, including the Paris text (190 n2): Mandeville tends to gather knowledge about foreign lands without transgressing the boundaries of his own body. His inclination to remain untouched by his experiences is entirely coherent, given that the aim of his eyewitness testimony is to reaffirm the values of his community. Always the observer, never the participant, Mandeville sees the East without taking it in, since he apparently remains impervious to eastern influences. The many exotic alphabets Mandeville transcribes are emblematic in this regard: they remain largely meaningless symbols, something a reader could literally see for himself and at the same time fail utterly to comprehend or appropriate in any meaningful sense. All of this ensures that, even while he transmits the East to his European audience, Mandeville is never identified as anything other than a western Christian. In a rather transparent move near the end of the account, the Egerton text further strengthens the ethical link between Mandeville and his western Christian audience by asserting that "our holy father the Pope has ratified and confirmed my book in all points" (222). We are clearly quite far from a claim to authority based on experience here.

Ultimately, Mandeville the individual, "experienced" traveler never supersedes Mandeville the representative Christian knight; the ethical eyewitness has absolute priority over the experiential eyewitness in the *Travels*. The only lessons Mandeville learns on this trip – even from an Egyptian sultan – are Christian lessons (in French, no less; 97-99). The most exotic thing he ingests is the water of a *fons juventutis*, which "they say . . . comes from Paradise terrestrial" (122) – that is, from a Christian source. Indeed, Mandeville hardly eats or drinks anything on his entire journey; his sensual relation to the East is overwhelmingly visual. If one were to remove from the Mandeville corpus all of the descriptions that depended upon more than purely visual scrutiny, one would leave most of the account intact. Mandeville's experiences never really course through his blood; indeed, they don't even get under his skin. Even the Valley Perilous, wherein dwell "devils," is a visual feast of "gold and silver and precious stones and many other jewels," or so he thinks, since he "never touched anything" there.[7]

Because Mandeville the eyewitness moves in a thoroughly Christian universe, he invites his audience into an ethically familiar

---

[7] The Paris text contains a much longer version of this episode, including a section in which Mandeville receives a wound so severe that he faints and has visions of "moults de merveilles, dont je nose parler" (392).

world, and not an "other" world. As a consequence, the weight of Mandeville's achievement lies not in his ability to mimic the rhetoric of experience; it lies, rather, in the virtuosic ways in which Mandeville was able to *bear* witness to the beliefs of an entire culture. (In this, he bears more than a passing resemblance to Dante's pilgrim.) It is precisely this privileging of *ethos* that justifies Iain Higgins's recent reading of Mandeville's book as a "representative witness to [medieval] Latin Christendom's actual and imagined relations with other cultures" (14). This does not mean, of course, that Mandeville never evinces a critical attitude towards Western Christendom. Rather, as the subsequent discussion of Marco Polo will help make clear, it means that he never flirts with any sort of identification with or assimilation of eastern culture. Carlo Ginzburg's account of a sixteenth-century miller's heterodox reading of Mandeville in *The Cheese and the Worms* suggests that the community Mandeville was addressing would in time disintegrate; no longer could Mandeville's stance be considered to approximate that of the increasingly broad range of people who would come in contact with his ever-more-popular book. There is thus nothing *inherently* orthodox about Mandeville's testimony; rather, its orthodoxy can only be determined with reference to its various audiences. Like any testimonial performance, Mandeville's *Travels* do not generate cultural meanings all on their own, but in dialogue with their addressees.

Mandeville's testimony shows that the eyewitness has not always grounded his credibility in his experience, even when he is supposedly testifying *about* experience. Rather than stake his authority on the premise that he knows what he is testifying about firsthand, Mandeville ensures that his audience will recognize his ethical status as their own.

"An Orientalized Venetian"

That Mandeville's version of the east was the more appealing to his western Christian audience than was Marco Polo's to his seems beyond question – that is, if the quantity of reproductions of Mandeville's account is any indication of its popularity and if we can link popularity with perceived credibility, or, better put, with audience sympathy. In her edition of Mandeville, Christiane Deluz reports that Mandeville's account survives in over 300 medieval manuscripts; the epoch of print produced eighty editions in eight languages between 1478 and 1592 (26). Polo, by contrast, survives in around 150 medieval manuscripts, and only really took off in print, with twenty-four editions during the sixteenth century (Larner 160).

John Critchley attributes the lack of influence of Marco Polo's travel account to its supposedly conventional character, and maintains that the book is full of commonplaces, not just about the East, but about the Tartars: "Polo's readers had their own picture of the Khan, which Polo reinforced" (98). Yet Polo's account was not simply ignored; it was actively disbelieved by his contemporaries. Such a reaction would be puzzling if, as Critchley claims, all of the "incredible stories were ones [his audience] had heard before" (83), unless there were other reasons for disbelieving them. Moreover, on those rare occasions when a medieval reader or scribe professes to believe Polo's account, the actual content of the *Travels* – its portrait of Mongol society or of Kublai Khan – is never cited. Even in the event that Polo's depiction of Asia was old news to his medieval audience, then, this depiction does not appear to have been the primary basis upon which the medieval public made judgments about his credibility.

In order to counter Critchley's view that Polo's account had little impact on his contemporaries, John Larner cites an early fourteenth-century French scribe who apparently had faith in Polo's account: "Ci commencent les rebriches de cest livre qui est appellez «Le Devisement du monde», lequel je Grigoires contrescris du livre du messire Marc Pol, le meilleur citoien de Venisse creant Crist" (*Devisement* 29, correcting Benedetto xxxiv; "Here begin the pages of the book called "Le Devisement du monde," which I Grégoire copied from the book of Mr. Marco Polo, the best Christian citizen of Venice"). Grégoire's brief comment does not tell us whether he found the contents of Polo's book novel and strange, or reassuringly traditional. Nonetheless, if this is indeed an attempt to present Marco Polo as a credible source, it is not, as far as one can tell, founded on the scribe's acceptance of his depiction of the Tartars. The scribe characterizes the book itself only in terms of its author, whom he deems a prominent citizen of a prominent republic, and a Christian. Whether one takes this comment to support Larner's view that Polo's book was considered important, or Critchley's contention that it was considered unremarkable, then, it clearly reinforces the proposition that the account's credibility depended on that of its author, who is presented here exclusively in terms of his *ethos* and not his experience.

We can observe a similar attention to ethical identity, and a concomitant neglect of the question of experience, in virtually all of the few surviving medieval evaluations of Polo's book. In the Italian preface to his 1320 Latin translation of the account, Francesco Pipino reassures potentially incredulous readers not by insisting that Marco saw everything for himself, but by asserting the integrity of all three travelling Polos:

> E acciò che le cose che noi non usiamo né avamo udite, le quali sono scritte in molte parti di questo libro, no paiano incredibili a tutti quelli che le leggeranno, si dinota e fa manifesto che 'l sopradetto messer Marco, rapportator di queste cosí maravigliose cose, fu uomo savio, fedele, devote e adornato d'onesti costumi, avendo buona testimonianza da tutti quelli che lo conoscevano, sí che pel merito di molte sue virtú questo suo rapportamento é degno di fede; e messer Nicolò suo padre, uomo di tanta sapienza, similmente le confermava; e messer Maffio suo barba (del quale questo libro fa menzione), come vecchio devoto e savio, essendo sul ponto della morte, familiarmente parlando affermò al suo confessore sopra la conscienza sua che questo libro in tutte le cose contenava la verità (cited in Ramusio 3.76-77)

> And so that the things that we are not accustomed to or have not heard of, that appear in many parts of this book, do not seem incredible to all those who read it, it is hereby noted and declared that the above-mentioned Marco, who gave the report of these almost marvelous things, was a wise, faithful and devout man of honest habits, which is attested by everyone who knew him, such that on account of the merits of his many virtues, this his report is worthy of credit; and Mr Nicolò his father, a man of great wisdom, likewise confirmed it; and Mr Maffeo his uncle (who is mentioned in this book), a devout and learned old man, affirmed in all good conscience, on his deathbed in private conversation with his confessor, that everything recounted in this book was true

Here, Marco is the object, not the subject, of testimony: everyone who knows him vouches for his integrity. He is wise, loyal, devout, and has honest habits. His father and uncle incarnate essentially the same qualities. Whereas Marco's account itself foregrounds the degree to which he was steeped in Mongol culture, Pipino, unlike Ramusio, never mentions this; nor does he cite any information from the account proper as evidence of its integrity.

Anyone who seeks to evaluate the credibility of Marco Polo's eyewitness narrator on the basis of his ethical stance will find that his *ethos* remains extremely elusive. He is briefly described in the prologue to the account of his travels as "a wise and learned citizen of Venice"; however, the rest of the book lends virtually no support to that claim, and indeed effectively serves to undermine it. Whereas Mandeville's initial address to the reader announces a journey to the center of the Christian universe, Polo's principal journey takes him to the farthest reaches of the East. And while Mandeville suggests that his journeys to the east were motivated by his duty as a "right heir of Christ" to travel to the holy lands, Marco Polo's travels throughout the Mongol empire are motivated by his service to the Great Khan. Of course, Marco's father and uncle do initially undertake a Christian mission, when the Great Khan reportedly asks them to request that the Pope send him a hundred Christian sages ("cent sages hommes de [nostre] loy crestienne"; 123). Nonetheless, while Niccolò and Maffeo do ultimately function as representatives of Latin Christendom, bringing holy oil and papal letters to the Great Khan, young Marco is merely along for the ride. The elder Polos are the ones described as having been charged with the original mission, and they are explicitly designated as the men who carry it out. When the two Dominicans accompanying the Venetian merchants on their second journey to the Mongol empire turn back in fear as war breaks out in Armenia, they transfer the letters and privileges with which they were entrusted to Nicolò and Maffeo, not to Marco ("il donnerent a mesire Nicolo et a mesire Mafe Pol toutes les chartes et tous les previleges que il avoient"; 127). Moreover, shortly after these documents are delivered to the Mongol emperor, Marco himself becomes an ambassador of the Khan ("quant le Seignour vit qu'il estoit si sages et de si biau portement, si l'envoia en son message"; 129). After the prefatory chapters, we hear nothing more about the project of bringing Christianity to the Far East.

It becomes increasingly clear that in transferring his ambassadorial allegiances from the Pope to the Great Khan, Polo has done much more than trade one sovereign for another; he has traded one *ethos* for another. The impression that Polo has "gone native" is only confirmed as the account proper unfolds. We are told that Marco mastered the customs, languages, and scripts of the Tartars and those they governed in marvelously short order ("Marc, le filz de monseignour Nicolo, aprist si bien la coustume des Tatars et lor langage et lor lettre . . . que ce fu merveilles. Et sachiez vraiement, il sot en pou de temps de pluseurs langages et sot de .IIII. lettres de lor escriptures"; 129). After we learn that Marco has thoroughly assimilated Mongol culture, we see Kublai Khan slowly emerge as both the physical and the metaphysical center of Marco Polo's account, in much the same way that John Mandeville's will be centered on Jerusalem. Where Mandeville plots virtually every phenomenon he recounts onto an explicitly Christian grid, Polo organizes his material with reference to the Khan and to the imperial city of Kin-sai. Towns and cities are more numerous, prosperous and civilized as the account nears the Mongol capital, and increasingly scarce, disordered and "barbarous" as Kin-sai grows distant.

Marco's alienation from his audience has several other facets. The network of exemplarity we can see in Mandeville – he is both imitating his Christian forefathers and setting an example for his Christian contemporaries – is lacking in Polo. Unlike Mandeville's exordium, Marco's prologue sets the traveler definitively apart from his medieval European audience. The scribe's portrait of the Venetian traveler indicates that Marco is the only one of his kind: "Since our Lord created Adam, our forefather, there has never been a man who knew as much nor researched as many different parts of the world as did Marco Polo. For this reason he thought that it would be a great pity if what he had truly heard and seen was not put into writing, so that people who had not heard or seen these things could know about them through this book" ("puis que Nostre Sire Diex fist Adam, [nostre] premier pere, ne fu onques homme de nul[e] generacion qui tant seust ne cerchast des diverses parties du monde comme cestui mesire Marc Pol en sot. Et pour ce pensa que ce seroit granz maus se ce ne feist metre en escrit ce que il avoit veu et oÿ par verité, a ce que l'autre gent que ne l'ont veu ne oÿ le sachent par cest livre"; 117-18). Marco's story is worth telling precisely because what it describes lies completely outside the boundaries of his audience's experience, and would presumably remain there were it not for "cest livre."

And this book, the prologue reminds us more than once, is the product of twenty-six years of firsthand experience in the East. As Polo (or rather his scribe, the writer of romances Rustigielo) reports, he went to Asia when he was about seventeen years old; he didn't return to the West until he was past forty. Thus, at the time he dictated his account of the East to his cellmate in a Genoese prison, he had spent more time in the East than in the West. While the appeal to the extent of Marco's own experiences in the East is clearly meant to enhance the authority of the account of those experiences, it ultimately exiles Polo from the community to which that account is delivered. In his venerable edition of the *Travels*, Sir Henry Yule called Marco Polo an "Orientalized Venetian" in connection with the somewhat peculiar, hybrid language of the original account (I:84). Indeed, within the account itself, Polo is rarely identifiable as a medieval Christian. Viewed from the perspective of medieval law, this fact, more than the status of Polo's account as innovative or derivative, most likely determined the relatively unenthusiastic reception of Marco's book in the Middle Ages. The Tartar *je ne sais quoi* Ramusio ascribes to Polo ultimately damaged his credibility in the eyes of his Christian contemporaries.

Polo's Tartar *ethos* is not the only element of his account that works to disrupt the ethical dialogue upon which credible testimony was based in the thirteenth and fourteenth centuries. While I have been talking about the text thus far as if its historical audience were roughly identical to the medieval Christians addressed by Mandeville, there are only intermittent indications within it that this was indeed the case (most notably when, early in the first of the account's three books, Marco describes two miracles he attributes to the Christian God). Whereas Mandeville's book literally maps out the physical territory and the corresponding values of the community he means to address, Polo's text ultimately offers very few bearings according to which the intended reader or listener may be situated. It opens with a call to "Emperors, Kings, Dukes, Marquises, Earls, and Knights, and all people who wish to know the different generations of men and the diversities of the different lands of the world." Despite its conventional nature, the first part of this phrase does of course project an identifiable audience: European nobles. But the scope of the address subsequently expands radically, extending to "all people" who are curious to know about other parts of the world. We might imagine that Polo's text thereby becomes theoretically available to a potentially much larger group of people than Mandeville's (and indeed, it is certainly more accessible to a modern reader than is Mandeville's book, for many of the same reasons it failed to convince a medieval European public). When we recall the medieval juridical model of testimony as a dialogic encounter among members of the same community, however, the appeal to the masses becomes rather problematic. By virtue of pretending to be able to address "all people," Polo's account ultimately addresses no single group in particular. (It is thus no surprise that the identity of Polo's historical intended audience remains a subject of scholarly debate.) Without a readily identifiable addressee, the testimonial dialogue that Polo's account is to stage loses the moorings that structure credibility in the medieval context.

The desire to know about the particular things contained in the account of Marco Polo's travels ultimately has its origins in the Mongol emperor, who, we learn, would rather hear about new things and learn about the customs of different places than have a report on the business undertaken on his behalf by his ambassadors ("J'ameroie miex a oïr les nouveles choses et les manieres de diverses contrees que ce pour quoi tu es alez"; 123). Marco's very motive for travel, as well as the reason he tries to register with some precision everything he sees on his journey, is the emperor's interest in hearing about the more remote corners of the realm; he thus becomes both an eyewitness and a narrator at the behest of the Khan. Consequently, when we read Marco Polo, we read material that is presented as having been originally intended for the Mongol emperor. If the non-noble members of Polo's audience found themselves cast in the prologue in the amorphous role of someone who wishes to know about the East, and in particular, the Mongol Empire, the body of the account attributes this role to Kublai Khan. There is a parallel established here between the Mongol emperor and Marco's European readers, since both become Polo's addressees by virtue of being people who are interested in hearing about the people and places of the Far East. If Marco serves as the Khan's eyes, those who receive the account of his travels are obliged to appropriate the Khan's ears. Polo's earliest readers were thus invited to make an imaginative identification with the Mongol emperor they may very well have resisted.

The call to give in testimony not only models a desire for that testimony; it also partially *authorizes* the testimony thus elicited.

The author of the call to testify acts as a legitimating point of origin with reference to which the testimony itself is justified as testimony. Thus, when Polo's narrator goes on to explain that the Khan's desire for news of the far-flung reaches of his empire led Marco to make a special effort to learn as much as he could about the people and places he encountered, so that he could tell the Khan about them when he returned to the capital ("car il moult desirroit a entendre estranges choses, si que pour ce, alant et venant, [Marco] y mist moult s'entente de savoir de toutes diverses choses selonc les contrees, a ce que a son retour le puisse dire au Grant Caan"; 130), Kublai Khan is positioned as the primary person before whom Polo means to bear witness. This would in fact explain why Polo's account lends him a Mongol *ethos*: Marco implicitly assumed that his original addressee would require such a stance from his ambassadorial witness. However, when Marco's testimony reaches a different audience with a distinct *ethos*, his ethical credibility will necessarily be compromised.

"JE, QUI VOUS FAIS CES VERITABLES CONTES"

The medieval juridical tendency to define the witness in terms of the moment in which he deposes entails a conception of testimony for which the dialogic situation of the testimonial utterance is central. In medieval narrative literature, as in the eyewitness travel account, the dialogue between narrator and audience implies an ethical relation that will determine the credibility of the material thus presented. The fictional mock-epics of François Rabelais explore the status of this dialogue at the end of the Middle Ages, and allow us to present a preliminary sketch of the trajectory of the ethical witness from the time of Mandeville into the beginning of the sixteenth century. In his first book in particular, the 1532 *Pantagruel*, Rabelais's adaptations of medieval popular tales grapple with the question of credible testimony, satirizing the ethical model while struggling to find an alternative to it.

Pantagruel was published under the pseudonym of Alcofribas Nasier, and Alcofribas appears in the book as the first-person narrator of the giant Pantagruel's adventures. Though *Pantagruel* and its sequels draw on a wealth of materials, Alcofribas explicitly relates his "chronique" to the *chroniques gargantuines*, medieval popular tales that still circulated both orally and in chapbook form in Rabelais's time. Perhaps the best way to isolate Rabelais's contribution to the debates surrounding credible testimony is to juxtapose his novel to its purported medieval source and attempt to take the measure of the distances between them.

The narrators of the various versions of the medieval *chroniques gargantuines* engage in a direct dialogue with their audience, with whom they share a common perspective on the world referred to in the tales. Direct, second-person address, which comes across as unusual and even innovative in the contemporary novel after centuries of print, is one of the fundamental elements of medieval storytelling. The *Chroniques Inestimables*, the *Vroy Gargantua* and the *Chroniques Admirables* all begin: "Tous bons chevalliers et gentilz hommes vous debvez sçavoir que au tems du bon roy Artus il estoit ung grant philosophe nommé Merlin" (116; "All good knights and gentlemen, you must know that in the time of King Arthur there lived a great philosopher called Merlin"). This opening positions the narrator as a second person who bears witness to his public ("vous debvez sçavoir" – a phrase that is repeated over and over in the Paris text of Mandeville's *Travels*). Mireille Huchon writes that a trait all of the versions of the *chroniques* share is their tendency to employ expressions such as "you would have seen" that imply a "hypothetical presence" ("renvoyer à une hypothéthique présence dans des expressions qui mettent l'accent sur la suprématie du témoignage oculaire: «vous eussiez veu»"; Lauvergnat 88). Though Huchon is referring to the potential presence of the listener in the world of the story as a hypothetical eyewitness to the adventures recounted therein, such expressions, with their direct address, also serve as indices of the copresence of poet and audience.

In addition to linking poet and audience, these opening lines establish another important relationship, that between the audience and the story world ("tous bons chevalliers et gentilz hommes" to the "tems du bon roy Artus"). This is a world, according to the prologue, about which listeners must necessarily have knowledge. The link between the word *sçavoir* and the actual phenomenon of knowing is here forged by the chronicle itself: *vous debvez sçavoir que...* points to the very words which follow it in the chronicle as that which will in fact constitute the knowledge of all good knights and gentlemen. If one reads or hears the chronicle, one will naturally know its contents; the opening of the *chroniques* thus creates its own ideal audience by collapsing the act of reading or hearing and the fact of knowing. This opening phrase, then, has the effect of controlling and containing, within the language of the story itself, the encounter between the "gentlemen" of the audience and the *chroniques*.

A third relationship, that of narrator to story world, is also implied in these opening phrases. We are made to understand that our narrator has never actually lived in this world; rather, his ability to narrate comes from the fact that he already knows the contents of the chronicle (just as the audience should know them). The origins of this knowledge are made explicit in the *Vroy Gargantua*, the *Admirables* and the *Grande et merveilleuse vie*, all of which contain a "prologue capital" that cites various prior sources for the story to follow. Such a prologue serves to accentuate the real distance between the narrator and the world of the story (since he apparently needs to rely on others' accounts of it) even as it presumably decreases the imaginative distance between narrator and audience, on the one hand, and the story world, on the other (since the narrator has gone to such great lengths to reconstruct it). The narrator's citation – from the Latin *citare*, "to call as a witness" – of numerous exterior sources tells audience members that they are not about to hear the individual and idiosyncratic testimony of the narrator himself, but rather, that of an entire tradition. The narrator's task is to reconstruct that tradition.

The narrator and the audience are ultimately put in the same position with respect to the world of the story: they share the same perspective on that world, and the poet literally shares it when he tells the tale. Narrator and audience are thus co-witnesses in terms of "seeing" the world of the story; when the poet tells the tale, he functions as a witness of/for the tradition. Neither the poet nor the audience are "third persons" with respect to that tradition, since it is, importantly, *their* tradition. But neither are they isolated individuals with respect to it. The tale does not belong to the poet, but to both the poet and the audience. The audience "must know" this story because it is in fact *their* story.

The ethical elements of oral epic narration thus go well beyond the mere fact of the physical encounter of narrator and audience. The idea that the "singer of tales" actively if subconsciously adapts traditional songs and stories to his particular context has long been accepted (Lord; Ong; Havelock); an oral poet modifies his material in response to the explicit reaction or implicit orientation of his audience. The oral tale is thus a profoundly dialogic production. This isn't to posit a utopian Middle Ages where groups of essentially anonymous people formed homogeneous communities in which all could participate equally, but rather to emphasize the degree to which oral poetry, like any live performance, involves a dialogic exchange between artist and audience.

As we have seen, John Mandeville, like the narrators of the *chroniques*, more or less assumes that his readers share his ethical perspective. Marco Polo, by contrast, manages to drive a wedge between himself and his public. Rabelais's narrator will also disrupt his ethical relationship to his audience, but in a far more self-conscious manner. Both the prologue and the main text of *Pantagruel* are full of retorts to the imagined objections of audience members, invective against uncharitable interpreters, and asides to potentially skeptical addressees. Alcofribas's adversarial posture serves to distance him from his audience; his defensive indignation suggests that his perspective is an isolated and alienated one. In *Pantagruel,* Rabelais stages the point of view of an individual that short-circuits the ethical dialogue between narrator and audience.

In the opening of the prologue to *Pantagruel*, Alcofribas Nasier seems to assume the narrative stance characteristic of the *chroniques,* in which an entire tradition is invoked to bear witness to the authority of the story to follow: "Tresillustres et Tresche-valereux champions, gentilz hommes, et aultres, qui voluntiers vous adonnez à toutes gentillesses et honnestetez, vous avez n'a gueres veu, leu et seu les *Grandes et inestimables Chronicques de l'énorme géant Gargantua*: et comme vrays fidèles, les avez creues, gualantement, et y avez maintesfoys passé vostre temps avecques les honorables Dames et Damoyselles, leur en faisans beaulx et longs narrez, alors que estiez hors de propos" (213; "Most illustrious and thrice valorous champions, gentlemen and others, who willingly apply your minds to the entertainment of pretty conceits and honest harmless knacks of wit; you have not long ago seen, read, and understood the great and inestimable Chronicle of the huge and mighty giant Gargantua, and, like upright faithfullists, have firmly believed all to be true that is contained in them, and have very often passed your time with them amongst honourable ladies and gentlewomen, telling them fair long stories, when you were out of all other talk"). [8] "Vous avez ... veu, leu, et seu ... et ... [creu]" simply asserts a series of propositions about the reader and a text, much like the "vous debvez sçavoir" of the *Inestimables*. Further on in the prologue, Alcofribas expresses his wish that everyone learn the *chroniques* by heart; he would turn every reader into a potential narrator: "Et à la mienne volunté que chascun laissast sa propre besoigne, ne se souciast de son mestier et mist ses affaires propres en oubly, pour y vacquer entièrement, sans que son esperit feust de ailleurs distraict ny empesché: jusques à ce que l'on les tint par cueur, affin que si d'adventure l'art de l'Imprimerie cessoit, ou en cas que tous livres perissent, on temps advenir un chascun les peust bien au net enseigner à ses enfans, et à ses successeurs et survivens bailler comme de main en main, ainsy que une religieuse Caballe" (213; "And I do heartily wish that every man would lay aside his own business, meddle no more with his profession nor trade, and throw all affairs concerning himself behind his back, to attend this wholly, without distracting or troubling his mind with anything else, until he have learned them without book; that if by chance the art of printing should cease, or in case that in time to come all books should perish, every man might truly teach them unto his children, and deliver them over to his successors and survivors from hand to hand as a religious cabal"). The oral transmission of the *chroniques* as depicted in Alcofribas's prologue is a process whereby the language of the circulating story replaces the discourse of its readers. When the chivalrous gentlemen are *hors de propos* – that is, when they have nothing (of their own) left to say – they may simply appropriate the *chroniques gargantuines*, making its *propos* their own. As Alcofribas describes it, the process of oral transmission entails that the individual narrator surrender that which is uniquely his ("sa propre besoigne ... son mestier ... ses affaires propres") in order to narrate. This process is thus predicated on the effacement of the narrator's own particular voice (he is "hors de propos" – "out of words") and of his personal history ("sa propre besoigne"). According to this model, the individual act of narration does not shape or modify the substance of the story, but rather perpetuates

---

[8] All references to Rabelais's writings in French are to Mireille Huchon's edition of the *Oeuvres complètes*, with page numbers given in the main text and the abbreviation *OC* used where necessary for clarity. English versions are taken from Urquhart's 1653 translation.

it. This model is entirely consonant with the type of narrator that we actually do see in the *chroniques gargantuines*.

The credibility of Alcofribas's first-person account, however, is ultimately predicated on competing claims that stand in tension with the model provided by the *chroniques*. After invoking the tradition of the popular tales, Alcofribas goes on to experiment with several different versions of narrative authority, all of which implicate distinct conceptions of the narrative witness. There are two significantly different variants of the most relevant passage, which together propose at least three possible models of a witness. In pre-1542 editions of *Pantagruel*, the passage reads as follows: "[Il] ne m'advint oncques de mentir, ou asseurer chose que ne feust veritable. J'en parle comme Saint Jehan de Lapocalypse: *Quod vidimus testamur.* C'est des horribles faictz et prouesses de Pantagruel, lequel j'ay servy à gaiges dés ce que je fuz hors de page jusques à présent" (215; "neither did it ever befall me to lie, or affirm a thing for true that was not. I speak of it like [St John of the Apocalypse]. Quod vidimus, testamur. It is of the horrible and dreadful feats and prowesses of Pantagruel, whose menial servant I have been ever since I was a page, till this hour"). John's narrative in Revelations comes from a vision given to him by Christ. In effect, John reads the narrative that Christ has written. If Alcofribas bears witness in the manner of St. John of the Apocalypse, he makes a claim, however parodic, for nothing less than divine revelation. This ultimately amounts to a position analogous to that assumed by the narrators of the *chroniques*, in that it assigns to the narrator-witness the role of the transparent mediator of a shared tradition.

As several readers of Rabelais have noted, however, the words "Quod vidimus testamur" are not from Revelations, but from the Gospel of John. In John 3, Jesus is trying to explain to the Pharisee Nicodemus how it is possible for a man to be born again. The verses leading up to the phrase Alcofribas cites are concerned primarily with setting forth the distinction between the spiritual and the earthly realms; it is in the spiritual realm, Jesus says, that man must be reborn if he is to enter the kingdom of God. Nicodemus, however, fails to grasp this distinction. Jesus responds, in the Vulgate: "Amen amen dico tibi quod scimus loquimur et quod vidimus testamur et testimonium nostrum non accipitis. Si terrena dixi vobis et non credetis: quomodo si dixero vobis celestia credetis" (King

James Version: "Verily, verily, I say unto thee, We speak that we do know, and testify that we have seen; and ye receive not our witness. If I have told you of earthly things, and ye believe not, how shall ye believe, if I tell you of heavenly things?"). Two very different modes of seeing are at issue here; the first is a physical, earthly seeing, "of the flesh"; the second is the New Testament kind of seeing Jesus has been trying to explain, which is "of the Spirit." Though some readers of Rabelais have taken Alcofribas's allusion to evoke the second, spiritual type of seeing (and thus of reading), it is not at all clear which of the two modes is designated by Jesus's "vidimus" in the Biblical verse.[9] Since Jesus's reference to his testimony of earthly things is in the past tense ("dixi") and his reference to his testimony of spiritual things is in the future perfect ("dixero"), one could argue that his present-tense "vidimus" in fact refers to some past act of earthly seeing. The Biblical allusion in early editions thus complicates, rather than resolves, the question of Alcofribas's status as *testis*. If Alcofribas is claiming to have "seen" in some spiritual manner, however, we must be prepared to read spiritually, that is, to seek the spirit behind the letter; this view would send us off on the search for hidden meanings – the very allegorical mode of reading that Rabelais describes so ambiguously in the prologue to *Gargantua*.

To complicate matters further, in the 1542 edition, Rabelais replaces the allusion to the two Johns with something quite different: "J'en parle comme un gaillard Onocratale, voyre dy je crotenotaire des martyrs amans et croquenotaire de amours: Quod vidimus testamur" (1238; "a lusty frolic onocrotary, I should say crotenotary of the martyrized lovers, and croquenotary of love"). Here we have Alcofribas's comic assertion of his personal probity, which invites us to read his testimony in light of his character. This is an unambiguous evocation of the ethical model of the witness we have been examining in the context of medieval law and travel testimony. If this is the model we are to apply, then we are dealing with a simple parody of testimony, and we can decide fairly easily that nothing Alcofribas says should be regarded as credible, or even credit-seeking.

All three of these models of the narrative witness – the divinely-inspired prophet; the author of allegories; and the tall tale-teller –

---

[9] Edwin Duval believes the primary function of the passage is to set up a general opposition between (Christian) revelation (that is, spiritual seeing) and (Jewish) law (linked to earthly seeing). See *The Design of Rabelais's Pantagruel* 6-11.

have antecedents that were well known to Rabelais's more learned reading public (in the Bible, Dante's *Divina Commedia*, and Lucian's *True History*, respectively). The prologue offers us one more alternative, however: the *serviteur à gaiges*, a witness who is meant to be imagined primarily as the human-sized companion of the giant whose chronicle he composes. It is the mise-en-scène of this last model of the eyewitness – an early version of what I have been calling the "epistemic witness" – that sheds the most light on the evolution of the discourse of witnessing in the early sixteenth century, and that ultimately accounts for the narrative innovation of Rabelais's book.

After the bold "Quod vidimus testamur" of the prologue, Alcofribas oscillates between two basic narrative positions. One is that of an eyewitness whose vision is both authorized and limited by the frontiers of his sense experience, and who is not necessarily able to understand or interpret what he experiences; the other is that of a historian with a broad knowledge of events and characters that extends far beyond anything he may have seen, touch, tasted or smelled, knowledge which he uses to shape the narrative into a coherent, synthetic form. By juxtaposing these two different types of narrator within the single figure of Alcofribas, Rabelais stages the broader conflict between epistemic and ethical witnessing, and between novelistic and epic narration.

The epic perspective requires a distanced observer capable of bringing together the elements necessary to construct a heroic story. This is the process we see described in the "prologues capitaux" to the *Vroy Gargantua*, the *Admirables* and the *Grande et merveilleuse vie*, where the narrator describes his archival research; it is also evident at the beginning of *Pantagruel*. Citing textual precedents – and not personal experience – as his justification, Alcofribas opens chapter one of *Pantagruel* with a comprehensive genealogy that extends back to the very origins of Pantagruel's race of giants around the time of Cain and Abel. He is concerned to establish "la première source et origine" of his subject, "au commencement du monde" (217), and thus to adopt the position of what Edwin Duval has called a "sacred historian," who reconstitutes the history of his ethical community.

In the chapters immediately following the genealogy, Alcofribas's role continues to be that of a historian whose function is to reconstruct a chronicle of Pantagruel's birth, childhood, and education. Early chapters contain frequent direct addresses to the reader, which serve to position Alcofribas in the world of his audience, rather than in the world of the giant Pantagruel. Despite his claim to have been Pantagruel's companion, Alcofribas does not appear as a character inside the story he is telling until chapter seventeen, where we find him walking down the streets of Paris with Pantagruel's friend, the trickster Panurge. As an epic narrator defined by his capacity to know the story he is telling, Alcofribas has no trouble in chapter sixteen recounting in detail Panurge's top sixty-three ways of obtaining money ("soixante et troys manières d'en trouver [de l'argent]"; 280). In chapter seventeen, however, Alcofribas is inside the story, at Panurge's side, and his ability to give a complete account of events – the aim of the narrators of both medieval epic and romance – appears to fail. He can only ask questions which position Panurge as narrator (e.g. "Dont avez-vous tant recouvert d'argent en si peu de temps?"; 286), and must now rely on Panurge to tell his own story.

This constitutes a significant shift in the narrator's relation to the story he tells. While the full title of the book and its opening chapters set up the story of Pantagruel as a comprehensive chronicle, Alcofribas's ability to sustain this type of narration is threatened at the very moment in which he is present as an experiencing eyewitness in the story. When Alcofribas enters the world of the characters in chapter seventeen, he must defer to Panurge's voice and to Panurge's narrative authority. This suggests that the epistemic eyewitness, immediately connected as he may be to a particular event, is in fact limited by this very immediacy. When Alcofribas limits his narrative testimony to that which he has seen for himself, the scope of his account narrows considerably. This in turn implies that the act of bearing ethical witness on behalf of a community, as do both the narrators of the *chroniques* and John Mandeville, is predicated on a certain distance with respect to the material thus transmitted; the expansive vision implicated by such a testimonial act slowly evaporates when the narrator gets too close to his subject.

After his close encounter with Panurge, Alcofribas exits the scene and reassumes his apparent omniscience. The fact that we have gotten a glimpse of him gathering material for his chronicle may have shaken our faith in the comprehensiveness of his mock-epic vision, but he quickly recovers from this lapse. In chapter 22, for example, he is privy to Panurge's amorous advances on the *haulte dame de Paris,* supposedly whispered to her in church. In chapter 28, as Pantagruel prepares for the duel with the evil Loup Garou that Edwin Duval positions as the "epic climax" of the narrative, Alcofribas enjoys relatively unlimited knowledge and mobility with respect to Pantagruel's world. He even draws attention to the ease with which he moves between Pantagruel's encampment and that of Loup Garou and Anarche: "Laissons icy Pantagruel avec ces apostoles," he says at one point, "et parlons du roy Anarche" (324). After a few paragraphs *chez* Anarche, he declares: "Maintenant, retournons au bon Pantagruel et racontons comment il se porta en cest affaire" (325). Such transitions manifest a narrative perspective conditioned by the generic norms of epic, norms which always put the narrator in a position to know, and which posit no other perspective outside of the one assumed by the narrative.

There is nothing strange about a narrator dutifully shuttling back and forth between hero and enemy in the context of the epic; however, these rather effortless shifts of focus are somewhat perplexing in light of Alcofribas's encounter with Panurge, where our narrator struggled to find out how Pantagruel's sidekick got his hands on so much money in such a short time. Most important, they are impossible to reconcile with Alcofribas's inability to see beyond Pantagruel's interior in chapter thirty-two. Every reader of Rabelais will recall the scene as this chapter opens: Having won the battle against Loup Garou, Pantagruel and his companions are off to finish the war against Pantagruel's arch-enemies, the Dipsodes, when they all get caught in a downpour. Alcofribas tells us that the giant unrolls his tongue as a sort of umbrella for his troops. Our *conteur* appears among them, and, seeing that there is no more room under Pantagruel's tongue, decides to climb up onto it and into the giant's mouth. At this moment, Alcofribas explicitly assumes both the position of an ethical witness who speaks directly to an audience, and that of an epistemic witness who has firsthand experience of the world of the story: "Je, qui vous fais ces tant veritables contes . . . cheminay bien deux lieues sus sa langue, tant que j'entray dedans sa bouche" (330-31; "I, who relate to you these so veritable stories . . . went along full two leagues upon his tongue, and so long marched that at last I came into his mouth"). Thus sheltered from the storm, Alcofribas encounters "un bon homme qui plantoit des choulx" (331), who verbally confirms the existence of an entire world inside the giant orifice. This world, as Terence Cave has noted, is far from exotic: "The points of reference are European, the religion is Christian, the cabbage planter a good imitation of a French peasant" ("Travelers" 40). Alcofribas, for his part, wastes no time settling down to enjoy the "beaulx grands jeux de paulme, belles galleries, belles praries, force vignes, et une infinité de cassines à la mode Italicque par les champs pleins de delices" (332). After running into trouble with some *brigands*, Rabelais's narrator finishes his stay in Pantagruel's mouth with a stint as a paid sleeper, "car l'on [y] loue les gens à journée pour dormir" (332), while a battle of giants rages outside between Pantagruel's troops and the Dipsodes.

Alcofribas's entry into the mouth of the giant raises complex questions about the status of a witness's experience relative to his *ethos*. Though the episode has numerous precedents in the *chroniques*, Rabelais's version explicitly problematizes medieval protocols of narrative testimony even as it freely adopts medieval themes. In the scenes where buccal voyages take place in the popular texts, Gargantua has either fallen asleep or is suffering from indigestion. It is important to note that in either case, he stops having adventures. Gargantua's sleep in effect stops his adventures cold; one might expect it to have a rather chilling effect on the narrative as well. However, the result is quite the contrary: Gargantua's naps provide material as vivid as any in the *chroniques*. The narrator does not simply stop narrating in the face of his protagonist's inactivity. Instead, he provides a glimpse of the interior of the giant's body, an interior which is necessarily hidden from view when we are invited to witness Gargantua's waking escapades. It is significant that it is only when these adventures are temporarily halted that is it possible for the narrator to assume a perspective which excludes the domain in which they take place. In light of this fact, Gargantua's slumber in the *chroniques* should be understood as a narrative strategy that puts his adventures on hold *so that* the narrative may adopt a different focus. The *chroniques* traditional narrative form, with its all-encompassing ethical vision, admits of no perspective outside of its own or of any point of view which would relativize it.

The *chroniques* commitment to projecting a unified point of view on the giant is made all the more evident by the fact that as soon as Gargantua does reawaken, some event occurs in the narrative that effectively serves to eliminate the interior point of view.

This elimination can be quite brutal; often, those who have fallen into the sleeping Gargantua's mouth are simply killed off when he wakes up. This is the case, for example, in the *Inestimables*. Some of the citizens of a city to which the giant has laid siege "tumboyent dedans la gueulle de Gargantua qui dormoit la gueulle ouverte . . . quand Gargantua fut esveillé il eut grand soif . . .: il alla à la rivière pour boire. . . . Lors les citoyens qui estoyent tombez en sa gueulle furent tous noyés" (138; "fell into the mouth of Gargantua, who was sleeping with his mouth open . . . when Gargantua woke up he was very thirsty . . . he went to the river to drink . . . whereupon the citizens who had fallen into his mouth were drowned"). Similarly, in the *Grande et merveilleuse vie*, "le Souldan qui avoit guerre contre les Chrestiens . . . trouva [Gargantua] contre une montaigne endormy la bouche ouverte pensoit que se fust une caverne et se mist dedans . . . mais se esveilla Gargantua et s'en alla boire à ung grant lac et churent tous dedans, et par la grace de Dieu furent noyez" (161; "the Sultan, who was engaged in a war with the Christians . . . found Gargantua on a mountain sleeping with his mouth open and, thinking it was a cave went in . . . but Gargantua woke up and went to drink at a great lake, and [the Sultan and his party] fell in and by the grace of God were drowned").

In the *chroniques gargantuines*, the protagonist's immobility creates a narrative situation in which a dimension of the giant previously hidden by the very perspective of the chronicle about him may be revealed and seamlessly integrated into that chronicle. The stories of swallowed citizens and sultans do not pull us away from Gargantua's story; rather, they are literally contained within that story, and thus can be understood simply as more of Gargantua's adventures – they just happen to take place while he's asleep. The relationship of the world in Pantagruel's mouth to the world outside of it in Rabelais's *Pantagruel*, by contrast, is not quite so neat. Whereas Gargantua's slumber allows the narrator of the *chroniques* to explore the giant's mouth without abdicating his position as chronicler of the giant's adventures, the buccal voyage in *Pantagruel* creates a complex, multi-layered narrative moment in which the narrator, Alcofribas, actually loses sight of his protagonist. Because Alcofribas commits himself to giving an account of the world in Pantagruel's mouth as an eyewitness defined by his experiences, and not by his ethical relationship to his audience, the question of his *individual* perspective comes to the fore.

Unlike the Gargantua of the *chroniques*, Pantagruel does not sleep through the narrative's detour into his mouth. Pantagruel is not only fully awake during Alcofribas's trip inside his mouth, he also continues to have adventures (six months' worth, in fact). What is more, the particular adventure that he has while Alcofribas tours his mouth is not just one among his many others: the battle between Pantagruel and the Dipsodes is in fact a key moment in the narrative of Pantagruel's *faictz et prouesses*. The crucial nature of this narrative juncture can be best explained by recalling Edwin Duval's epic reading of *Pantagruel*. Duval calls the book an "epic New Testament," and characterizes its overall narrative structure as "the forward-moving, teleological design of the epic quest." [10] In Duval's reading, Pantagruel's victory in chapter 29 over the invading Dipsode army led by Loup Garou effectively closes the heroic biography of the enlightened giant: "The heroic exploit performed by Pantagruel at the epic climax fulfills a prophecy contained in the first two chapters and brings about the final resolution toward which the entire book has moved."

At this point in the narrative, however, Pantagruel has won an important battle, but not the war. At the beginning of chapter thirty-one, immediately after he has vanquished Loup Garou and his troops, Pantagruel proposes to "prendre d'assault tout le Royaulme des Dipsodes" (328). Anticipating an easy victory, he starts making plans to install colonists from overcrowded Utopia in Dipsode territory. The description of the departure of the Utopian troops invokes a scene from the Old Testament: "Ainsi commencerent à marcher droict en Dipsodie en si bon ordre qu'ils ressembloyent es enfans d'Israël quand ils partirent de Egypte pour passer la mer rouge" (328). Now the stage is truly set for the culmination of Pantagruel's "epic New Testament," as Duval has described it. The children of Utopia are about to conquer the Dipsodian forces of darkness and install Pantagruel as enlightened king. And indeed, most of the vanquished Dipsodes welcome Pantagruel with open arms.

Most, but not all: there is a group of resistors, the Almyrodes, who refuse to surrender. As chapter thirty-two of *Pantagruel* opens, the Utopian army is poised to attack the recalcitrant Almyrodes. Victory is swift: by the end of chapter thirty-two, Pantagruel

---

[10] All citations from Duval here are from *A New History of French Literature* 157. Duval fully develops this thesis in *The Design of Rabelais's Pantagruel*.

and company have conquered the entirety of Dipsodie. But this summary is somewhat misleading. The story it tells is not exactly the story that Alcofribas tells us. The triumphant conquest of the Almyrodes is never actually reported – much less described in any detail – by our intrepid narrator. Indeed, Alcofribas gives absolutely no information about Pantagruel's final battle. Instead, the hero himself must tell his narrator that victory has been won. The entire story of this conquest is relegated to one line spoken by Pantagruel upon Alcofribas's exit from the mouth-world: "Quand il me apperceut, il me demanda: «Dont viens-tu, Alcofrybas?» Je luy responds: «De vostre gorge, Monsieur.» –Et despuis quand y es tu? dist il. –Despuis (dis je) que vous alliez contre les Almyrodes. –Il y a (dist il) plus de six moys. . . . Nous avons avecques l'ayde de dieu conquesté tout le pays des Dipsodes" (333; "As soon as I was perceived by him, he asked me, Whence comest thou, Alcofribas? I answered him, Out of your mouth, my lord. And how long hast thou been there? said he. Since the time, said I, that you went against the Almirods. That is about six months ago, said he. . . . We have with the help of God conquered all the land of the Dipsodes"). The scant attention paid to Pantagruel's victory is all the more remarkable in light of the fact that Pantagruel's campaign, as Duval's reading can be used to suggest, is positioned as the ethical climax of the very narrative which leads up to it. Alcofribas essentially blocks the epic trajectory of the giant's biography when he strolls off the battlefield and into Pantagruel's mouth, taking the story along with him. Pantagruel may still very well be a (mock-) epic hero – after all, he does win his war – but Alcofribas is most certainly not an epic narrator.

In Rabelais's version of the voyage into the giant's mouth, we are explicitly made to understand that we are at the mercy of the narrator's vision. Of course, one is always forced to rely on a narrator's vision of a fictional world; the *chroniques*, however, do not betray a consciousness of this fact. In *Pantagruel*, we are invited to take cognizance of Alcofribas's perspective *as* a perspective, since his point of view is not equivalent to the totalizing vision proposed by the *chroniques*. Nor is it the parodic perspective of the Lucianic eyewitness of the *True History*, a narrator who never intimates that his point of view has limitations. Lucian's eyewitness in fact has much in common with the narrator of epic. Like the epic poet, Lucian never posits any reality outside that which his eyewitness narrator sees; the perspective of that narrator is thus never problematized, is in fact never really constituted *as* a perspective. It is simply a transparent window onto a fictional world.

Alcofribas's narrative perspective, by contrast, is positioned as individual, idiosyncratic, and relative. While mortal combat rages in Pantagruel's world, Alcofribas has retreated to the relatively peaceful confines of the world in Pantagruel's mouth. When Alcofribas enters Pantagruel's mouth, his narrative perspective no longer mediates the (mock-) traditions of a (mock-) ethical community, but rather the contingent experiences of an isolated individual. The isolation of Alcofribas's perspective is staged within this episode: the world in which Pantagruel has his adventures is not simultaneously put on hold, as Gargantua's world is in the *chroniques*, when the narrator disappears into the mouth of the giant; rather, it simply continues on without him. In other words, when he sends Alcofribas scurrying along Pantagruel's tongue, Rabelais does not incorporate the world in Pantagruel's mouth into the world of Pantagruel's mock-epic adventures. Instead, he creates an entirely new diegetic world which relativizes the one in which all the other chapters of the book take place.

The problematic nature of the relation between the two diegetic worlds in *Pantagruel* is reinforced by the fact that all of the characters in the book, save Alcofribas, remain ignorant of their respective other worlds. When our narrator reemerges, his exchange with Pantagruel consists not of an account of the contents of the giant's mouth, but rather of an accounting of his own bodily functions during his stay among the *Gorgias*. Alcofribas gives the cabbage-planter even less information about Pantagruel's world. The two perspectives are not simply smaller parts of a larger whole, as they are in the *chroniques*. In *Pantagruel*, giving credible testimony about one world renders one incapable of speaking authoritatively about the other. Alcofribas's performance in *Pantagruel* 32 suggests that at the very moment he stakes his most compelling claim to an authoritative, firsthand vision of Pantagruel's world, he can no longer fill the role of the medieval narrator whose totalizing perspective mediates the *ethos* of an entire community.

Rabelais offers us no unambiguous criteria according to which we may compare the two perspectives created by Alcofribas's visit to the world in Pantagruel's mouth. He leaves the conflict between them unresolved; neither perspective is ultimately privileged in *Pan-*

tagruel. The epistemic perspective of the individual is never integrated into the broader ethical world posited by most of the book; rather, it is simply, strikingly juxtaposed to it. As a result, we have no gauge by which to measure the value of Alcofribas's eyewitness testimony.

Like Rabelais's traveller-narrator, eyewitness historians in the sixteenth century will openly struggle to articulate a perspective that is simultaneously individual and particular, yet sanctioned by a community. The same problematic is staged in concentrated form in the 1564 *Cinquième livre* (the last in Rabelais's series of novels).[11] One of the stops on the fictional voyage recounted in the book is a "school of testimony" run by a chap called Hearsay ("ouy-dire"). Readers have often been nonplussed to find the likes of Ludovico de Varthema, Pedro Cabral, and Jacques Cartier among those taking lessons in witnessing there. All of them were well-known eyewitness historians, and none had (or have) a reputation for exaggeration. Why are these eyewitnesses represented at the feet of "Ouy-dire," with his seven tongues split into seven pieces that speak seven different languages?

As the author of the *Cinquième livre* clearly recognizes, all testimony, even that of eyewitnesses, is transmitted primarily as hearsay. The eyewitness may see for himself, but those to whom he testifies do not (otherwise his testimony would lose its privilege). Eyewitness testimony thus presupposes human mediators in an intersubjective dialogue. As the next chapter will argue, a crisis of "hearsay" – which is nothing other than the breakdown of the ethical mode of testimony – has become obvious by the time the *Cinquième livre* is written and published. The figure of the eyewitness does not provide a resolution to this crisis, but is rather caught up in it. How is one to evaluate the eyewitness testimony of a complete stranger? How is one to adjudicate among the reports of multiple such eyewitnesses – say, seven different witnesses writing in seven different languages? As what one hears becomes increasingly divorced from one's own experience, how is one to know what to make of what one hears (or reads)?

---

[11] The open question of the book's authorship is of little relevance in the context of the present enquiry. The *Cinquième livre* can tell us as much about conceptions of witnessing in sixteenth-century France as can the books we are sure Rabelais wrote.

CHAPTER THREE

EXPERIENCE

BINOT Paulmier de Gonneville left Honfleur in 1503 on the *Espoir* with the intention of undertaking a commercial voyage to the Portuguese East Indies. The ship was blown off course and ultimately landed in what the crew's account of the trip, the *Relation authentique*, describes as a "nouvelle terre des Indes," and what subsequent scholarship has concluded was Brazil. When the *Espoir* returned to Europe in 1505, it was attacked by pirates just off the coast of Normandy. The expedition lost everything in the attack, including the journals of their voyage. When Gonneville and his crew lodged a formal complaint in order to seek compensation for their loss, the King's prosecutor requested that they supply an account of their voyage, as well as of its unfortunate end, to the office of the admiralty. They did so, and their official deposition is what is now known as the *Relation authentique*.

The *Relation authentique* is the first French eyewitness account of the New World. However, one looks in vain in Gonneville's relation – as one does in the letters of Christopher Columbus, Amerigo Vespucci or Hernán Cortés – for the kind of self-conscious promotion of practical experience that is usually associated with firsthand accounts of the New World. It has become a cliché of scholarship, as Anthony Grafton summarizes the view, that "naked experience take[s] the place of written authority" as a source of knowledge over the course of the sixteenth century in Europe thanks in significant part to New World historiography (5). Though Grafton somewhat exaggerates the claim in the course of putting it into question, it is nonetheless true that eyewitness histories of the New World are seen as having played a crucial role in establishing the epistemological authority of experience alongside, if not necessarily over, the store of knowledge inherited from both pagan Antiquity and the Christian Middle Ages.[1] Yet Gonneville never uses the term "experience"; indeed, the entire relation is written in the third person.

In order to understand the place and function of the notion of "experience" in Gonneville's *Relation*, it is necessary to take account of the juridical context in which it originated. As an official record of a deposition, it was written out by a court functionary. That alone, one might propose, would be enough to explain the absence of the first person in the account: the court clerk translated what was originally a first-person report into impersonal, objective "information." But that act of translation tells us some important things about the status of eyewitness testimony in early sixteenth-century law courts. That the clerk did not transcribe this testimony *verbatim* suggests that the grammatical form of a testimony was not seen as integral to its content. This is confirmed by the fact that witness depositions given in the vernacular were often still transcribed in Latin at this point. Thus, the rhetoric of first-person experience could and did remain absent from the juridical deposition, even as firsthand experience was considered to be the best source of knowledge according to juridical theory.

---

[1] Grafton convincingly demonstrates that even authors who openly mock the limitations of the Ancients in matters geographical on the basis of their own experience draw heavily on long-established anthropological and cosmographical paradigms in their histories of America. However, it is worth noting that his study of New World historiography emphasizes authors writing in the learned tradition of humanism. Indeed, José de Acosta, the author of Grafton's leading example of a firsthand account of the New World that is heavily indebted to ancient texts, explicitly claims that his work unites the "*filosofía*" of an educated man with the experience resulting from "mucho trato con los mismos indios" (57; "many interactions with the Indians themselves"). While Grafton's characterization of Acosta's historiographical program can usefully be extended to the writings of (mostly Spanish) humanists like Bartolomé de Las Casas or Francisco López de Gómara, it does not address the role of experience, nor outright ignorance of learned tradition, in many of the best-known vernacular eyewitness accounts of the New World. The writings of Jacques Cartier and Jean de Léry in France or of Bernal Díaz del Castillo in Spain tend to hew very close to firsthand experience and to resist the drive to intellectual synthesis that ultimately leads the humanist authors back to the authoritative texts of Antiquity. Though these writers, like their humanist counterparts, retain most of their own cultural assumptions in their writings about the New World – how could they not? – they also struggle to come to terms with the possibilities and limitations of eyewitness testimony based primarily in experience.

As testimony, Gonneville's deposition was comprised of a dialogue between himself and juridical authorities in the Office of the Admiralty at Rouen. The Admiralty of France is one institution that resisted centralization throughout the sixteenth century, despite repeated royal efforts to bring maritime matters under the control of Paris. Those who bore the title Admiral of France were never able to exercise their authority in the provinces. When Henri, duc de Montmorency, became Admiral of France in 1612 and was able to assume the admiralty of Guyenne two years later, this represented an unprecedented extension of the power of the office. (Soon thereafter, the office was abolished and recast as the office of the *Grand-maître, chef et surintendant général de la Navigation et du Commerce de France*, and taken over by none other than Richelieu in 1626 [see Buffet 257-282].) The context for the testimony given in the *Relation* is thus a concretely local one, and not the more abstract encounter between an individual and "the law" that will gradually come to characterize the experience of giving testimony in the modern nation-state.

The process by which Gonneville's relation acquires the epithet "authentique" – that is, legal – takes place outside the document itself, through the formalities that grant its status as an authentic witness deposition. More important, though, is the fact that the grounds on which Gonneville's eyewitness testimony is considered *credible* are intimately intertwined with those on which it is deemed *legal* (and thus *authentique*). The ethical situation in which Gonneville's deposition was composed neither required nor facilitated the elaboration of a rhetoric in which experience functioned as a source of testimonial credibility. Gonneville's deposition itself indicates that his account has in effect *already* been accepted as credible by the members of his own community before it assumes its legal form.

Near the end of the testimony transcribed in the *Relation* is a list of all of those who returned with the expedition. Though several sailors had been lost, at least one soul had been gained, since Gonneville and his companions brought back a native prince from the new land in which they had sojourned, and had baptized him with Gonneville's given name, Binot. The roster of returning mariners concludes thus: "Plus l'indien Essomericq, autrement dit Binot, qui audit Honfleur et par tous les lieux de la passée, estoit bien regardé, pour n'avoir jamais eu en France personnage de si lointain pays: estant les gens de la ville aises de voir leurs compatriotes revenus de tel et si grand voyage, et marrys des cas malencontreux advenu quasiment au seüil de l'hostel" (109; "And the Indian Essomericq, otherwise called Binot, who in the aforementioned Honfleur and all along the way was well regarded, since there had never been in France a person from such a distant land: the people of the city being relieved to see their compatriots returned from such a great voyage, and dismayed at the unhappy events that took place virtually on the threshold of their safe haven"). Gonneville's legal testimony incorporates an account of the fact that the inhabitants of Honfleur have witnessed Gonneville's return from afar, have seen Essomericq for themselves, and have expressed dismay about the pirate attack that is, in the end, what the *Relation* is meant to address. What is being asserted in this part of Gonneville's deposition, then, is not merely Essomericq's reputation ("bien regardé" as he reportedly was), but more importantly, Gonneville's status as a "compatriot" of the people of Honfleur. In their deposition, Gonneville and his companions specify that they have borne witness to the members of their community before they testify before the law. The fact that Gonneville's deposition includes such a testimonial *mise-en-abîme* suggests that, in order to become the basis for authoritative testimony, Gonneville's experience had first to be mediated by his community. At bottom, the ethical relationship between Gonneville and his compatriots is what confers upon Gonneville the status of a reliable witness before the law.

Though Gonneville's firsthand experiences in a "nouvelle terre des Indes" are of course the *referent* of most of Gonneville's testimony, they are not its ground; Gonneville's status as a reliable witness is conferred primarily by the members of his immediate community on the basis of their ethical relationships. This perhaps explains why the *Relation authentique* contains virtually no references to experience explicitly characterized as such, and is in this respect very similar to the accounts of Polo and Mandeville. The capture of Essomericq, for example, is recounted as a deed, an event – but not as an experience: "Et parce que c'est coustume à ceux qui parviennent à nouvelles terres des Indes, d'en amener à Chrestienneté aucuns Indiens, fut tant fait par beau semblant, que ledit seigneur Arosca vousist bien qu'un sien jeune fils qui d'ordinaire tenoit bon avec ceux de la navire, vînt en Chrestienneté" (101-102; "And because it is customary among those who reach new territories in the Indies to bring some Indians back to Christian lands, it was arranged that by means of a ruse, [the chieftain] Arosca would agree that a son of his who got along well with the ship's crew come to Christian lands"). While Gonneville and his companions are obviously the agents of Essomericq's capture, their deposition on the topic is not cast in the first person and does not overtly claim a privileged point of view. This is because, as we learned from Beaumanoir, the deposition proper is not the place where the witness asserted his authority to speak.

A growing body of work in the history of science emphasizes the empirical bent of much skills-based, non-elite knowledge in the Middle Ages and Renaissance, long before the official "scientific revolution" of the seventeenth century (see for example Dear; Ogilvie; Smith). Thus, it is likely that one of the sources for the *discourse* of experience – that is, a record of experience that makes no explicit, self-conscious claims for the epistemic potential of experience – in firsthand accounts of the New World was the practice-based tradition of the seafarer. Before the European designation of the Americas as a New World, and particularly in the context of a thoroughly text-based, humanist historiographical tradition interested first and foremost in the political and moral lessons of the past, there would have been little occasion for the practical lore of the sailor to intervene in the writing of History. Thus, the fact that Norman sailors may have been fishing off the coast of Brazil in the early fifteenth century would have simply been of no consequence to the Historian. The two distinct discourses – the one empirical and "experience"-based, the other rhetorical and text-based – existed alongside one another, and there was apparently no need felt to reconcile their distinct epistemological premises.

Once it was widely accepted that Columbus had indeed encountered a "fourth part of the world," marine experience necessarily found itself implicated in the broader discourses of history and cosmography. But it would take some time before this development would provoke a direct confrontation between the discourse of experience or of seeing for oneself, on the one hand, and the discourses of "philosophy," "rhetoric," or "history" on the other. The explicit appeal to the epistemic superiority of experience – what I shall call the *rhetoric* of experience – is actually a rather late arrival on the scene of New World historiography. The most forceful claims for the epistemic reliability of experience over other forms of gaining knowledge, such as those made in the account of Jacques

Cartier's second voyage, start appearing in the 1540's, fully fifty years after the *mundus novus* had been christened.

When it became clear that the discourse of practical experience required a rhetorical and philosophical justification that it had previously done very well without (certainly in merchant and seafaring circles, as the writings of Columbus and of Marco Polo attest), eyewitness historians were in a position to draw on the protocols of juridical testimony. There can be no doubt that anyone reporting on a voyage to the New World would have been familiar with juridical protocols relating to witness depositions: by the sixteenth century, all of the European countries from which such voyages were made required that legal accounts of them be given to the office of the admiralty, which comprised a separate jurisdiction within the context of increasingly nationalized systems of justice. Given a relative familiarity with the experience of giving legal testimony in the seafaring community, it is perhaps not surprising that the turn to experience as a primary source of testimonial *credibility* (as distinct from *knowledge*) that one can observe in eyewitness accounts in this period evolves in tandem with piecemeal, unsystematic modifications in the procedures for gathering and evaluating witness testimony in French lay courts over the course of the sixteenth century. The shift cannot be explained merely by proposing that experience had suddenly been granted a new epistemological authority in light of the historical encounter with the New World. As the legal manuals show, firsthand experience had long been considered a superior source of knowledge on the part of witnesses. Rather, firsthand experience is explicitly positioned as authoritative in sixteenth-century French eyewitness accounts of the New World because the rhetoric of personal *ethos*, still important in theory, had by mid-century lost a significant measure of its practical applicability in the context of an increasingly centralized system of justice administered from Paris. Thus, while experience had long been recognized as a source of practical knowledge, it was only in the mid-sixteenth century that a self-conscious *rhetoric* of experiential knowledge became necessary.

In the medieval era, the credibility of witnesses and testimony was founded primarily on the network of ethical relationships that formed the witness's immediate community. In medieval travel literature as in the medieval lay courts, testimony is directly addressed to a particular audience who must recognize the witness in order to accept his testimony. This will remain the theoretical model for witnessing and testimony into the sixteenth century in France. However, over the course of this same period, the witness and his audience will become increasingly estranged in both the legal and the literary context. As circumscribed feudal communities gradually give way to larger and more abstract collectivities, it becomes more difficult to determine the *renommée* of all of those with whom one might have social and juridical intercourse. Moreover, as heterogeneous groups are absorbed into larger social entities, the question of a community's shared *ethos* becomes an increasingly vexed one.

Whereas testimony as hearsay is fundamental to medieval ethical relationships – to the very notion of *renommée* or reputation – the mechanisms for policing the communal ethical judgments vehicled by hearsay are in a state of flux in the sixteenth century. This doesn't mean that hearsay is abandoned; it means that the ways in which community judgments had been incorporated into the structures of cultural authority were no longer seen as adequate, and that those judgments were no longer capable of establishing satisfactory versions of the truth. Certainly, hearsay persisted (and persists) as a site of cultural authority, but as it became less exclusively associated with actual hearing and speaking among members of a circumscribed ethical community, it became increasingly difficult to manage.

O TEMPORA, O MORES

Over the course of the sixteenth century, the tension between the practical requirements of a not-yet-nationalized system of justice, on the one hand, and the ethical criteria for managing witnesses that emerged out of the feudal context, on the other, reached a crisis point.[2] As the typical witness deposition conformed less and

---

[2] Green (*Crisis* chapter 4) observes many of the same developments I do in his discussion of the consequences of centralization for the folklaw of England. Green sees an uneasy hybrid of centralized, written practice and local, oral practice in the 14th century. He suggests that as justice became more centralized, it did indeed become more disinterested (since one was no longer necessarily tried by one's peers) but since the English jury was originally predicated on familiarity and "interest" on the part of the jurors, procedural means for reaching "disinterested" verdicts were lacking. I would argue, however, that rather than forcing a reformulation of testi-

less to the model of the direct oral encounter in a relatively circumscribed community upon which medieval procedure had been based, the ethical notion of *renommée* or reputation that had grounded testimonial proof in both folklaw and the medieval inquisition became increasingly difficult to enlist as the principal criterion for accepting or rejecting witnesses. Nonetheless, since France's justice system was not yet truly nationalized at the beginning of the sixteenth century, there had not yet developed a satisfactory institutional alternative to the medieval criteria for evaluating witnesses. The tensions between feudal ethics and the administrative requirements of a centralized system of justice crucially condition the changing fortunes of the figure of the witness over the course of the sixteenth century in France.

The gradual breakdown of feudal mechanisms for establishing the credibility of testimony eventually leads to a wholesale disparagement of witnesses in the juridical literature of sixteenth-century France. The Renaissance jurist Jean Boiceau articulates this attitude in terms of a more general crisis of *bonne foy*: "si la preuve par témoins, dont la foy estoit simple et inviolable autrefois, est devenuë suspecte & dangereuse dans la suite des temps, il ne faut pas faire une reproche à l'antiquité de ce qu'elle en est servie . . . mais il faut en accuser plûtost les moeurs corrompuës de nostre siecle . . . on pourrait en cet endroit s'écrier avec Cicéron: O temps, ô moeurs, tant il est vray que la bonne foy & cette innocence des premiers siecles est rare à present . . . son témoignage [de l'homme] qui estoit autrefois tres-religieux, se trouve entierement corrompu dans les moindres affaires dans lesquelles on est obligé de s'en rapporter à luy" (n.p. "if proof by witnesses, whose [good] faith used to be simple and inviolable, has become dangerous and suspicious over the course of time, one shouldn't reproach antiquity for having made use of it . . . but one should rather blame the corrupt mores of our time . . . one could cry out here with Cicero: "Oh the times, oh the mores," so true is it that the good faith and innocence of the first ages has become rare . . . [human] testimony, which used to be

---

mony in terms of abstract truth, the nationalization of the English system made of jurors the judges of facts in a way that maintained a consensual notion of truth. The notion of truth as consensual has obvious affinities with the truth-establishing practices of the Royal Society as they have been described by Steven Shapin in *A Social History of Truth*, chapter five, "Epistemological Decorum: The Practical Management of Factual Testimony."

sacred, has become entirely corrupt in even the most minor affairs in which one is obliged to take recourse to it").

Boiceau is here justifying a well-known provision of the 1566 ordinance of Moulins. The ordinance restricted the use of witnesses in civil cases to matters where only small sums were at issue – a provision that is usually summarized with the formula "lettres passent témoins," in order to contrast it with the characteristically medieval hierarchy that favors witnesses over documents. Both the ordinance and Boiceau's lament indicate that the credibility of witness testimony was felt to have reached a nadir in mid-sixteenth-century France. Even Henri III's 1579 order to establish written birth, death, marriage and burial registers, ostensibly a case of the extension of state control over private information, is presented as motivated by a desire to avoid proof by witnesses ("pour éviter les preuves par témoins"; Isambert 14: 251). This attitude will be reiterated in the seventeenth century, when Jean Danty justifies the promulgation of the ordinance of Moulins by claiming that the abuse of testimonial good faith, on the increase since the time of Moses, had reached "excessive" levels in France in the sixteenth century, thus obligating Charles IX to act.[3] But can we really attribute the increasingly widespread tendency to avoid witness testimony where possible to the fact that, as Boiceau and Danty would have us believe, sixteenth-century Frenchmen were constitutionally less trustworthy than their forbears?

The ordinance of Moulins suggests that the crisis of faith in juridical testimony more likely stemmed from the dysfunction of the institutional mechanisms by which the reliability of witness testi-

---

[3] "Ce fut . . . pour prévenir le desordre que pouvoit causer dans la societé civile l'incertitude des faits que Moyse, le premier des Legislateurs, prescrivit aux hommes la maniere de faire la preuve de la verité par la déposition de deux témoins, & l'on ne peut disconvenir, que cette preuve, comme la plus simple & la plus naturelle, ne fût aussi la meilleure en ce temps-là, parce qu'il y avoit de la bonne foy parmi les hommes; mais les moeurs se sont tellement corrompuës dans la suite des siecles, le mensonge & la calomnie sont devenus si frequens, que c'est avec raison, que cette preuve ne trouve plus la même créance. Et s'il n'a pas esté possible de la rejetter entierement en matiere de crimes, parce qu'ils ne se peuvent prouver d'ordinaire que par témoins, c'est avec beaucoup de sagesse, qu'elle n'a esté admise en France en matiere de conventions, que dans celles de peu de consequences, ou seulement dans les cas où elle sert à fortifier la preuve par écrit. L'abus même qu'on en faisoit passa juqu'à un tel excès dans le dernier siecle, que les Parlemens envoyerent des Deputez au Roy Charles IX. pour s'en plaindre, ce qui l'obligea de la restreindre par l'article 54. de l'ord. de Moul., dont la disposition a esté renouvellée depuis par celle de 1667" (34).

mony had formerly been established. The first article of the ordinance reads: "Pour obvier à la multiplication des faicts . . . subiets à preuve de tesmoins, & reproches d'iceux, dont adviennent plusieurs inconveniens & involution de proces . . . de toutes choses excedans la somme ou valeur de cent livres pour une fois payer, seront passez contracts par devant notaires & tesmoins" ("In order to obviate the multiplication of facts . . . subject to proof by witnesses, and [to obviate the multiplication of] reproaches of [witnesses], which results in numerous inconveniences and procedural entanglements . . . for any matter in which it is a question of a one-time payment of more than one hundred *livres*, [written] contracts will take precedence over [the testimony of] notaries and witnesses"). Rather than describe witness testimony as inherently unreliable, the ordinance of Moulins deems proof by witnesses administratively unmanageable. According to the ordinance, the reason the use of witnesses must be restricted is that proof by witnesses, and in particular the process of establishing the credibility of witnesses (via objections or "reproches"), results in "plusieurs inconveniens & involutions de process." The administrative requirements of evaluating witness testimony had apparently come to seem impracticable or at least excessively burdensome; consequently, proof by witnesses was perceived as an inefficient means to reach a satisfactory juridical verdict.

Even as the procedures for evaluating witness testimony failed in practice, however, the presuppositions on which they were based continued to animate juridical theory. The notion of the feudal community that could still legitimately inform Beaumanoir's thirteenth-century customal could by the sixteenth century no longer serve as the basic structure on which legal practices were predicated. Nonetheless, the body of legal practices that presupposed such a community was not simply discarded. Instead, jurists strained to adapt them to what had become very different circumstances.

Witnesses in the sixteenth century could, like their medieval counterparts, be disqualified for a number of reasons relating to their social standing and reputation. In his 1546 *Traité des tesmoings et des enquestes*, Guillaume Jaudin states outright that "en tesmoignage le bon renom, honneste vie, & preud'hommie du tesmoing vient à regarder sur toutes choses" ("the most important consideration in testimony is the good reputation, honest life, and *prudhommie* of the witness"). In his 1609 annotations to Jean Imbert's *Practique judiciaire*, Pierre Guenois gives an extensive list of legitimate objections to witness testimony. They turn out to be none other than the old medieval *reproches* based on socio-ethical status. Witnesses are disqualifed for reasons like the following:

> Quand les temoins sont ennemis mortels & capitaux . . . 2ment s'ils sont parens de la partie qui le produit . . . 3ment s'ils sont domestics . . . Quarto, s'ils sont voleurs, homicides, &c. ou bien ont commis quelque autre crime capitale ou portant infamie publique . . . Quinto, s'ils sont convaincus de parjure . . . Sexto, s'ils sont convaincus d'avoir porté autrefois faux tesmoignage . . . 7o, s'ils sont infames . . . 14o, s'ils n'ont l'aage requis pour porter tesmoignage . . . 16o, s'ils sont hermaphrodites, par le droict canonique . . . 17o, s'ils sont furieux ou insensez, & hors de leurs bons sens . . . 18o, s'ils sont hermaphrodites . . . 20o, s'ils sont blasphemateurs ordinaires du nom de Dieu (318-19)

> When witnesses are mortal and capital enemies [of the accused] . . . if they are relatives of the party that calls them . . . if they are domestic servants [of the party that calls them] . . . if they are thieves, murderers, or have committed some other capital crime that renders them infamous [entailing a loss of legal status] . . . if they have [ever] been convicted of perjury . . . if they have ever been convicted of giving false testimony . . . if they have been deemed infamous . . . if they are not yet of the age required to give testimony . . . if they are hermaphrodites . . . if they are blasphemers of God's name

The grounds for reproach that both Guenois and Jaudin give are consonant not only with those of customary law, but also with the *droit écrit* that developed out of Roman law. Many of the same principles are enunciated by the medieval glossaters and their sixteenth-century epigones, as indicated in a Latin collection of treatises on testimony collected by Francesco Ziletti (Zilettus) and published at Venice in 1584-86. These writings both confirm what we have already seen in the medieval period – namely, that the inquest's theoretical focus on the facts behind a case did not necessarily result in the abandonment of ethical for epistemological considerations in the evaluation of witness testimony – and demonstrate the persistence well into the sixteenth century of both a theoretical and practical commitment to ethical criteria.

In order to understand why the introduction of the inquest did not immediately alter the fundamentally ethical status of testimonial proof in medieval lay courts, it is important to acknowledge that the potential "rationality" of inquisitional procedure was by and large *not* what recommended it to those who adopted it. It would be difficult to argue that royal legislation designed to eliminate the old proofs in favor of the inquest in French lay courts sprang from a desire for more rationally-grounded juridical verdicts: as Beaumanoir's customal makes clear, the impulse behind the introduction of the inquest into French lay procedure was Louis IX's attempt to assert royal control over feudal courts in the mid-thirteenth century.

Though one cannot yet speak of a single, unified "French" procedure by the end of the sixteenth century, sixteenth-century French sovereigns, especially François I and Charles IX, significantly expanded the role of the inquest in the law courts with the Saint-King's aim of juridical centralization in mind. In both civil and criminal cases, the sixteenth-century French inquest assigned an officer of the government to both gather evidence and pass judgment on it. As John Langbein points out, a series of statutes in the 14th century had isolated the public interest in criminal prosecution and made it the charge of the *procureur du Roi*, who, by the sixteenth century, was the only one allowed to initiate "serious criminal sanction" even when there was a formal private complainant (*Prosecuting* 217).[4] The inquest, which required that all phases of procedure assume written form, could accommodate and indeed facilitate the centralized administration of justice across a large swath of territory that incorporated several different feudal communities. By contrast, the old forms of justice, with their emphasis on orality and on the face-to-face confrontation, were practicable only in fairly circumscribed settings. More than any drive towards rational proofs per se, then, it is this contrast – between a quasi-national, and thus bureaucratically-mediated procedure on the one hand, and a local, face-to-face encounter among familiars on the other – that deter-

---

[4] In *Torture and the Law of Proof*, Langbein argues that "the consolidation of the nation-state and judicial power provided a stable, institutional context in which the system of free judicial evaluation of the evidence could flourish" (56). For Langbein, this process culminates in France in the eighteenth century. The use of torture is a signal example of the priority of state control of the administration of justice over any commitment to grounding juridical verdicts in rational proofs.

mined the evolution of juridical procedure, and thus of juridical witnessing and testimony, in early modern France.

When we foreground the political motivation behind the spread of inquisitional procedure in France, the divide between inquisitional theory and actual juridical practice becomes somewhat more intelligible. Despite the significant expansion of the inquest in France from the fourteenth to the sixteenth centuries, the criteria for evaluating witnesses remained largely unchanged and primarily ethical up through much of the sixteenth century. As long as ethical criteria for evaluating witnesses continued to function satisfactorily, there was no impetus to change them. This meant that the ethical model of the witness had to break down utterly and completely in practice before it was relinquished in theory. As the ordinance of Moulins implies, this breakdown was felt to have occurred on a large scale by the middle of the sixteenth century.

There are fairly concrete reasons why the medieval mechanisms for establishing the credibility of witnesses were no longer functioning satisfactorily in this period. In the sixteenth century, parties in a legal dispute were more likely to come from different (feudal) communities than they were in Beaumanoir's time. This fact is indexed in several pieces of legislation. Article 166 of the ordinance of 1539 Villers-Cotteret eliminates the *droit d'asile*, according to which a defendant could request that legal proceedings against him take place "au lieu de son domicile" – that is, in his home jurisdiction. The *de facto* jurisdiction of the sixteenth-century court was thus not restricted to the community in which it was located, but covered anyone who happened to become involved in a legal dispute there. Similarly, Article 35 of the ordinance of Moulins officially establishes the judge in place where a crime was committed (as opposed to the judge presiding where the criminal resides) as the best one to handle the case. Such legislation could only make it more likely that a sixteenth-century inquest would involve persons that were not necessarily well known to one another. As a consequence, it became increasingly difficult for a party to enlist the basic criterion of *renommée* when he was invited to lodge objections against witnesses, for the simple reason that he often did not "recognize" those witnesses.

By the time we reach the sixteenth century, the traditional objection based on reputation appears to have become utterly impracticable in a large number of juridical settings. Thus, at the Etats-

Généraux of 1560, the Tiers-Etat protested against Article 154 of the ordinance of Villers-Cotteret, since it "compels accused persons immediately to allege their objections to the witness, which is a great hardship, and often results in the innocence of many being imperilled." Paul Guilhiermoz demonstrates that as early as the fourteenth century parliamentary judges would sometimes go ahead and issue a verdict without bothering to investigate objections against witnesses (121-2). In a study of heresy trials, Bernard Schnapper argues that there existed by the sixteenth century a body of continental legal doctrine that allowed testimony from witnesses that previous theory had systematically excluded. Schnapper acknowledges that it is difficult to determine to what degree such doctrines were put into practice, given the lack of documentation, but he ultimately sees a movement in early modern French jurisprudence towards the elimination of the notion of the reproachable witness.

Duels, as Beaumanoir's customal makes clear, were the medieval inquest's solution to the problem of the witness who is irreproachable because utterly unknown. This quintessential embodiment of feudal, aristocratic justice is described as outside the bounds of normal procedure in sixteenth-century legal manuals. Echoing complaints that had been around for centuries in the context of canon law, but whose sentiment had only recently triumphed on a nationwide scale in civil law, a mid-century jurist expresses revulsion for the old proofs (that is, ordeals, including the duel): they were "excogitées par l'instigation du diable, desquelles on n'usoit que pour tenter Dieu: ont partant les droicts Ecclesiastiques & Canoniques à bonne & juste cause iceux abolis, & mis à neant. Et de ce n'a depuis plus este usé" (Damhoudere 47r; "thought up at the Devil's instigation, and were used only to tempt God: thus were they abolished and eliminated, with good and just cause, in ecclesiastical and canon law. And it has not since been employed"). Similarly, in the *Recherches de la France*, Etienne Pasquier seems astonished that anyone would seek justice by means of the *gage de batailles* (Book 4, chapter 1). Thus, at the same time that disputes between members of different regional communities became more frequent, resistance to the duel grew, particularly in royal, juridical and intellectual milieux.

Unfortunately, sixteenth-century legal doctrine had little to offer in the way of an alternative to the duel as a means for settling disputes among relative strangers. French courts appear to have continued to subscribe to the ethical model of the witness in this period, and to have simply made ever more modifications to procedure without consciously developing a new theoretical basis upon which such conflicts could be adjudicated. Nevertheless, these administrative changes – despite their obviously improvisational character – eventually did effect a transformation in the way the witness was conceptualized. The unsystematic responses of the secular courts to the administrative challenges of evaluating witness testimony in the context of a quasi-national jurisdiction would ultimately pave the way for the emergence of a theoretical alternative to the rhetoric of *ethos* as a source of testimonial authority.

Credible v. Lawful Witnesses

Up through most of the fifteenth century, as I have suggested, French lay courts continued to work primarily from the model of the witness as deponent. This model makes one's status as a credible witness coextensive with the act of testifying under oath. As the fifteenth century comes to a close, however, witnesses and testimony will be managed with increasing frequency in terms that drive a wedge between credible witnesses, on the one hand, and lawful deponents on the other. In the more or less feudal context in which Beaumanoir was writing, there would necessarily have been an almost total overlap between the categories of the "credible" and the "lawful" witness, since a witness's credibility was established prior to his taking the oath and thus becoming a lawful witness. In the sixteenth century, as we shall see, the categories of the credible and the legal witness no longer overlapped to the extent that they had in the past. These conditions in turn force a redefinition of credibility. This does not mean that a specific interest in credibility only arose in the sixteenth century; rather, it shows how specific procedural transformations had the (unintended) effect of creating a distinction between credible and lawful witnesses.[5]

---

[5] In *Probability and Certainty*, Barbara Shapiro notes that "the distinction between credible and lawful witnesses became increasingly common, particularly in the latter part of the seventeenth century" (185), as part of a "transition to evaluation of testimony for credibility" (186) in England. What she means, I take it, is that

One can track the progress of the divide between lawful and credible testimony – a gap that is initially temporal, but finally perceived as ontological – by tracing the fate of the testimonial oath as it can be gleaned from the writings of the Parisian jurist Jean Imbert.[6] Imbert's *Practique judiciaire*, initially published in 1543 and annotated and reissued throughout the remainder of the century, along with his 1566 *Institutes de praticque en matiere civile et criminelle*, give a practicing jurist's perspective on judicial procedure that gives us insight into the impact of royal legislation on the actual functioning of French law courts in the second half of the sixteenth century. Imbert gives descriptions (and critiques) of all phases of procedure according to the norms of the Paris *Parlement,* with particular reference to the ordinances of 1498 and 1539. Imbert's text has the advantage of incorporating a more descriptive element than the ordinances themselves, which are necessarily prescriptive (though much information can be gleaned from them).[7]

There is a fundamental distinction between the type of testimonial oath characteristic of folklaw and the testimonial oath of inquisitional procedure. Folklaw oaths like the *serment purgatoire* consolidate testimony into a single moment of truth, because the oath and the testimony it guarantees are coextensive. As Richard Firth Green notes in his study of the notion of "truth" in Ricardian England, "Such an oath did not initiate proceedings, it terminated them; it was not a preliminary to making one's case, but the culmination of it" (92). It is easy to see the structural resemblance between the first type of testimonial oath and the duel or the other ordeals. Both consist first and foremost of a form of personal engagement that simultaneously founds, performs, and bears witness to a state of affairs. The inquisitional oath, by contrast, consists in a *promise* to tell the truth at some future time. This kind of oath

---

testimony was increasingly evaluated in terms of *epistemic* credibility. She further notes that "oaths, in general, were not taken as seriously as they had been in earlier centuries" (186). Shapiro never quite explains what may have motivated these transformations.

[6] For an overview of the historical evolution of the oath in various Western legal systems from Greco-Roman antiquity to the present, see H. Silving, "The Oath."

[7] A more concise description of the sixteenth-century criminal inquest can be found in Etienne Pasquier, *L'Interprétation des Institutes de Justinian*, chapter XVIII, "Ordre judiciaire en matière criminelle." Sixteenth-century comparisons of French and Roman law, such as François Hotman's well-known *Anti-Tribonian*, tend to discuss broad legal principles as opposed to concrete procedures.

thus divides testimony into a series of temporally distinct moments. As the inquisitional process in France acquired ever more layers of official, written mediation, the idea of a moment of juridical truth, so clearly embodied in the purgatory oath (as well as in ordeals and duels), and translated in the early inquisition's face-to-face encounters and relatively speedy rendering of judgment, gives way to a procedure that routinely took weeks or months to render a judgment and under which those involved in a legal case might never even confront one another in person.

Regarding the status of the oath in 12th-14th-century France, Jean-Philippe Lévy remarks "Peu d'institutions ont eu au Moyen-Age une fortune plus grande... on peut dire que des serments sont alors prononcés à tout instant" (*Hiérarchie* 131; "few institutions enjoyed such great success... one could say that in that period oaths were sworn at every turn"). By contrast, Imbert reports that the Paris parliament no longer accepted the (purgatory) oath of either defendant or plaintiff as decisive in cases where proof is insufficient, "pour raison de la grande facilité que les hommes du jour-d'huy ont de jurer & faire serment: qu'ils n'ont telle reverence ne religion à un serment ou jurement judiciaire, qu'au temps passé ils avoient" (1609 [339]; "because of the ease with which men nowadays swear or utter an oath: they no longer have the religious reverence for oaths or judicial swearing that they had in the past"). Imbert's sense that the oath had once held a sacred status that it no longer enjoyed is reflected in the evolution of the form of the oath itself. The actual words of the oath had undergone some noteworthy changes since Beaumanoir's time, when it explicitly represented one of the ways in which secular justice maintained its link to divine judgment. Beaumanoir gives the testimonial oath thus: "Vous jurés, se Dieu vous aït, et li saint et les saintes, et les saintes paroles qui sont en ceste livre, et li pouoirs que Dieus a en ciel et en terre, que vous dirés verité" (1228/134; "You swear, so help you God and the saints, and the holy words that are in this book, and the powers God possesses on earth and in heaven, that you will tell the truth"). According to Imbert, the testimonial oath consisted in nothing more than the promise to tell the truth, with the right hand raised but not necessarily on the Bible: "Et feront faire ledict serment aux tesmoings lays la main dextre levée en haut... & n'est poinct necessaire qu'ilz touchent les sainctes evangiles de nostre Seigneur Jesus Christ" [175; "And secular witnesses shall take the oath with their right hand raised . . . and it is not at all necessary that they touch the Holy Gospel of our Lord Jesus Christ"]. But the changing form of the oath is surely a symptom, and not the cause, of the decline in the power of oath-swearing to establish "truth." In order to get a sense of *how* and *why* the oath lost its sacred status, we need to look closely at the evolution of the juridical practices in which the oath was implicated.

As Beaumanoir notes, Saint Louis's thirteenth-century legislation generously granted disputants two full days to prepare their case and gather their witnesses, in contrast to previous custom, where what is to be proven must be proven within the first twenty-four hours ("ce qui est offert a prouver . . . doit estre prouvé a la premiere journee"; 107). It is fair to say that Louis's extra day would have been utterly inconsequential in the context of a sixteenth-century inquest. Between Beaumanoir's time and Imbert's, the production of a witness deposition had slowly been transformed from a relatively circumscribed, discrete phase of procedure into a long, drawn-out process. In the 1550's, Pierre Ayrault, a vigorous critic of sixteenth-century procedure, expressed a longing for the days when "le procès se faisoit tout à un instant, et comme en un seul tableau, la verité pour l'une et pour l'autre partie se presentoit devant les juges" ("trials used to take place within a very short, circumscribed period of time in which the judges would instantaneously take in all of the aspects of a case and see the truth of the matter displayed before their very eyes, like a picture"). The dilation of the sixteenth-century inquest, by contrast, appears to have led participants to perceive the several moments of testimonial engagement therein as increasingly heterogeneous. In particular, one crucial modification in procedure – the gradual displacement of objections to witnesses, or what the juridical literature calls *"reproches"* – has significant repercussions that will fundamentally alter the status of the oath and eventually transform the figure of the witness.

According to Beaumanoir's thirteenth-century customal, the preliminary, face-to-face confrontation of the parties and their witnesses had represented a decisive moment for the witness in early inquisitional procedure, since it was at that time that his competence to testify was determined and that he publicly swore the testimonial oath. By contrast, Imbert notes that in the sixteenth century the opposing party was often not present when the witnesses against him took the testimonial oath, much less invited to intervene to halt their testimony: "Et par les ordonnances du Roy Charles VII . . . et du Roy Louis XII . . . il faut appeller la partie adverse a la production & reception des tesmoings, & ne suffit d'adjourner le procureur en cause . . . combien qu'en plusieurs lieux, comme a la Rochelle, il y ayt coustume escripte par laquelle il suffit d'adjourner le procureur. Toutefois nous usons bien en ce pays de Poictou, en tous les sieges royaux, qu'a l'appel ou l'audience de la cause en jugement, & en presence du procureur de partie adverse, l'on peut produire & faire recevoir & faire jurer tesmoings, sans que ladite partie y ayt esté adjournée" (176-7; "And according to the ordinances of King Charles VII . . . and of King Louis XII . . . it is necessary to call in the opposing party for the production and reception of witnesses, and it does not suffice to call in the opposing party's legal representative . . . even though in several jurisdictions, as at La Rochelle, there exists written law to the effect that it suffices to call in the legal representative. In any case in all of the royal courts in Poitou, we follow the procedure according to which, at the time the case is put before the judge, one can legally bring in witnesses and have them take the oath in the presence of the opposing party's legal representative, without the said party having been called in"). As Imbert's descriptions suggest, while the oral encounter described by Beaumanoir at the end of the medieval period remained a juridical ideal, it had disappeared in sixteenth-century practice. No longer was the swearing of the oath necessarily or even usually a moment in which the witness came face-to-face with the opposing party in order to face potential objections; rather, it had become a judicial formality that those involved could attend by proxy. Article 37 of Louis XII's ordinance of June 1510 states that it was required that a defendant be present at the taking of the oath by the witnesses; however, the ordinance indicates that such a requirement was necessary precisely because too many court examiners had the habit of receiving and swearing in witnesses without calling in the party against which the inquest is being undertaken ("ont accoutumé recevoir et faire jurer les témoins sans appeller la partie, contre laquelle se fait l'enquête"; Isambert 11:592).

The fact that the testimonial oath in the sixteenth century was frequently taken in the absence of the opposing party, and prior to any confrontation with that party, both indicates and perpetuates a deterioration in the power of the oath to serve as an index of communally-determined credibility in this period. Again, a return to Beaumanoir's thirteenth-century customal helps to elucidate the increasingly problematic status of the sixteenth-century testimonial oath. In the medieval procedure Beaumanoir describes, the oath constitutes an evidentiary frontier: before taking the oath, the capacity of the witness to give in evidence – and thus, his very status as a witness – is in suspension, pending the potential reproaches against his person that the opposing party will be allowed to lodge. After the witness has taken the oath, however, his testimony can no longer be contested. In fact, a party was not even required to give over a copy of the written depositions of witnesses to the opposing party, since, as Beaumanoir explains, "en la court laie l'en ne puet riens dire contre le dit des tesmoins puis que li tesmoing sont passé sans estre debouté de leur tesmoignage; ainçois convient que jugemens soit fes seur le dit des tesmoins" ("in lay courts one cannot say anything against the statements of witnesses, since the witnesses have testified without having been disqualified; thus it is appropriate that judgments be founded on the statements of witnesses"). Thus, on one side of the oath, we have an ethical evaluation of the witness; on the other, we have his deposition which is simply not subject to dispute. Indeed, the publication of witness depositions was officially discontinued in 1276, just six years after St. Louis's death (Guilhiermoz 74). In the procedure Beaumanoir describes, then, the granting of permission to take the testimonial oath brings to a close the process of evaluating a witness's credibility.

The position of the oath within the sequence of steps that produced a juridical deposition began to shift in the fourteenth century. It became possible to request a delay of the phase of the inquest in which objections to witnesses were to be lodged, in order to allow a party time to develop and justify his *reproches*. Meanwhile, however, the inquest itself would go forward: the witness would take the testimonial oath and give in testimony while potential objections against his person were still pending. In his study of late medieval inquisitional procedure, Paul Guilhiermoz describes the gradual displacement of the *reproches de témoins* over the course of the fourteenth and fifteenth centuries: Initially, the accused could request a delay of objections until after the witnesses had deposed, as long as all parties to a case had formally to agreed to the extension; by the mid-fifteenth century, however, the deferral of objections no longer required the special consent of the parties (*Enquêtes*

81-82). In mid-sixteenth-century practice, according to Imbert, the confrontation with the accused and the concurrent objections of witnesses virtually never preceded the production of the deposition. Essentially following the ordinance of 1539, Imbert explains the process of the *recolement et confrontation*:

> Quand lesdicts tesmoings comparent, le juge prend leur serment, & separéement: & leur faict faire lecture de leur deposition, en l'absence du criminel. Puis l'un apres l'autre les confrontera audict accusé: fera jurer & affermer lesdicts accusé & tesmoings par serment, & sçavoir s'ils se cognoissent l'un l'autre. Apres sommera le criminel de dire & proposer contre ledict tesmoing, les reproches qu'il a à dire contre luy, autrement qu'il n'y sera plus reçeu: & demandera audict tesmoing, si lesdicts reproches proposez contre luy sont veritables. En fin il fera faire lecture audict tesmoing de sa deposition, en la presence dudict prisonnier, & luy demandera si elle est veritable, & s'il y persiste. Et le tout sera diligemment rediger par escrit. . . . Note que le criminel est montré au tesmoing, à celle fin qu'il cognoisse si c'est de luy qu'il a parlé, & qu'il a chargé par sa deposition (40r)

> When the witnesses appear, the judge takes their oaths individually, and has their deposition read out to them in the absence of the accused. Then he confronts them one after the other with the accused: he has both the defendant and the witness swear an oath, and state whether they know one another. Afterwards he will ask the defendant to state any objections [*reproches*] he wishes to make against the witness, otherwise no objections will be heard: then he will ask the witness if the objections brought against him are founded. Finally [the judge] will have the witness's deposition read out to him in the presence of the defendant, and will ask him if it is truthful, and if he still stands by it. And the whole process will be diligently put down in writing. . . . Note that the defendant is brought before the witness, in order that the witness may know whether he was in fact the man he spoke of and accused in his deposition

Imbert's final comment here indicates that the moment in which the judge reads out the witness's ratified written deposition in the presence of the accused could be the first time in the course of the entire proceeding that witness and accused come face to face. It may even be the first time the accused learns the witness's name, since the witness list was frequently kept secret by the judge in order to minimize the risk of subornation (Imbert 189). Pasquier describes the same order of events, and presents the face-to-face encounter of witness and accused as a possibility, not a necessity: if the accused denies the facts about which he is interrogated, the judge must bring witnesses in for further questioning, but need not confront them with the accused ("si l'accusé desnie les faicts sur lesquels il est interrogé . . . il sera ordonné par le juge que les tesmoings seront amenés pour estre récollés; et, si besoin est, confronté"; *Interprétation* 782).

Even in cases where the witness was obliged to confront the accused, this confrontation took place only after his testimony has been signed, sealed and delivered under oath. And it is at this moment, and only at this moment, that the accused could propose his objections to the witness. In other words, it was only after witness testimony had already assumed written (and often substantially edited) form that the sixteenth-century witness underwent a test of credibility. Since objections to witnesses were always lodged only *after* those witnesses had already given in their testimony, witnesses routinely swore oaths and delivered testimony before they were ultimately deemed legally capable of testifying in a particular case. Obviously, if witnesses who have testified under oath are subsequently subject to objections, the oath itself can no longer function as an index of credibility. Because the mechanisms for establishing credibility prior to allowing witnesses to take the oath and testify were no longer practicable by the sixteenth century, witnesses were *legally* testifying without first having been deemed *credible*. It is thus not surprising that the swearing of the oath is no longer considered coextensive with an act of good faith, as had been the purgatorial oath, since it is no longer a ritual in which only those previously determined to be of good faith are allowed to participate (as it was for Beaumanoir).

In the context of sixteenth-century procedure, testimony given under oath was still open to question, either by the witness himself during the *recolement* or by the defendant if he lodged a charge of subornation at the *confrontation*. The oath itself had become embroiled in temporal contingency: rather than a stable evidentiary frontier beyond which all statements were held to be credible, the oath in sixteenth-century French procedure was perennially subject to annulment pending information that could only come to light after the oath had been uttered. As Pierre Ayrault laments, "the very first assertion which the witness has made use of in deponing [i.e. the oath] exists no longer when we come to our confirmations and ordinary confrontations" (III/3/38; cited in Esmein, 170). The testimonial "moment of truth" performed by the purgatory oath and approximated in the testimonial oath as it was administered in early years of the inquisition is stretched to the breaking point in sixteenth-century procedure. As a consequence, the hierarchy between the credibility of the witness and that of his testimony would be inverted.

Whereas the presence of strangers in juridical proceedings had given the initial impetus to the gradual temporal expansion of the inquest in the fourteenth and fifteenth centuries, by the sixteenth century, it could be said that the dilation of legal proceedings themselves, and in particular the drawing out of the process of deponing, began to make it difficult to think of the witness as the embodiment of a stable, enduring ethos. Moreover, no amount of extra time granted to a party could realistically be expected to allow him to form the kind of relationship with a witness that the old ethical objections against witnesses presupposed. The result of these circumstances was that objections to witnesses were rarely made on ethical grounds in the sixteenth century. Rather, an objection of an entirely different kind became more frequent.

The relative brevity of the testimonial encounter in medieval procedure left little opportunity for the subornation of witnesses; moreover, such a charge would in any case be brought *before* the witness in question would be allowed to testify. When Beaumanoir touches briefly on the matter of witness corruption, after a long list of other reasons to disqualify witnesses that are presented at much greater length, he feels compelled to explain why it might not be a good thing for a witness to accept a bribe: "car perius seroit que cil qui recevroit don ou pramesse ne deist autre chose que verité par couvoitise" (1185; "because there would be a risk that the person who receives a gift or a promise thereof would say something other than the truth due to greed"). By contrast, sixteenth-century commentators assume readers' familiarity with the concept of subornation and build an entire form of procedure around it: the *procès extraordinaire*, which is carried out entirely in secret.

The long delays between the witness's initial deposition and his appearance at the *recolement et confrontation* that were typical in the sixteenth century were perceived as providing opportunities to influence witness testimony. Article 110 of the ordinance of 1498 had already cited the risk of subornation as a justification for undertaking an inquest behind closed doors: "Quant aux prisonniers ou autres accusez de crime, ausquels faudra faire procès criminel, ledit procès se fera le plus diligemment et secretement que faire se pourra, en maniere que aucun n'en soit averti, pour éviter les subornations et forgemens qui se pourroient faire en telles matieres" (Isambert 11:365; "in the case of prisoners or others accused of a crime, and subject to criminal prosecution, legal proceedings shall be undertaken in the most diligent and secret manner possible, such that none are made aware of then, in order to avoid the subornations and forgeries that may occur in such matters"). The fear of subornation led some judges in Imbert's time to avoid the publication of the names of witnesses. Imbert describes additional deviations from official procedure motivated by this fear. Though Article 153 of the ordinance of Villers-Cotteret specifies that the judge must confront the accused only with those witnesses that stand by their accusation when the judge reads their deposition out to them, Imbert says that "plusieurs juges de grand experience confrontent tous tesmoings, tant ceulx qui chargent, que ceulx qui ne chargent point, afin que le demandeur partie civile ne puisse cognoistre si ses tesmoings chargent ou non, & que voyant que ses tesmoings ne chargent point, il face son effort d'en suborner" (473; "several of the most experienced judges confront the defendant with all of the witnesses – both those who accuse him and those who do not – so that the plaintiff is unable to be sure whether his witnesses charge the accused, and so that, seeing that some of his witnesses do not charge the accused, he does not attempt to suborn them"). Imbert's observations suggest that subornation of witnesses was still possible at the confrontations, a possibility that presupposes that the witness could have the opportunity to modify his testimony even at this late stage of the proceedings.

In order to understand how subornation emerged as an object of increased concern in the sixteenth century, it is important to realize that the charge of subornation was the only option available to a party who had been unable to articulate objections to the witness upon first confronting him. Once the witness's deposition was read out, the accused in a sixteenth-century inquest could no longer object to the witness on ethical grounds. The only way one could object to a witness after having heard his testimony was, according to Imbert, "si l'on veut maintenir la deposition faulse, & le tesmoing avoir esté suborné & corrompu" (204; "if one wants to deem the deposition false, the witness having been suborned and corrupted").[8] The protocols of the sixteenth-century inquest thus effectively encouraged objections to witnesses on the specific grounds that they had been suborned. Since the charge of subornation was made after the defendant had heard the testimony against him, and since he was allowed a certain amount of time to prepare a case to support his accusation (whereas he was allowed virtually no time to prepare his reproaches), claiming that an unfavorable witness was suborned was the only procedural recourse for a defendant who was not well acquainted with the witnesses who confronted him.

As an alternative to the test of character, proof of subornation requires no prior familiarity with the witness so charged. Consequently, it is eminently useful in a system of justice obliged to adjudicate disputes among parties not necessarily well known to one another. Moreover, as a concrete (criminal) *act*, subornation – as opposed to a more abstract *attribute* like social standing or *renommée* – is precisely the kind of thing that the inquest is designed to investigate. Thus, it was not only the lack of fit between feudal ethics and the inquest, but also the synergy between the protocols of inquisitional procedure and the concept of subornation that led to a veritable obsession with subornation in both legal manuals and royal legislation in the sixteenth century. As the sixteenth-century witness was called upon to testify in an increasingly abstract and anonymous context in which his ethical status gradually lost its feudal moorings, the very notion of *ethos* itself was in the process of being reformulated, and along with it concepts of what made a testimony reliable.

Ethos *degré zéro*

Perhaps the most famous Renaissance treatment of the problem of reliable testimony is to be found in Michel de Montaigne's 1580

---

[8] Imbert/Guenois 1609: Guenois glosses this as "nous ne recevons à faire preuve que les tesmoins ont deposé en faux sinon au cas que le tesmoin soit accusé de corruption ou subornation" (334).

essay "Des cannibales." [9] This essay is usually read as touting the epistemic superiority of concrete, firsthand experience over theoretical extrapolations – a view that is certainly consonant with Montaigne's brand of skepticism. Once we recognize that this position is not particularly controversial from the perspective of juridical practice, however – particularly if we bear in mind Montaigne's professional activities as a magistrate – such a reading requires considerable modification. At the very least, we must follow the lead of André Tournon and recognize legal discourse as one of the sources of Montaigne's epistemology.[10] The essayist's approach to gathering information about the New World amounts to an application of juridical theory about testimony to the writing of geography and history – and indeed, "tous autres subjects" (205). Montaigne does more than merely import such criteria into his essay, however; he actually takes part in the reshaping of the figure of the witness, a process originally begun in the law courts. Rather than proposing a revolutionary view of the epistemic potential of experience, Montaigne's depiction of the ideal witness constitutes a radical rethinking of the role of *ethos* in guaranteeing the reliability of testimony.

Near the beginning of the essay, having proclaimed that the "tesmoignage de l'Antiquité" (the "testimony of Antiquity," represented by writings attributed to Aristotle and Plato) doesn't contain any information about the New World, Montaigne claims that he has learned about the New World from an eyewitness, a man who has spent ten or twelve years in Antarctic France. Though Montaigne is careful to specify that his witness has firsthand knowledge of America, his ensuing description of his eyewitness does not showcase the man's epistemic capacities. Indeed, when Montaigne pauses to characterize his firsthand source, the question of knowledge – and thus, of experience as a superior source of knowledge – simply drops out of the picture:

---

[9] All French citations of Montaigne are taken from Pierre Villey's edition of the *Essais*. I give volume, essay, and page number. English translations are taken from Donald Frame's one-volume translation of the complete works of Montaigne and are indicated by page number only.

[10] Tournon has written extensively on Montaigne's activities as a jurist and their relation to the *Essais*, most notably in *La Glose et l'essai*. He deals more specifically with the question of testimony in "L'Essai: Un témoignage en suspens," which briefly addresses "Des cannibales" (131-32).

> Cet homme que j'avoy, estoit homme simple et grossier, qui est une condition propre à rendre veritable tesmoignage: car les fines gens remarquent bien plus curieusement et plus de choses, mais ils les glosent; et, pour faire valoir leur interprétation et la persuader, ils ne se peuvent garder d'alterer un peu l'Histoire: ils ne vous representent jamais les choses pures, ils les inclinent et masquent selon le visage qu'ils leur ont veu; et, pour donner credit à leur jugement et vous y attirer, prestent volontiers de ce costé là à la matiere, l'alongent et l'amplifient. Ou il faut un homme très-fidelle, ou si simple qu'il n'ait pas dequoy bastir et donner de la vray-semblance, à des inventions fauces; et qui n'ait rien espousé. Le mien estoit tel (I.31.205)

> This man I had was a simple, crude fellow – a character fit to bear true witness; for clever people observe more things and more curiously, but they interpret them; and to lend weight and conviction to their interpretation, they cannot help altering history a little. They never show you things as they are, but bend and disguise them according to the way they have seen them; and to give credence to their judgment and attract you to it, they are prone to add something to their matter, to stretch it out and amplify it. We need a man either very honest, or so simple that he has not the stuff to build up false inventions and give them plausibility; and wedded to no theory. Such was my man (152)

Both kinds of witnesses Montaigne describes here – the simple man on the one hand and clever people on the other – have firsthand sense experience of the things about which they testify. What recommends the simple man over his clever counterpart is thus not his "experience"; nor is it any kind of enhanced perception of the truth on his part, since the clever witness sees more things and sees them better. Moreover, the essayist never claims that the simple man he lauds *knows* more than do the "clever people" he criticizes; indeed, it is the latter who "observe more things and more curiously."

Given some of the elements of Montaigne's negative characterization of "clever people" – in particular the references to persuasion and amplification – it is tempting to see a rejection of rhetoric in his praise of the testimony of the simple, crude man. But the essayist's critique goes far beyond the question of rhetoric to grapple with the increasingly vexed question of a witness's *ethos*, as well as that of the appropriate contribution of an eyewitness to "l'Histoire."

Clever people "bend and disguise [things] according to the way they have seen them"; in other words, clever people have a point of view that they transmit along with the things they have seen. Both their perceptions and their testimony bear an ethical imprint that necessarily alters "les choses pures." The simple man, by contrast, does not alter things in the process of transmitting information about them. His ability to do this rests upon his utter lack of ethical identity. Though Montaigne does attribute a few general qualities to his witness, his syntax leaves us wondering just which of them are meant to apply to the simple man. He in effect proposes that we need a man who is *either* X *or* Y, *and* Z, and his man was...what exactly? This technique reinforces our sense that the simple man has no specific characteristics at all, since he appears to have no personal inclinations whatsoever. This unassailable character turns out to be a man without qualities – a man to whom nothing is *propre*. Montaigne manages here to invoke the very *idea* of character, without ever allowing the witness an identity of his own.

In "Des cannibales," the ideal witness should not only be unable to construct a rhetorically compelling argument; he must in fact remain entirely absent from the site of his testimony. The best witness, the perfect mediator, is the one that enables us to see through him to "les choses pures." *Fines gens* put too much of their own point of view into their account of things ("ils les inclinent et masquent selon le visage qu'ils leur ont veu"). Montaigne's *homme simple et grossier*, by contrast, becomes authoritative precisely by erasing any trace of himself, both in his encounter with the New World and in his account of it. His credibility is predicated not on the content, then, but precisely on the *emptiness* of his character. It is by now fairly well known that Montaigne took most of the information contained in "Des cannibales" not from conversations with *hommes simples et grossiers* but from books.[11] He omits mention of these sources, however, allowing only that he has spoken with his crude, simple witness. This is because no source Montaigne would

---

[11] In Chapter 9 of his 1911 *L'Exotisme américain dans la littérature française au XVIe siècle*, Gilbert Chinard documents Montaigne's unacknowledged borrowings from, among others, López de Gómara, Benzoni, and Léry. See also the essay by Bernard Weinberg, "Montaigne's Readings for 'Des Cannibales'," in George B. Daniel, Jr., ed., *Renaissance and other Studies in Honor of William Leon Wiley* (Chapel Hill: U of North Carolina P, 1968, 261-279).

name – whether it be a philosopher like Plato, a humanist historian like Francisco López de Gómara, or even an eyewitness like Jean de Léry [12] – could possibly meet the standards of blankness and purity the essayist requires. Montaigne in fact draws on all three of these sources in "Des cannibales," but names only Plato – and then only to reject him as a source of reliable geographical information about America.

Montaigne's witness is utterly irreproachable thanks to the fact that we don't know his name, we don't know where he's from, and we don't hear a thing he says. It has been suggested that early eyewitness histories allowed for the emergence of an explicitly subjective perspective on the world, and as such, could be read as one of the precursors of modern autobiography.[13] Montaigne's characterization of the ideal witness clearly challenges this notion, since his witness's lack of biography – indeed, his complete lack of identity – is presented as crucial to the reliability of the testimony Montaigne supposedly receives from him. This analysis is borne out by the fact that the simple man makes only the briefest of appearances in Montaigne's text; he disappears as soon as he is introduced. To linger with this witness, to allow him to speak, would be to risk turning him into a deponent whose *renommée* would then have to be investigated. Rather than engage in what had become the inconvenient and entangled enterprise of assessing the ethical character of a witness, Montaigne will propose that what makes a testimony reliable is his witness's capacity simply to disappear behind "les choses pures."

The simple man thus testifies without leaving a trace of himself. Just how Montaigne's witness does this has everything to do with the fact that his testimony is ultimately mediated by a second per-

---

[12] See Chinard, Weinberg, and Pierre Villey, *Les Sources*.

[13] In his short piece on Léry and Thevet in *A New History of French Literature*, Michel Jeanneret suggests that while Thevet's cosmography remains mired in classical citations, Léry's *Histoire* manifests a personal, subjective take on the New World. In her book *The Witness and the Other World: Exotic European Travel Writing 400-1600*, Mary Campbell argues more broadly for a more or less causal relationship between eyewitness travel narratives and the emergence of first-person autobiography. She suggests that the narrative innovation of Columbus's *Journal* was to have introduced "private experience into geographical narrative" (192). For Campbell, this representation of what she calls private experience "open[s] up the travel account to a subjectivity and narrativity new to the form and essential to its later masterpieces. The autobiographical and experiential bent and the ample sensibility of the modern genre bear the stain upon them of original sin: it was in the self-love of conquering heroes that the travel memoir was born" (209).

son. Rather than present his witness with the challenge of representing pure experience, Montaigne himself will provide a second-person perspective on the simple man that will enable him to recreate the ethical dialogue on which pre- and early modern testimonial discourse was founded. Montaigne makes clear that his witness gave testimony to him personally, in an oral encounter in which Montaigne deemed him credible. Thus, the burden of establishing the credibility of the witness in "Des cannibales" lies not with the witness, but with the essayist. The witness may be the one who has experienced the New World, but it is Montaigne who establishes the authority of the simple man's testimony.

This becomes all the more clear when we realize that "Des cannibales" turns out not to be about the witness's experiences at all, but rather revolves around an ethical comparison between the New World and the Old. After establishing the source of his information about Antarctic France, Montaigne returns to the philosophical question with which the essay is primarily concerned: "je trouve, pour revenir à mon propos, qu'il n'y a rien de barbare et de sauvage en cette nation . . . sinon que chacun appelle barbarie ce qui n'est pas de son usage" (I.31.205; "to return to my subject, I think there is nothing barbarous and savage in that nation . . . except that each man calls barbarism whatever is not his own practice"; 152). The essayist pursues his reflections on the matter by appealing to an explicitly Platonic view of the superiority of nature over art (206); by rueing the fact that Plato and Lycurgus will never know the peoples of the New World; and finally, by casting his entire description of America as an imaginary conversation with Plato himself ("C'est une nation, diroy je à Platon . . . "; 206). At this point, Montaigne's simple man has disappeared into an anonymous, amorphous group of witnesses ("à ce que m'ont dit *mes tesmoings*"; 207), and we never get to hear from a single one of them. Rather than quote from their testimonies, Montaigne cites from the works of Propertius, Virgil, Juvenal and Claudian.

Montaigne's return to the Ancients, after his initial ostentatious dismissal of them in his search for information about the New World in "Des cannibales," does not render his essay any more or less "reliable" as a depiction of sixteenth-century America. What it does do is give us significant insight into what the essayist and magistrate understood to be the place and function of eyewitness testimony in the production of a judgment, be it legal or philosophical.

The simple man, we recall, is a good witness precisely because he does *not* pass judgment on the object of his testimony, but rather communicates it in its "pure" form. Conversely, Montaigne discounts the testimony of *fines gens* on the grounds that they interpret what they see – in other words, he finds it problematic that they make judgments about their experiences. And yet, when he laments the fact that the discovery of America came too late to be known by Plato and Lycurgus, it is because they were men "qui en eussent sceu mieux juger que nous" (206; "able to judge them better than we"; 153). Clearly, the ethical stance of the ancient philosophers determines the value of their judgments. In order to make sense of Montaigne's apparent equivocation here, we must again recognize that for the magistrate, the function of the witness and that of the judge are to be kept strictly separate. If for Montaigne, the ideal witness transmits raw empirical data untainted by his own point of view, the judge, by contrast, is obliged to assume a position and issue a verdict. In "Des cannibales," with the help of his ancient sources, Montaigne rather uncharacteristically assumes the role of judge, synthesizing the data of the anonymous firsthand testimonies he has supposedly heard into an unambiguously damning verdict on the moral state of European civilization.[14]

Montaigne thus shifts the ethical burden of this testimony about the New World onto himself, whilst delegating epistemic authority to his anonymous witness. Thanks to the transparent simple man, Montaigne is able to know the New World as well as if he had seen it for himself; thanks to Montaigne, the testimony of the simple man can play a role in an ethical judgment. Even though we are supposed to see through him, the simple man cannot disappear altogether if Montaigne is to legitimately assume the position of judge. Montaigne's *ethos* is all over "Des cannibales": if he were to present *himself* as a witness, he would surely be found guilty of hav-

---

[14] In his classic study, "Un cannibale en haut de chausses: Montaigne, la différence et la logique de l'identité," Gérard Defaux focuses on Montaigne's posture of epistemological purity – what Defaux terms "le vieux rêve critique de l'approche innocente" (928). Given the material studied here, I'm not convinced that this dream was at all characteristic of French culture before Descartes. Rather, I think Montaigne was struggling to articulate a new approach to testimony in "Des cannibales." Montaigne's struggle with the question of the ethical character of the witness suggests that the lesson Defaux draws from his essay – that "toute lecture, toute interprétation n'est au fond que traduction" (956) – was in fact the prevailing view of testimonial "readings" and "interpretations" in Montaigne's time.

ing "ben[t] and disguise[d] things according to the way [he had] seen them."

The dialectic of testimony and judgment in "Des cannibales" indicates that neither the testimony of the simple man nor the independent judgments of any single individual (in particular those of Montaigne himself, "si frivole et si vain") would alone be sufficient to ground a legitimate verdict. Thus, the essay suggests that testimony and judgment, if utterly distinct, are mutually dependent. The judge requires the testimony of (preferably firsthand) witnesses as a basis for his verdict; at the same time, witnesses cannot articulate judgments without compromising the integrity of their testimony. The mutual dependency of testimony and judgment here indicates that Montaigne has managed to salvage (or invent) a dialogic structure for his textual rendering of the testimony of an anonymous witness, thereby preserving the intersubjective quality of testimonial discourse even in the absence of an identifiable testimonial subject.

By maintaining a strict distinction between the witness and the judge and by privileging eyewitness testimony, Montaigne hews closely to juridical theory and practice in "Des cannibales." As I have insisted, the use of eyewitnesses in the process of formulating judgments was hardly novel in pre- and early modern culture. What is new in Montaigne's time, however, is the increasing reliance on *anonymous* witnesses: witnesses who have neither a readily identifiable ethical status, as did witnesses in the feudal era, nor a culturally sanctioned authority, as did those authors (like Plato and Aristotle) whose testimony had traditionally served as a resource for writing and thinking about geography, history, and "tous autres subjects." The testimony of the anonymous witness cannot be evaluated on the basis of his character; instead, the ethos of such a witness emerges from his testimony.

The Credibility of Witnesses v. the Credibility of Testimony

In the sixteenth century, as we have seen, what was formerly a preliminary test of a witness's legal capacity to testify had become a *post facto* attempt to evaluate a potentially unfamiliar witness who had already testified under oath, largely with reference to his very testimony. In other words, whereas previously, his testimony had been evaluated on the basis of his *renommée*, now the reputation of the witness was frequently constructed *on the basis of his testimony*. When the ethical test of character precedes the taking of the testimonial oath, as it did in the early years of the lay inquisition in France, the evaluation of the witness precedes and thus underwrites his testimony. When that temporal order is inverted, a witness's ethical "character" will instead become a *product* of his testimony rather than its foundation.

We can observe a modified instance of this inversion in the hierarchy of the criteria used to evaluate witnesses and testimony in Gonneville's *Relation authentique*. While Gonneville's reputation appears to have constituted the legal basis for his testimony, that reputation is itself a function of Gonneville's firsthand experience. There are no references to the community's perception of Gonneville's ethical character – the very element central to the construction of the reliable witness in the accounts of Polo and Mandeville – in the *Relation authentique*. What sets Gonneville's *Relation* apart from the writings of Polo and Mandeville is the fact that Gonneville's credibility appears to be considered by all concerned to be a *product* of the reputation he acquired as someone who had particular kinds of experiences, and not some foundational condition that predates those experiences. In other words, Gonneville is not characterized in the *Relation* as an essentially reliable person, whether as a Poloesque "learned citizen" of Honfleur or as a Mandevillian soldier of Christ; rather, he appears to have been deemed a reliable witness as a *result* of his experiences in the New World.

The catch here, of course, is that Gonneville's personal history as an eyewitness is effectively identical to the testimony that such a history is meant to authorize. The history of the eyewitness is not in any way prior to eyewitness history; the two revolve around each other. In the local, oral setting of Gonneville's *Relation*, however, these two poles do not give rise to circular self-referentiality, but rather to dialogue. Gonneville's personal history is ultimately fixed by his community (and cast as reputation), based on its members' interactions with him. Similarly, Gonneville's eyewitness testimony acquires its credibility (in the eyes of his community, and thus with respect to the local judicial authorities) as a result of its predication on Gonneville's own reputation. A major feature of this dialogic structure, as we have noted, is that Gonneville is still recognizable as a specifically second-person witness. He gives in testimony directly to a readily identifiable, ethically definable community.

The addressee of a testimony, as I have suggested, is in effect its co-author, and in this sense plays the role of a witness himself. This witness to the witness participates in the ethical dialogue through which the pre-modern *testis* is legitimated as a deponent. For John Mandeville, this function is fulfilled by those who consider themselves members of the Christian community to whom he addresses the account of his travels; for Marco Polo, I argued, this position was occupied by Kublai Khan. The lack of any stable French-sponsored enterprise in America, along with the inability of French sovereigns to contain the religious conflicts that coursed through France throughout the sixteenth century, sapped the power of abstractions like "France" or "Christianity" to ground an ethically persuasive testimonial stance in French eyewitness accounts.[15] The majority of French travelers to the New World in the sixteenth century were not sent by the French king or his representatives; consequently, they had nobody to report to. Therefore, it was unclear who their partners in the testimonial dialogue were. As both his own ethical identity and that of his addressee have become increasingly ill-defined, the French witness tends to lose his dialogic bearings, and thus, his capacity to give testimony that can be deemed credible according to ethical criteria. The case of the French Huguenot settlement in Florida is exemplary in this regard, both for the way in which accounts of it attempt – and fail – to characterize it as a collective "French" enterprise, and for the way in which the accounts themselves were received by Charles IX.

In the *Histoire memorable de la reprinse de la Floride* (1568), an anonymous firsthand account of Dominique de Gourgues's 1567 trip to exact revenge for the Spanish attack on the French occupants of Fort Caroline the previous year, we learn that when Gourgues's party landed and began seeking local allies to support the undertaking, the native Floridians wanted to be reassured that Gourgues's men were "vray François" and not Spanish or Por-

---

[15] In *Inventing Renaissance France*, Timothy Hampton paints a compelling portrait of sixteenth-century France as a community in perpetual crisis (see especially chapter one, "The Garden of Letters"). Hampton's book explores the consequences this fragmentation of community has for literary forms in the period. Whereas the present discussion focuses on the difficulties of dialogue within France, Hampton's concentrates on French dialogues with extramural "Others."

tuguese. The natives reportedly came up with a rather unusual test of nationality: if the members of Gourgues's party were true Frenchmen, as they claimed to be, then they should sing Psalms in French to prove it. (The natives reportedly even called out a few requests.) Upon hearing this, Gourgues commanded his people to sing some Psalms, which they promptly did, in Clément Marot's vernacular translations. It all ends well, according to the author of the *Histoire*: "Lesquels Psalmes chantez par les François asseurarent les Sauvages d'estre vrais François" ("The Psalms sung by the French assured the Savages that they were indeed true Frenchmen").[16]

This scene must have had a curious impact on its original readers. Appearing in the midst of the second and third in a series of armed conflicts between Catholic and Protestant factions in France that would continue even after the Edict of Nantes in 1598, it suggests that one test of authentic Frenchness is the ability to sing Psalms in the vernacular – an activity explicitly associated with Protestantism. The Wars of Religion (as they were already known in the sixteenth century) made Gourgues's claims to represent French necessarily polemic: to characterize oneself as a "true Frenchman" in the context of the civil wars was to call one's religious adversaries traitors to the nation.

The French nation, such as it was, was not initially much interested in Jean Ribaut's Florida enterprise, much less Dominique de Gourgues's revenge plot. It was well known that those who had been attacked and killed by the Spanish at Fort Caroline were Protestants, and Charles IX was not about to join battle with Phillip II over them. Gourgues essentially set off on his own, with neither Charles's support nor his blessing; when he returned to France, having successfully attacked the Spaniards, Charles refused to see him. Though Ribaut's expedition to Florida had been undertaken at the behest of the Admiral of France, the Protestant Gaspard de Coligny, by the time Goulaine de Laudonnière's account of

---

[16] This account is published in Suzanne Lussagnet's *Français en Floride*. The passage I have paraphrased reads "disant que, s'ils estoyent vrais François, comme ils disoyent estre, qu'ils chantassent des Psalmes ainsi qu'avoyent fait par cy devant les capitaines Laudonnière et Jehan Ribaud et ceux qui estoyent avec eux quand ils habitoyent à la Floride. Quoy voyant, le Capitaine Gourgues commanda à ses gens de chanter Psalmes à la louange de Dieu, ce qu'il firent . . . promptement. . . . Lesquels Psalmes chantez par les François asseurarent les Sauvages d'estre vrais François" (243). Lussagnet identifies the three Psalms requested by the Floridians as 43, 50 and 91 (243n2).

these voyages was published (along with Nicolas Le Challeux's description of the Spanish attack) in 1586, Coligny had been brutally assassinated in the Saint Bartholomew's Day massacres. Despite receiving repeated appeals on behalf of the surviving kin of those killed at Fort Caroline, Charles IX never saw fit to take military action against the Spanish for what even Catherine de Medicis termed a "massacre." Not surprisingly, then, Laudonnière's editor could think of no more suitable dedicatee than Sir Walter Ralegh. The enthusiastic reception of Marot's Psalms in Florida notwithstanding, the attempt to turn Ribaut's Huguenots into representative Frenchmen failed miserably. Instead, they became Protestant martyrs.[17]

French accounts like this one stage witnesses who try, but ultimately fail to create the illusion of an ethical relationship with their readers. Jean de Léry, by contrast, will explicitly abandon a pretention to ethical dialogue, and claim to offer an account of the New World based solely on his experiences. Léry published a firsthand account of his stay in French Brazil that is frequently cited as one of Montaigne's primary sources of information about the New World (indeed, Gilbert Chinard asserted that "il n'y a pas un détail [chez Montaigne] sur la vie des Cannibales que nous ne trouvions dans Léry" [196]; "there is not a single detail about cannibal life [in Montaigne's essay] that we do not find in Léry"). Montaigne borrowed much more than anthropological data from Léry, however, for it is in Léry's *Histoire d'un voyage faict en la terre de Bresil*, first published in 1578, that we find the prototype for the essayist's simple man. There is a crucial difference between Montaigne's witness and Léry, however: whereas the testimony of the all but absent simple man is mediated by the ethical presence of the essayist, Jean de Léry was on his own.

Léry originally made the trip to Brazil in 1556 as part of a Huguenot contingent sent by Calvin from Geneva to the French colony at Guanabara, which, under the direction of Nicolas Durand de Villegagnon, was to be a model of religious harmony far from the simmering conflicts between Catholics and Protestants that later exploded into full-fledged civil war in France. However, religious disagreements emerged between the Huguenots and Villegagnon, and

---

[17] The Spanish accounts of the attack acknowledge a confessional motive. Menéndez himself reports sparing a few of the French because he had determined they were Catholic. For the Spanish sources, see Eugenio Ruidíaz y Caravia, *La Florida, su conquista y colonización por Pedro Menéndez de Avilés*.

the Huguenots were eventually expelled from the colony. Subsequently, two purportedly eyewitness accounts, one by the Catholic André Thévet in his 1575 *Cosmographie Universelle*, the other by Léry in his *Histoire* (first published in 1578), competed to give the authoritative story of the colony. Léry's account thus pits two eyewitness testimonies against one another. Simply claiming that he *was* an eyewitness was consequently not sufficient if Léry was to convince his audience that his testimony was more reliable than Thevet's.

Léry was no public figure when he published the *Histoire*. As Geoffroy Atkinson notes, "Léry n'avait pas un nom, ni un rang, capables d['en] faire imposer la lecture" to the broad audience that the book eventually reached (*Nouveaux* 41; "Léry had neither the name nor the status to compel the reading of his book"). For all practical purposes, Léry was a stranger to most of his audience when he published his *Histoire*. Furthermore, as a Huguenot, he would not have been able to exploit the notion that he was a representative Frenchman at the height of the religious wars in France. In contrast to Mandeville or Gonneville, then, Léry is not addressing a community that recognizes him either in terms of his personal *renommée* or in terms of his overall *ethos*. Léry's situation thus replicates what was increasingly that of the witness in the juridical domain, whose reputation can no longer serve as an index of truthfulness because it can no longer be satisfactorily determined.

The introduction, exploitation and suppression of the eyewitness in "Des cannibales" reveals the degree to which *renommée* lingers as a theoretical criterion for evaluating witnesses even when the reputation of witnesses remains largely obscure in practice. For his part, when he attempts to establish the reliability of his eyewitness account of the short-lived French colony in Brazil, Léry feels compelled to address the question of his *renommée*, if only to beg the reader to set the matter of his reputation aside: what one should ask of his testimony, he writes, is "si ce que j'ay dit . . . est vray ou non; car c'est là le poinct, et non pas à la façon des mauvais plaideurs, esgarer la matiere en s'informant qui je suis" (88; "whether what I have said . . . is true or not, for *that* is the point; and not, in the style of bad lawyers, to confound the issue by seeking to know who I am"; lviii).[18] Only a bad lawyer, Léry suggests,

---

[18] References to Léry in French are to Frank Lestringant's edition. English versions are cited from Janet Whatley's translation, though they are sometimes modified to reflect a more literal rendering.

would make the irrelevant detour into questions of *renommée* when evaluating witness testimony – questions that could only lead, as the ordinance of Moulins had indicated, to "plusieurs inconveniens & involution de proces."

In medieval folklaw, let us recall, the question of the witness's experience was secondary to the question of his status in his community. In the early inquisition, as well as in medieval eyewitness travel literature, we saw how the question of the witness's status still retained priority over the question of his experience, even when his experience became an object of the court's interest in the context of inquisitional procedure. Subsequently, the evolution of the ways in which testimony was introduced into judicial deliberations led to a gradual abandonment of the effort to evaluate a witness's ethical status, and a correspondingly intensified focus on the evaluation of his deposition, now an entity apart. This is the kind of testimonial act we see invoked in Montaigne's "Des cannibales" and in Léry's *Histoire*. Rather than an interlocutor in the ethical, intersubjective dialogue that had been the foundation of pre-modern testimony, Léry's eyewitness is left alone with nothing but his experiences – experiences that constitute the very testimony they are meant to authorize.

Léry is no more "experienced" than Gonneville was (in fact, he spent significantly less time in the New World than Gonneville had), yet he foregrounds firsthand experience in an extremely self-conscious manner in his account. Unlike those who presume to write about America as a whole, he announces that his intention is to "seulement declarer ce que j'ay pratiqué, veu, ouy et observé" during his stay in Brazil ("simply to declare what I myself have experienced, seen, heard and observed"; 3). Léry makes this statement, however, not because he has suddenly discovered how much knowledge one can gain from experience; rather, he divorces the issue of "truth" from the question of his character because he is quite unable to appeal to his own ethical authority as a witness. Whereas the authority of medieval eyewitness testimony was predicated on the ethical stance of the witness that delivered it, the authority of Léry's *Histoire d'un voyage faict en la terre de Bresil* is constructed entirely on the basis of the testimony it offers. What the *Histoire* ultimately aims to provide is a testimony *without* an ethically identifiable witness: what Montaigne calls "*les choses pures*," and what Léry will term "*science*."

The Site of Witnessing: From Here to There

Where previously, witnessing had been a matter of "being here" to testify, now the emphasis has shifted to a focus on "being there" to see something one subsequently reports on. The immediacy of the testimonial encounter is transferred from the moment of bearing oral witness to the moment of a privileged eyewitness vision outside the confines of that encounter. We no longer see the witness before our eyes (and here, "Des cannibales" is an instructive example, since Montaigne places himself so squarely between the witness and us, who supposedly receive the simple man's testimony); rather, we are supposed to be shown some past moment that the witness has experienced, and that his testimony will re-present or make proximate, even as the witness himself remains distant. Such "testimony without a witness" encourages the possibility of thinking of experiences as detachable from the people who have them – that is, as objective occurrences or events that have a claim to truth regardless of who testifies about them. When the witness fades into the background, his experience (in the ideal form of "les choses pures") can come to the fore.

Paulmier de Gonneville's *Relation authentique* showed how a report of firsthand experience, even of the new and exotic, could be authorized by a dialogue between the eyewitness and his addressees – addressees who thus become, in effect, the co-authors of his testimony. Whereas Gonneville could enlist his "compatriots" as witnesses to his credibility, in much the same way that the reliability of Montaigne's "simple man" is vouched for by Montaigne, Léry has no such interlocutor; nor does he see fit to invent one. At the time Léry composed his *Histoire*, the ethical relationships on which medieval juridical consensus had historically been founded were disintegrating. Ultimately, however, the breakdown of the ethical model opens up a space in which the epistemic foundation of eyewitness testimony, which had been secondary to its ethical foundation, can assume a new priority. Despite the fact that firsthand experience – particularly visual experience – had long enjoyed epistemic prestige in the law courts, the belief that a witness's credibility should be predicated first and foremost on his experience was a new one in the sixteenth century. Though firsthand experience and empirical knowledge had long been linked, concern for empirical knowledge of facts had been subordinated to an interest in the ethical status of the parties involved in juridical proceedings. It is only when testimony itself comes to be considered a *primarily* epistemic rather than a *primarily* ethical discourse that (epistemic) experience will become both the subject and the very ground of testimony. This is precisely what happens, albeit in fits and starts, over the two centuries or so that separate Marco Polo and John Mandeville from Jean de Léry.

It may sound like a commonplace to suggest that eyewitness historians of the New World privileged "experience" over "booklearning." It is important to note, however, that in this respect, they do not differ all that much from historians who remained on the European continent. Even Francisco López de Gómara, so much maligned by eyewitness historians because of his own lack of "experience," acknowledges that experience has shown the Spaniards what philosophy was unable to: "Niegan todos los antiguos filósofos de la gentilidad el paso de nuestro hemisferio al de los antípodas. . . . Empero está ya tan andado y sabido, que cada día van allá nuestros españoles a ojos (como dicen) cerrados; y así, está la experiencia en contrario de la filosofía" (17; "All of the pagan philosophers of Antiquity deny that it is possible to go from our hemisphere to the antipodes. . . . And yet this is now so common and well known, that our Spaniards go there every day with their eyes closed (as one says); thus is experience contrary to philosophy"). López de Gómara's choice of words here is illuminating; the experience of the Spaniards is authoritative not because it refers to a moment of new and unprecedented vision, but rather because it is something these men can do with their eyes closed ("a ojos cerrados"). For López de Gómara, "experience" does not designate a realm outside of tradition and habit; rather, "experience" is defined, precisely, by repetition. López de Gómara thus assimilates "experience" to that which is well-known, defusing the potential novelty of the New World experience by positing it as habitual and even automatic; indeed, it is already the object of common knowledge ("tan andado y sabido"). While experience is defined in opposition to philosophy here, it does not acquire an authoritative valence on that basis alone; rather, experience becomes authoritative only when it attains the status of common knowledge. Thus, we have not yet reached the point where the experiences of the witness are construed primarily as those of an *individual*.

Even Michel de Montaigne, whose second-longest *essai* is an extended reflection on the peculiarities of individual experience, enlists López de Gómara's view of experience as collective in order to accredit his description of the New World. In "Des cannibales," the eyewitness's experiences, initially set apart from the traditional wisdom represented by Plato and Aristotle, quickly become the experiences of the French nation or European society or even mankind as a whole as the essay progresses. In one of his many hymns of praise to New World societies in this essay, Montaigne writes that "ce que *nous voyons par experience* en ces nations-là, surpasse ... la conception et le desir mesme de la philosophie" (255, emphasis mine; "what *we actually see* in these nations surpasses ... the conceptions and the very desire of philosophy"; 153). Similarly, the Tupi are characterized by a "nayfveté ... pure et simple, comme *nous la voyons par experience*" (255, emphasis mine; "a naturalness so pure and simple as *we see by experience*"; 153).

When experiences are perceived as largely shared or shareable, there is no reason to address the question of experience in terms that oppose it to "tradition" or "common knowledge" – in other words, no reason to cast it in terms of an individual as opposed to a collectivity. López de Gómara and Montaigne do not present experience here in terms of ineffable singularity, but rather explicitly as something that could and did "belong" to an entire nation. Rather than something "unrepeatable," experience could in fact be defined by repetition. There is thus no necessary link between the notion of "experience" and the first-person singular. Such a link, however, will eventually be forged by eyewitness testimony that is born, diffused and received exclusively in writing.

CHAPTER FOUR

THE FIRST PERSON

THE material medium of the legal witness deposition in France changes significantly between the era of folklaw and the sixteenth century, from an essentially non-linguistic act accompanied by a formulaic oral statement, to the written record of a fundamentally oral transaction, and finally, I argue here, to a document that was potentially more authoritative than its oral antecedent. Moreover, the grammatical form that the written deposition assumed tended to suppress the dialogic encounter out of which it had emerged, thus making it increasingly difficult to think of the witness as a second person. Ultimately, the reconceptualization of witnessing occasioned by qualitative changes in the relative status of the oral and the written witness deposition effectively transformed the witness from a second person into a first person in the sixteenth century.

The priority granted to orality in so much medieval literature is consonant with attitudes towards the relative reliability of witnesses and documents in medieval law. The oral encounter was considered to be ethically superior to the exchange mediated by writing in the medieval juridical context. The oral testimony of witnesses continued to trump the evidence of written documents in the lay courts after the introduction of inquisitional procedure in France. Medieval legists tended to generalize the maxim "témoins passent lettres," drawn from *Novelle* 73: "Dignior est vox viva testium quam vox mortua instrumentorum" – or, as Jean Boutiller's fourteenth-century *Somme rurale* puts it, "tesmoins de vive voix, passent lettres."[1] The motivations for this preference for witnesses over docu-

---

[1] See Lévy 84-105. The Roman source had said only that *témoins instrumentaires* surpassed the written act they had witnessed; but the superiority of witnesses

ments went beyond a purely ideological attachment to juridical tradition, since there were also practical reasons to favor witness testimony over written evidence. Because witnesses had been an essential part of folklaw procedure, a system of controls had developed to gather and evaluate oral witness testimony. No such system was in place for the written document, due, no doubt, to its very scarcity in juridical proceedings. Moreover, the techniques that were used to test a witness's good faith, such as the threat of a duel, were not transposable to the written document. In other words, oral witness testimony functioned to produce satisfactory verdicts in a way that written documents could not in the medieval period.

By the time we reach the sixteenth century in France, however, the hierarchy between the witness and the document has been reversed, as the ordinance of Moulins stipulates. As I suggested in the previous chapter, one motivation for the ordinance of Moulins's call for restrictions on the use of witness testimony was the impasse that resulted from the ethical confrontation between witnesses and defendants who were not well known to one another. This "inconvenience" stemmed not only from the fact that parties to a juridical dispute were frequently not in the position to make meaningful ethical judgments about the witnesses they faced, but was also a consequence of the form of the juridical deposition itself.

The Decline of Orality

Like most other elements of inquisitional procedure that were foreign to medieval folklaw, writing was not embraced in French lay courts in the years immediately following Louis IX's establishment of the secular inquest. Beaumanoir explains that in canon law, one is required to present one's complaint in writing, but "de tout ce ne fet on riens en cort laie, selonc nostre coustume, car on ne plede pas par escris.... Et convient que li home par qui li jugemens doit estre feis, retienent en lors cuers ce sor quoi il doivent jugier" (15; "we do not do anything like that in the lay courts, according to our

---

becomes generalized in the early 1200's. In this period, writes Lévy, the legists simply adopted the principle to all occasions, and considered Roman cases where written proof was represented as preferable to witness testimony as so many exceptions to the general rule that posited the superiority of witnesses.

custom, because we do not enter pleas in writing. . . . And it is appropriate that the men who are to judge a case retain by heart the matter that they are to judge"). He goes on to say that since some disputes produce so much information that a judge's memory might fail to retain it all, judges can take notes if they so choose – but they aren't required to write down anything. Similarly, if the parties are in dispute over several different points, they "*poent* baillier en escrit ce qu'il entendent à prouver" (15). Writing is completely optional here; it has no particular juridical value in and of itself. It serves mainly as a means of information storage and retrieval in the context of a juridical encounter that is fundamentally oral. Beaumanoir further suggests that witness testimony in the late thirteenth century could be transmitted by the *auditeur* to the judge orally when he specifies that no court functionary should hear witnesses alone, "car s'il les ooit seus, et il portoit le dit des tesmoins en jugement, *ou par escrit, ou sans escrit*, et partie le debatoit," one would have to start the procedure all over again (17).

Paul Guilhiermoz maintains that there was a significant gulf between canon and lay procedure in fourteenth-century France with regard to the use of writing ("Il y a . . . une véritable abîme entre le rôle que l'écriture jouait dans la procédure canonique et celui dont elle dut se contenter dans la procédure française"; "Persistance" 22). Despite the introduction of writing by the parties in the form of the "articles" into which they were to organize the points of their dispute, the inquest was still always preceded by an oral debate. In his handbook for lawyers, however, Jean Imbert suggests that the authority of oral procedure holds sway only in the domain of trivial disputes in the sixteenth century: "Un juge avise bien, que pour une chose legere et de petite valeur, il ne face un long proces, mais le plus sommairement qu'il pourra, comme examinant les tesmoings verballement, sans en faire un proces par escrit" (17r; "A judge does well when, in the case of something inconsequential where little is at stake, he does not undertake a lengthy trial, but rather [handles the case] in the most summary way possible, by for example examining witnesses orally, without turning it into a written procedure"). Similarly, "ne se baillent reproches ne salutations de tesmoings par escript en un proces qu'il faut sommairement discuter, quand il est question de petite chose: mais faut que tout soit faict verbalement: l'examen des tesmoings, les reproches, & salutations d'iceux & en la presence des parties" (21r; "reproaches and appearance of witnesses are not recorded in writing in summary proceedings that bear on petty matters; rather, everything should be done orally: the examination of witnesses, the reproaches, and their appearance before the court and before the parties"). The orality that is at the heart of medieval testimony is here associated with a relative lack of legal importance, since the purely oral examination of witnesses is reserved for cases that are believed to be of little consequence. [2] Moreover, Imbert's account of the *procès par écrit* makes clear that its written dimension does not function merely to generate and maintain an official record of what could be construed as at bottom an oral procedure. Rather, writing is, through and through, the very medium of the administration of justice in the sixteenth-century *procès par écrit*, so pervasive as to displace the face-to-face encounter as the primary vehicle of witness testimony. The status of the face-to-face encounter and the oral deposition that underpin early written procedure had changed by Imbert's time, leading to a qualitative shift in the ways in which writing functioned in the administration of justice. This shift, in turn, had a profound effect on the way witnesses and witness testimony were used and understood.

In *Medieval French Literature and Law*, Howard Bloch argues that the expansion of writing in legal proceedings had a significant impact on French vernacular literature in the 12th-14th centuries. Bloch reads the tales told by the Knights of the Round Table at King Arthur's court as "depositions" explicitly represented as being recorded by one of Arthur's clerks, and argues that the consignment to writing is what ultimately permits the testimony of the knights to endure as literature. What I would draw attention to here, however, is the fact that the writings of Arthur's clerks are grounded in an originary orality – an orality that will continue to authorize witness testimony well beyond the introduction of the inquisition in the thirteenth century. There is, significantly, always a scene of oral testimony at the origin of the deposition-cum-chivalric

---

[2] The ordinance of 1498 is at least partly concerned with the distinction between ordinary (open, oral) procedure and extraordinary (closed, written) procedure. Esmein asserts that even as the ordinance was published, "the extraordinary procedure had become ordinary" (148) – that is to say, the *procès verbal* was more a theory than a practice, since most cases were handled according to extraordinary procedure. In modern French usage, the *procès verbal* is the official record of the verbal interactions between a suspect and officers of the law.

tale. As Bloch observes, "in order to assume significance within a social context," the knights' adventures "must first be recounted publicly" (209). The writing here is ancillary; what is essential for the credibility of the knights' testimony is that they depose in person to their own community. Indeed, the fact that the knights enjoy a certain status in their community is what puts them in a position to testify in the first place. They are recognized in the ethical sense by those who receive their original oral "deposition." The resulting written record does not *confer* credibility on the testimony of the knights, but *draws* its own authority from that possessed by the oral deposition.[3] Bloch goes on to describe a subsequent transformation of the knightly testimony, this one based entirely in writing: the material recorded by Arthur's scribes is represented as having been recovered and edited by the author of the Pseudo-Map Cycle. Even in this second-order written version, however, the oral encounter still ultimately grants legitimacy to the written document, since the putative referent – indeed, the very *matière* – of all of this writing is the knight's oral deposition.

As I suggested in chapter one, the linguistic manifestation of the compurgatory oath constitutes the very substance of the compurgatory witness's testimony as a performative act of ethical solidarity. The introduction of inquisitional procedure modifies but does not radically alter the performative dimension of the compurgatory model. Though inquisitional testimony had an epistemic basis, the written record of such a deposition had only a derivative authority; the "original" deposition, and hence the actual testimonial act, was the oral statement under oath. Guilhiermoz cites from the thirteenth-century *Grand coutumier de France* the articulary formula "[X] dient et proposent, *et autrefois ont dit et proposé de bouche par devant vous*" ("[X] say and propose, and formerly said and proposed orally before you") or some variant thereof that foregrounds the original oral encounter that the written document merely records

---

[3] Most studies of writing in medieval culture have sought to modify classic Ong-McLuhan technological determinism (and I would argue that Ong himself never really espoused the extreme version of this view; he merely paid close attention to differences that had previously been little studied). See e.g. Michael Clanchy, who cautions against the view that writing had taken over from orality in late-medieval England: "Dependence on symbolic gestures and the spoken word persisted in law and literature, despite the growth of literacy . . . pre-literate habits of mind persisted long after documents became common" (*From Memory to Written Record* 226). Green, *Crisis*, also evinces this view.

("Persistance" 27). Similar formulae were used when judges invited parties to submit their complaint in writing (to "bailler par escript . . . leurs faiz et raisons aujourd'huy en jugement pardevant nous plaidiez"; 28), again implying the originary oral encounter from which the written elements of early inquisitional procedure were derived. Any part of the plea or of the written articles that were later determined to have strayed from the oral original was rejected. Guilhiermoz gives evidence for this all the way into the 15th century, and notes that the practice of referring written records back to oral responses was abandoned only in the sixteenth century ("ce fut seulement au XVIe siècle que l'usage d'accorder les articles tendît à disparaître"; 31).

The conditions under which the witness deposition acquired juridical legitimacy in the sixteenth-century inquest led to increasing uncertainty about whether the initial oral statement, on the one hand, or the written version of that testimony, on the other, constituted the substance of a witness's testimony. A witness's obligation to reiterate his testimony several times over the course of months, itself in part a product of the increased use of extensive written mediation in juridical proceedings, inevitably produced variations that looked suspicious to increasingly literate-minded lawyers. The "problem" of variation did not affect forms of testimony such as the purgatory oath or the duel. Nor was what we would today consider significant variation between oral testimony and written record considered meaningful immediately upon the introduction of writing into legal procedure via the inquest, since writing served then merely to record, and not truly vehicle, witness testimony.

As we have already seen in the previous chapter, the complex mediation that resulted from the expansion of written procedure served to distance a witness's oath, which was of course always given in person, from his testimony, which had become first and foremost a document. Whereas a sixteenth-century witness was expected to confirm a deposition he may initially have given in weeks or indeed months before, the initial deposition and ultimate confirmation of witness testimony in the inquest described by Beaumanoir occurred at essentially the same time. Up until about the mid-fifteenth century, the witness's written deposition was immediately read out to him by the recording officer himself and affirmed or amended before it went into the dossier and on to the judge. One presumes that the witness himself had little input into the finished product beyond his initial oral statement, since, in the *pays de droit écrit*, witness depositions were written up in Latin until the end of the fourteenth century; in areas governed by customary law, they were recorded in either French or Latin. The written document thus necessarily "varied" from the oral original, since it was frequently in a language other than the one in which the witness had deposed. This reinforces the notion that the medieval written deposition was a *record* of testimony, not testimony itself.

A 1490 ordinance requiring the use of the vernacular for the writing up of witness depositions suggests that the distance between the oral deposition and its written record was by this time perceived as a meaningful discrepancy. According to the ordinance, the vernacular is to be used so that witnesses are able to understand their depositions, which were to be recorded in the "language and form" of the oral deposition, "tel que lesdits tesmoins puissent entendre leurs deposicions et on les leur puisse lire et recenser en tel langage et forme qu'ils auront dit et deposé" (quoted in Guilhiermoz, *Enquêtes* 78). Article 47 of Louis XII's ordinance of June 1510 states "Pour obvier aux abus et inconveniens, qui sont par cidevant advenus au moyen de ce que les juges desdits païs de droit escrit ont fait, les procès criminels desdits païs en latin, et toutes enquestes pareillement, avons ordonné et ordonnons, afin que les temoins entendent leurs dépositions et les criminels, les procès faits contre eux que doresnavant tous les procès criminels et les enquestes en quelque matière que ce soit, seront faites en vulgaire et langage du païs où seront faites lesdits procès criminels et enquestes, autrement ne seront d'aucun effet ou valeur" (Isambert 596; "In order to obviate the abuses and inconveniences which have heretofore resulted from the judges of the said districts of written law having conducted the criminal actions of the said districts, as well as the inquests, in Latin, we have ordained and hereby ordain that henceforth all criminal actions and the said inquests ... shall be done in the vernacular and the language of the district, so that the witnesses may understand their depositions and the criminals the proceedings against them" [Esmein 148n1]). Here we see that a witness may not previously have been able to understand his own written testimony when it was presented to him for confirmation. We should not assume, however, that the order to use the vernacular here indicates a conscious desire for a more intimate link between the original oral deposition and the written record of testimony. In fact, the ordinance implies that the good faith of the witness who deposes orally is no longer sufficient to constitute credible testimony. Thus, it has become necessary that the oral deposition take the form of a faithful transcription. No longer merely the record of an oral original, written testimony was to be an improved (because fraud-proof) version of a *temporally* prior oral statement – an oral statement whose *ontological* priority over the written record was thereby threatened. No longer the defining moment of the testimonial encounter, the authority of the oral deposition has been compromised.[4]

In the sixteenth as in the thirteenth century, witnesses who had taken the oath were interrogated individually outside of the courtroom by a team of legal functionaries who recorded the deposition in writing. This written deposition became a part of the dossier eventually presented to the judge presiding over the case, who virtually never interrogated the witnesses himself. Beaumanoir indicates that in thirteenth-century procedure, *auditeurs* were to write down witness testimony, seal it, and deliver the document to the judges. Imbert, however, describes an additional step that intervened in the production of a sixteenth-century witness deposition. The written deposition is not treated as evidence in this period until it is read out by the judge and the document affirmed or amended by the witness in a subsequent phase of the inquest. Imbert's remarks about this step, which occurred at the *recolement de témoins*, suggest that the sworn deposition might undergo important changes at this point: "Le tesmoing n'est point tenu par son recolement & confrontation, de persister en sa deposition redigée par escript par l'information: & peut impunément varier, & muer sa deposition, s'il voit qu'elle ne soit veritable, ainsi qu'elle est escripte, combien qu'il soit juré par l'information" (474; "The witness is not required, when confronted with the accused, to stand by his deposition as it is officially recorded in writing: he can change it without penalty, and modify his deposition if he sees that it is not truthful as

---

[4] This is a clear contrast to the English jury model, where, according to the 1555 Marian Commital Statute, witness testimony became lawful evidence only at the moment it was given by the witness at a public oral jury trial. Since it was not yet considered "legal," testimony gathered preliminarily by court examiners was not given under oath and needed only be written down "within two days" – hence merely paraphrased as to its perceived content, not scrupulously recorded (see Langbein, *Prosecuting* 81-2).

written, despite the fact that it has been certified by the court"). In his 1609 annotations to Imbert's manual, Pierre Guenois confirms that there was continuing controversy on the question of whether a witness could renounce a signed deposition, as well as over whether one should officially re-interrogate a witness when he does not stand by his original deposition at the *recolement*. Moreover, Guenois confesses uncertainty about the appropriate procedure to follow if a witness changes his story: which deposition should prevail? (718).

The fact that Imbert suggests that a witness can "impunement varier" when confronted with his own written testimony underlines the ambiguity of the relationship between writing and orality in sixteenth-century French law. Such evidence highlights an awareness of a potential conflict between the oral statement under oath and the written deposition, a conflict that pits two distinct notions of testimonial truth against one another. In feudal law, because the credibility of a testimony is a function of the ethical status of the witness who gives it, "truth" is produced in and by the oral deposition given by a witness who is legally irreproachable. The written version of such a testimony possesses an authority that is strictly derivative and wholly dependent on that of the original oral encounter. As this approach to testimony becomes increasingly impracticable, for all of the reasons I have been discussing, jurists no longer recognize the oral deposition as constituting a testimony's "moment of truth." The proliferation of depositions from the same witness in the same case precludes any one of them functioning as an authoritative original. The act of comparing and collating these several statements about the "same" thing encourages the development of a conception of the truth of the matter that is independent of any given deposition, and to which the deposition should remain faithful.

When the mid-century jurist Philibert Boyer discovers that witness testimony changes over time, he requires an explanation. He blames "perfidie" on the part of the witness, thus reinforcing the negative view of witnesses that permeates sixteenth-century French juridical literature: "lorsque l'ordonnance [de 1539] fut faite, les faux tesmoins n'estoient pas en si grande abondance qu'ils sont à present.... Quand il advient qu'aucuns tesmoings se desdisent, ou augmentent ou diminuent à leurs depositions, il faut necessairement qu'il y ayt de la perfidie" (226r-227v; "when that ordinance was made, false witnesses were not as abundant as they are now.... When it happens that a witness disavows his testimony, or augments or shortens his deposition, there must necessarily be some perfidy involved"). As Boyer's disparaging remarks suggest, the differences between the oral and written versions of a juridical deposition were increasingly being treated as troubling inconsistencies. Jean Imbert also mentions the tendency of witnesses to modify their testimony in the context of the sixteenth-century inquest. Like Boyer, he finds this phenomenon disturbing. Whereas Boyer had blamed the "perfidie" of witnesses, Imbert suggests that the problem lies with court functionaries who fail accurately to transcribe the testimony of witnesses: "on ha trouvé par plusieurs fois que les sergens & notaires, qui besongnent es informations, ne mettent au vray le dire du tesmoing. Et pource que grand nombre de tesmoings oyz par l'information se desdisent, & dient n'avoir deposé le contenu en leurs depositions: le juge debvroient ordonner que le sergen & le notaire viendroyent en personne.... Car aujourd'hui ce crime pullule tant, qu'il n'y ha si homme de bien, qui ne soit mis en peine & en danger par ces sergens & notaires" (474; "it has frequently been found that the sergeants and notaries who transcribe depositions do not faithfully record what the witness says. And due to the fact that so many witnesses who depose before these court functionaries later recant their testimony, and claim not to have deposed what is contained in their [written] deposition, the judge should order that the sergeants and notaries appear in person.... Because these days this crime is so rampant that even the best man is not immune to difficulty and danger at the hands of these sergeants and notaries").

It is of course difficult to discern from such general remarks the degree of variation that is at issue. However, an anonymous sixteenth-century jurist implies that even slight discrepancies were considered meaningful when he describes peasants who, for fear of compromising themselves, refused to reiterate their oral declarations, stating only 'what is written is well written' ("paysans qui, craignant de se compromettre, refusaient de réitérer leurs déclarations, se bornant à dire «quod scriptum est bene scriptum esse»").[5] The jurist Pierre Ayrault even suggests that when judges questioned

---

[5] Quoted in Allard, *Histoire de la justice criminelle au XVIe siècle*, 259; Allard names the source but not the author.

witnesses about the substance of their testimony, many requested to hear their written depositions read out in order to reply (III.3.38; quoted in Esmein, *History* 170). In other words, the written deposition was sometimes considered the authoritative "source" to which the live witness sought to conform. The increasing uncertainty regarding the relative authority of the oral versus the written deposition put the very ontological status of testimony into question. When had a witness in fact given his testimony? At the moment he deposed orally, or at the moment he certified a written record of his oral deposition? This uncertainty, as we shall see, will eventually allow for the elaboration of a rhetoric of testimony that dispenses with the concept of the oral encounter altogether.

Mediating Testimony

In his exhaustive study of French voyages of exploration and settlement in the fifteenth and sixteenth centuries, Charles-André Julien notes that the French initially learned about America through both reading and conversation. Of course, as Julien goes on to observe, "le rôle de la diffusion orale qui fut, sans nul doute, le principal, échappe presque totalement à nos investigations" (*Voyages* 320; "the role of oral diffusion, which was no doubt primary, almost entirely escapes investigation"). Despite our inability to recover and thus to study these conversations about America, however, it is important to recall that they took place. Moreover, as the case of Gonneville suggests, even written testimony about the New World could still conform to a primarily oral paradigm into the sixteenth century.

We should thus not discount the influence of actual oral exchanges on the rhetoric of testimony in the sixteenth century; likewise, we should not underestimate the theoretical prestige that orality continued to enjoy. Indeed, one way in which the credibility of testimony was instantiated in print was via the staging of an oral encounter within the text. We have already seen this technique employed in somewhat attenuated form in Montaigne's essay on the cannibals, where we are made to understand that the simple man gave his *veritable tesmoignage* to Montaigne in person. Montaigne explicitly presents the ideal testimony of the New World in this essay as oral, and ostentatiously denies having consulted any books on the subject at all. Of course, basing the credibility of a written text on a necessarily inaccessible oral antecedent, and thus positing the priority of the oral with respect to the written, eventually undermines the authority of the written text. Consequently, this was not a sustainable solution to the problem of witnessing in print.

Rather than appeal to the authority of a prior oral encounter, many eyewitness historians sought to enlist the traditional prestige of oral testimony by attempting to create an "orality effect" by means of an explicit claim to rhetorical ineptitude.[6] Montaigne himself evokes this response to the problem of mediating eyewitness testimony in print in "Des cannibales": though he never allows his simple man to speak directly in the essay – the witness is, we should recall, never quoted – Montaigne assures us, in his inimitably convoluted way, that his source is reliable at least partly because the simple man has no rhetorical resources at his disposal. Jean de Léry will use this technique as well, claiming in the preface to his *Histoire* to be writing for "ceux qui aiment mieux la verité dite simplement, que le mensonge orné & fardé de beau langage" (98; "those who prefer the truth simply stated over lies dressed up and adorned in fine language"; lxii). But Léry's eyewitness history also provides compelling evidence that the degraded status of the oral juridical deposition and the correspondingly enhanced authority of its written counterpart had an impact on witnessing and testimony beyond the confines of the law courts, as he abandons the rhetoric of orality for something altogether new. Constructing his eyewitness account according to presuppositions about testimony that emerge from the law courts, Léry will elaborate a rhetoric of witnessing that is particularly well-suited both to the printed text and to the post-feudal, post-Reformation society of sixteenth-century France.

Léry's *Histoire* is never represented as having been recounted orally to anyone. Though he does allude ever so briefly in his prologue to having recounted some of his experiences to friends and

---

[6] This term has, not surprisingly, been used to describe the rhetoric of Michel de Montaigne's *Essais*. See George Hoffmann, *Montaigne's Career* (Oxford UP) 55. I would argue, however, that the term is (ironically) ill-suited to describe the style of "Des cannibales," one of the most coherent, focused, and unretouched essays in the collection.

acquaintances, he makes it clear that these conversations did not result in the book we are about to read. Unlike Montaigne, then, Léry does not stage a face-to-face encounter between the witness and his addressee. Instead, what we see in the prologue to the *Histoire* is a witness in search of his testimony – that is, we see Léry hunting for the written source on which his printed testimony is to be based. Rather than posit a non-textual antecedent for his eyewitness account, Léry suggests that the most authentic version of his testimony is in fact a written one.

Attempting to explain why he has waited twenty years after his return from Brazil to publish his story, Léry writes that his "mémoires" from the voyage were written "in Brazilian ink and in America itself." Michel de Certeau seizes on the material immediacy of this image in his classic reading of the *Histoire*: "as his preface already indicates, the tale is fabricated from "memoires . . . written in Brazilian ink and in America itself," a raw material doubly drawn from the tropics, since the very characters that bring the primitive object into the textual web are made from a red ink extracted from the *pau-brasil*, a wood that is one of the principal imports to sixteenth-century Europe" (218). Certeau in essence proposes that Léry's Brazilian field notes partake of the substance of Brazil itself, a substance that is thus "caught" in Léry's own text. What Certeau glosses over, however, is the complex relation between Léry's admittedly material *mémoires* and the eyewitness testimony presented in the *Histoire*, a relation Léry himself describes in great detail in his prologue.

Like many writers of his epoch, Léry turned his work over to a scribe who produced the initial manuscript version of his *Histoire*. Whether Léry gave this person his notes or some other written incarnation of the book is ultimately an idle question here, since, as Léry informs us, this manuscript gets lost. Luckily, however, Léry recovers some drafts of that same manuscript that he had left with the person who transcribed it for him. A second manuscript was produced from those drafts (presumably by a scribe, though Léry doesn't say), but this version gets left behind due to the extenuating circumstances of the religious wars in France. The original manuscript is "finally recovered" when Léry tells the story of its wanderings to a man who recognizes the manuscript in Léry's tale and happens to know where it has ended up. As Léry tells it, the recovery of this "original" manuscript allows him finally to compose and publish the *Histoire d'un voyage faict en la terre du Bresil*. Rather than publishing his notes, written "in Brazilian ink and in America itself," or writing up another manuscript from them, or drawing directly on his memories of his experiences in Brazil, Léry positions this errant manuscript as the authoritative source for his book. Léry's prologue thus resurrects the medieval "found manuscript" topos where we would least expect it – in an eyewitness account of the New World. There is a twist, however, since, unlike Arthur's clerks, Léry does not claim to be reconstructing an originally oral relation.

Against the judicial background I have discussed, Léry might have supposed the printed text of the New World eyewitness account to appear *less* mediated than the oral deposition, since the inquisitional deposition was perceived as becoming entangled in several layers of potentially corrupting institutional mediation before it was allowed to play its role as evidence in a case. As Imbert's comments suggest, writing *per se* was not necessarily considered a potential agent of the corruption of witness testimony; rather, it was the human mediators who threatened to distort a witness's deposition. Léry's testimony is inextricable from its written version(s), which, far from deriving from an oral origin, exist entirely independent of any oral encounter with a potentially corrupting other. The very substance of Léry's testimony is a document which has acquired an existence independent of the witness who supposedly produced it. Ironically, it is Léry's very absence as a deponent that will lead to the emergence of the first person in his testimony.

Just before he underlines that the events described in the *Histoire* are "matieres de [son] propre sujet," Léry explains that, "à mon petit jugement, une histoire, sans tant estre parée des plumes d'autruy, [est] assez riche quand elle est remplie de son propre sujet" (96; "in my modest judgment, a history that is not bedecked with the plumes of others is rich enough when it is full of its own subject"; lxi). The "plumes" to which Léry refers here are of course the rhetorical flourishes, in the form of citations, that characterized the traditional, third-person histories against which the early eyewitness accounts defined themselves. Just below the surface of this metaphor is the *plume* as pen, the paradigmatic instrument of written mediation; Léry prunes his account of the mediation of others in order to take the pen into his own hand. By doing so, he abandons the rhetoric of orality for the rhetoric of first-person experience.

Léry's act of witnessing, as distinct from the testimony of the medieval inquisitional witness, is not coextensive with the act of deponing, but with a past firsthand experience that assumes priority over the present in which Léry testifies. As the witness deposition becomes more and more explicitly mediated by writing, the notion of authenticity, which had formerly derived from the moment in which a witness gave in his testimony (as in Gonneville's *Relation authentique*), now derives from the fidelity of the written text to something beyond itself. Instead of being seen and recognized, Léry is the one who *sees*.

Whereas for Gonneville, the emphasis would have been on "being here" in Honfleur among people who knew him, for Léry the emphasis has shifted to "being there" to see something but testifying via writing or print. As a consequence, instead of being "present" at the moment of bearing witness, Léry's presence is meant to bear principally on the moment of a privileged eyewitness vision. It is no longer a matter of having the witness before our eyes, or of conjuring up an image of the deponing witness in textual form, so that we readers may act as witnesses to the witness. Rather, what Montaigne describes and what Léry ultimately executes is a testimony whose end is to put the witness's *experiences* before our eyes, so that we may also see what the witness has seen. The witness himself must thus remain transparent.

Léry's testimony will re-present Brazil to us, even as he himself remains distant. This encourages the possibility of thinking of Léry's experiences, like his manuscript, as detachable from Léry – that is, as objective occurrences or events that have an existence independent of him. The witness fades into the background in order that his experiences can come to the fore. In the folklaw model, let us recall, the question of the witness's experience was secondary, and the question of his identity central. In Gonneville's *Relation authentique*, we saw how the question of the witness's identity still retained priority over the question of his experience, even when his experience became an object of interest in the context of inquisitional procedure. In other words, the answer to the question "who speaks?" was central in folklaw, where "speech" amounted to an affirmation of solidarity or a willingness to put one's very life at risk; it continued to be important even after the introduction of inquisitional procedure. The evolution of the ways in which testimony was mediated, however, induces the gradual withdrawal of the ethical witness, who cedes his ground to the written report of his experiences. Consequently, the ethical question of who is speaking is ultimately subordinated to the epistemological question of how a witness has acquired knowledge of the matters recounted in his testimony.

THE FIRST PERSON

In 1576, Pierre Ayrault explicitly laments the fact that one can no longer "see" the witness in his deposition, since the oral encounter in which he gives in his testimony is never represented in the document generated by the court: "Is it reasonable to credit what one judge and a hired clerk report as to the testimony of ten or twenty witnesses? Such depositions do not show either what is said by the deponent or how he says it.... Nothing can be said in reply ... the witness, according to the way he is examined ... testifies for the prosecution or the defense" (*L'ordre et formalité* III.3; cited in Esmein, *History* 170). Ayrault's criticisms of written procedure bring out the contrast between the overtly dialogic character of pre-modern oral testimony and the increasingly monologic nature of the sixteenth-century witness deposition. His protestations against writing recall those put forth by the character of Socrates in Plato's *Phaedrus*, namely, that the written word cannot accommodate dialogue. The written deposition is unsatisfactory not only because nothing can be said in reply to it, however. Ayrault also contends that the written deposition suppresses the dialogue that produces witness testimony in the first place, since it reveals nothing about "the way [the witness] is examined." It does not report the oral dialogue in which testimony originates.[7]

As Ayrault's comments imply, witness depositions were not word for word transcriptions of the inquisitional interrogation; they were usually in the third person, and, as we have seen, not even

---

[7] One cannot help but wonder if Montaigne read Ayrault, since the essayist's comments on the superiority of oral exchange in general and with respect to witness testimony in particular (in, for example, "Des boyteux") are strikingly similar to those of the jurist. It seems clear, in any case, that Montaigne's attitudes toward the oral encounter are related to the experiences he would have had trying to evaluate written witness depositions as a magistrate, as Tournon has argued.

necessarily in the vernacular before the end of the fifteenth century. The suppression of the dialogic origin of juridical testimony in the written deposition, like the delay or outright omission of the face-to-face encounter between witness and accused in the sixteenth-century inquest, discourages the conceptualization of the witness as a second person. Gonneville's *Relation authentique* demonstrates this: Although it is clearly an eyewitness account of an overseas voyage, the *Relation* is not composed in the first person, but the third. It is punctuated throughout with the expression "Disent que . . . ," as in its opening line: "Et premièrement, disent que traficquant en Lissebonne, il Gonneville et honnorables hommes Jean l'Anglois et Pierre le Carpentier . . . firent complot d'ensemble . . . envoyer une navire [aux Indes orientales]" ("And first, they say that while on business in Lisbon, Gonneville and the honorable men Jean L'Anglois et Pierre le Carpentier decided to outfit a ship for the East Indies"). The third person governs the account throughout, whether the subject at hand is the ship's inventory or a description of "choses singulières inconnues en Chrestieneté." In the *Relation authentique*, we have an eyewitness testimony from which the grammatical first person remains absent.

Of course, the use of the first person would not in and of itself imply a focus on the isolated individual that will eventually become the subject of modern testimony. The referent of the first-person plural, "we," is always ambiguous with respect to the interlocutor because it may or may not be intended to refer to the addressee; "we" can mean a group of people to which "you" do not belong; it can encompass only the speaker and his or her interlocutor; or it can implicate a larger group to which the addressee is also understood to belong. The first-person plural thus serves to indicate several different types of affiliations between an individual and a group and between individuals. By the sixteenth century, when the nature of these affiliations is undergoing rapid change, "we" in fact becomes the narrator-witness of choice in writing about the New World, by both eyewitness and non-eyewitness writers. As a pronoun that can implicate both a first-person experience and an ethical identity, the first-person plural acts as a mediating term between the first-person singular witness who sees what nobody else has seen, on the one hand, and the second-person witness, whose identity as a witness depends upon the presence of an interlocutor.

The writings attributed to Jacques Cartier offer a striking example of a grammar of testimony that asserts simultaneously the presence of a privileged, experiencing eyewitness, that of a group of firsthand witnesses, and that of a larger ethical community whose members are not all firsthand observers.[8] Cartier's case is especially interesting for an analysis of such rhetoric, since several manuscript and printed versions of his *Voyages* exist, yet none has been definitively attributed to Cartier himself. Chapter One of the first voyage is entitled "Comme le capitaine Jacques Quartier partit avec deux navires de St. Malo, et comme il arriva en la Terre Neufve appelée la Nouvelle France, et entra au Port de Bonnevue" ("How Jacques Cartier left St. Malo with two ships, and how he arrived in that part of the New World called New France, and entered the port of Bonnevue." The second bears the heading "Comme nous arrivasmes en l'Isle des Oiseaux, et de la grande quantité d'Oiseaux qui s'y treuvent" ("How we arrived on the Isle des Oiseaux, and of the great quantity of birds there"). The change from third to first person, it turns out, had been effected in the course of the very first sentence of the first chapter: "Après que Messire Charles De Moüy ... eut fait jurer les Capitaines, Maistres et Compagnons des Navires, de bien et fidelement se comporter au service du Roy très chrestien, sous la charge du Capitaine Jacques Quartier, nous partismes ... du Port de Saint Malo ..." ("After M. Charles de Moüy ... had the ship's crew swear to conduct themselves in such a way as to serve the very Christian king, under the captaincy of Jacques Cartier, we departed ... from the port of St. Malo"). While most of the first voyage is narrated in the first-person plural, there are a significant number of passages in the first person singular and several in the third person with respect to Cartier (where he is referred to as "le Capitaine").[9] The second voyage is similarly constructed, except that there are no longer any instances of the first person singular, and "le Capitaine" has become "nostre Capitaine." The absence of

---

[8] Cartier's first voyage took place in 1534; the earliest published account of it appeared in Ramusio in 1556; the earliest surviving French version was published at Rouen in 1598. I quote here from the *Relation originale du voyage de Jacques Cartier*, which gives the 1598 French text.

[9] The "modernized version" of Cartier's text (Julien 1992) subtly registers both the ambiguity of the original pronouns: all of the *"nous"* rhetoric in the chapter titles of the sixteenth-century editions is "modernized" into *"ils"* in the newer edition.

"je" in the Second Voyage is especially striking, given that this text is prefaced by a first-person singular letter to François I in which the letter's author specifically argues for the superiority of the eyewitness perspective in cosmographical matters. [10] "*Experientia est rerum magistra*," he writes, consciously citing an Aristotelian dictum even as he encourages François to question the beliefs of the "saiges Philosophes du temps passé."

It is generally agreed that Cartier did not write this letter, which is not included in most of the manuscript versions of the text. Nevertheless, the aim of the letter is to situate Cartier with respect to François, and thus to elaborate the position from which Cartier speaks as a witness to the royal audience that has requested his testimony. After praising François for stamping out the Protestant "heresy," the letter's author goes on to discuss French explorations in the New World. The referent of the first-person plural continually shifts: Initially, the criterion of (Catholic) faith is what determines membership in the community conjured by Cartier's letter; this community's most prominent member appears to be none other than the King of Spain. But when the letter speaks more directly about Cartier's own travels at the behest of the French King, a specifically French collectivity would appear to be evoked. When the letter subsequently addresses the question of what had heretofore remained unknown to "us," it is clear that he does not only have Catholics in mind. Despite the explicitly anti-Protestant stance that permeates this prefatory letter, Cartier's testimony appears to aspire to legitimacy in the eyes of a fairly broad community, one that would include French readers of all faiths. Cartier is thus simultaneously positing and denying affiliation with French Protestants under cover of the first-person plural pronoun, an ambivalence that reveals the difficulties that attach to constructing an ethical position from which to give eyewitness testimony in a printed publication in sixteenth-century France. In the account which follows this letter, the notion of experience is linked to the writing subject in a purely rhetorical fashion: "nous" never consistently co-

---

[10] It is a tribute to the rhetorical force of the first-person singular pronoun in the modern period that, according to Robert Le Blant, one of the arguments used by scholars to demonstrate that Cartier indeed authored these writings is the fact that "on trouve de temps à autre dans le texte un exposé à la première personne" (91; "one finds now and then in the text passages in the first person").

incides with a particular eyewitness, nor even with a concrete group of eyewitnesses, but remains an abstraction whose referent constantly shifts throughout the narrative.

One of the narrative functions of this "nous" is to bridge the distance between the New World and the Old, and thus to posit an ethical relationship between witness and addressee of the type we saw in Mandeville's *Travels*. If "nous" means "we Frenchmen," then the French reader becomes implicated in the text which bears witness to the New World. Another function of this pronoun, however, is to serve as an index of a first-person experience that potentially excludes the audience: "we left the port of St. Malo"; "we arrived on the Isle des Oiseaux." The first-person plural thus mediates between a characteristically medieval form of collective, ethical testimony, on the one hand, and a modern model for which the epistemic experiences of a particular individual will become central. We have already seen this hybrid form of testimony in Montaigne's essay on the cannibals, where the experiential testimony of the simple man dissolves into the ethical judgments of Montaigne, judgments he makes on the basis of experiences he characterizes as collective. Though he is careful to attribute his information to someone who has the relatively uncommon credential of firsthand experience of Antarctic France, Montaigne acts as the spokesperson for an entire community: even though his judgments are critical of European culture, they are not meant to be read as the idiosyncratic rantings of an individual, but as statements that have an ethical force *for* Europeans.

Like the Montaigne of "Des cannibales," Francisco López de Gómara, the official historian of the early Spanish conquest of America, will also yoke ethical and experiential witnessing together by means of the first-person plural pronoun. In his enthusiastic praise of someone he identifies as the inventor of the compass, one Flavio de Malfa, he exclaims: "Quien más a Flavio debe somos españoles, que navegamos mucho" (19; "We Spanish owe the most to Flavio, since we navigate so much"). The energy of López de Gómara's first-person plural, like that of Montaigne, flows in a direction opposed to that of the "nous" in Cartier's eyewitness text: "navegamos" allows López de Gómara to insinuate himself into the narrative of the New World as a member of an abstract collectivity, the Spanish nation, without ever having to set sail. It is difficult to glean from Cartier, Montaigne or López de Gómara just which mode of testimony – ethical or experiential – should be understood to be privileged by the first-person plural. Rather, the two types of witnessing form an ambiguous "we" whose relationship is never made clear. This is not meant to suggest that any of the three – the eyewitness (or his scribe), the essayist or the historian – were being deliberately shifty, however. It indicates, rather, that the ground upon which the authority of eyewitness testimony was constructed was itself shifting. Was it primarily ethical or primarily epistemological?

In his account of his sojourn in Brazil, Jean de Léry recognizes the ambiguity of the first-person plural, explicitly attacking the use of "nous" in André Thevet's *Cosmographie universelle*. In the *Cosmographie*, Thevet accuses Léry and his Huguenot companions of having disrupted the French settlement at Guanabara. Questioning Thevet's authority to write about the events at Guanabara, Léry singles out an episode quite unrelated to the supposed Huguenot revolt. Léry's strategy is to probe the elements of Thevet's "nous": "je luy demande en premier lieu, si ceste façon de parler tout expresse dont il use: assavoir, *Les Sauvages irritez de telle tragédie, peu s'en fallut qu'ils ne se ruassent sur nous, et missent à mort le reste*, se peut autrement entendre, sinon que par ce *nous,* luy se mettant du nombre, il veuille dire qu'il fut enveloppé en son pretendu danger" (65; "I ask him in the first place whether this deliberate expression that he uses, "The savages, incensed by such a tragedy, nearly rushed upon us and put the others to death," can be meant otherwise than, by this "us," to include himself in this supposed danger"; xlvii). Léry suggests that it is not enough for Thevet to create a community out of himself and his companions via the use of the pronoun "nous"; it is instead necessary that Thevet demonstrate his presence among his fellow travelers each time he uses the first-person plural. In other words, Léry does not accept appartenance in a community – here, the community of Frenchmen, largely Catholics, who joined Villegagnon in Brazil – as a license to speak on behalf of that community. He attacks Thevet's use of the first-person pronoun as an attempt to absorb the experiences of his companions into his own account of experience. Thevet's brush with death is thus reduced to nothing more than "ceste façon de parler tout expresse dont il use." Thevet's "nous" is ultimately an unconvincing, outmoded sign of ethical appartenance, and not the grammatical vehicle of experience that Léry demands. Indeed, Léry will go on to maintain that the *primary* index of reliable testimony is firsthand experience.

At the end of his prologue, Léry refers back to his criticism of Thevet's use of "nous." He is not unaware of the implications that his attack on Thevet's rhetoric has for his own project. Having denigrated Thevet's attempt to use "nous" to refer to an ethical community, and not to a group of eyewitnesses, Léry takes pains to assure his readers that he will do no such thing. In fact, Léry will not use "nous" at all. Resolutely refusing to speak on behalf of anyone but himself, Léry explains "a fin qu'on ne m'objecte qu'ayant ci-dessus reprins Thevet, et maintenant condamnant encor ici quelques autres, je commets neantmoins moy-mesme telles fautes: si quelqu'un di-je trouve mauvais que quand ci-apres je parleray de la façon de faire des sauvages (comme si je me voulois faire valoir) j'use si souvent de ceste façon de parler, Je vis, je me trouvay, cela m'advint, et d'autres choses semblables: je respon, qu'outre (ainsi que j'ay touché) que ce sont matieres de mon propre sujet, qu'encores comme on dit, est-ce cela parlé de science, c'est a dire de veüe et d'experience" (97-8; "so that one does not object that, having rebuked Thevet on that point, and now reproving others, I am committing the same faults: If someone finds it ill that hereafter, when I speak of savage customs, I often use this kind of expression – "I saw," "I found," "this happened to me," and so on (as if I wanted to show myself off) – I reply that not only are these things matters of my own subject but also that I am speaking from knowledge, that is, from seeing and experiencing for myself"; lxi). Léry's use of the first-person singular, he tells us here, is meant to confirm that he is staking the authority of his testimony on firsthand experiences.

We should recall here that Paulmier de Gonneville also spoke from experience, yet his testimony ultimately took on a form quite dissimilar from that of Léry. Even when experience began to rival ethos as a source of testimonial authority, as it did in Gonneville's *Relation authentique*, it did not necessarily produce the monologic rhetoric of the modern, first-person eyewitness. The *Relation* retains the inherently dialogic character of pre-modern testimony; Léry, by contrast, adopts a polemically first-person stance in his account.

Léry's defense of his use of the first-person singular implies that what is novel (or at least controversial) about his account is his use of precisely those utterative markings identified by Michel de Certeau as articulating the "place" from which the classical eyewitness historian speaks. According to Certeau's analysis of Book IV of Herodotus's *Histories*, the kind of rhetoric Léry justifies here makes possible "the fabrication and accreditation of the *text as witness of the other.*" Such phrases are, in other words, "the utterative markings ("I saw," "I heard," etc.) and modalities ... which, with regard to the 'marvels' recounted, organize the place at which [the eyewitness historian] would like to make himself heard and believed" (*Heterologies* 68). Certainly, what Certeau calls the "utterative markings" in Herodotus are in abundant evidence in Léry's text. In the passage under consideration here, however, Léry tries to explain where those phrases come from. Thus, the indices of first-person experience do not function as modalities in the rhetoric of Léry's prologue. Rather, "je vis" itself is the *object* of Léry's authenticating discourse. In other words, Léry's "je vis" does not constitute an experiential mode of expression; it is, ultimately, the very thing expressed ("I had an experience"). That to which Léry's preface is to bear witness is not Brazil; it is nothing less than Léry's *status as a witness*. Rather than the "text as witness of the other," then, we have a text which testifies first and foremost that an act of witnessing has indeed taken place.

For Léry, witnessing is no longer bearing witness, but having experiences; thus, the "stuff" of testimony is not the act it performs in the here and now, but the experiences it recounts in the then and there. The act of testifying about those experiences has now become the secondary, derivative act. As Léry's *Histoire* demonstrates, it has now become possible to conceive of the substance of testimony as something completely distinct from the act of testifying. As an experience, Léry's act of witnessing takes place in Brazil, not in France. His testimony, by contrast, is an attempt to situate that experience in terms that would be considered credible by his French audience. Although Léry states explicitly that his primary reason for publishing the *Histoire* is to dispute another account of the short-lived French colony in Brazil, he does not give testimony to a judicial official; rather, he takes his case directly to the public. This is all the more remarkable in that Léry is responding to a public allegation of sedition against the governor of the colony made by the king's own royal cosmographer, André Thevet, in his 1577 *Cosmographie universelle*. One would certainly assume a more pressing monarchical interest in Léry's case than in something like Gonneville's pirate attack, and a corresponding desire on Léry's part to clear his name in an official manner. Yet Léry's preface indicates that a printed publication aimed at a broad readership was his preferred medium of refuting Thevet's allegations. Moreover, although Thevet initially appears to play the role of Léry's addressee, Léry does not maintain a dialogue with him beyond his prologue. Léry's *Histoire* is thus constructed as an account with neither a real nor an implied interlocutor. "The readers" could be just about anyone, anywhere. Instead of a testimonial dialogue, Léry's testimony takes on the monologic character that is the hallmark of modern testimony.

CHAPTER FIVE

PRESENCE

SIXTEENTH-CENTURY books, unlike medieval manuscripts, always existed in multiple copies, often in the same place (that is, at the same bookseller's or in the same city). As Terry Cochran remarks in his discussion of the relationship between print and modernity, "the existence in multiple copies allows for no original to which the discourse [thus vehicled] can be reduced."[1] This situation is only compounded when a work exists in more than one edition. Like the judicial witnesses of sixteenth-century France who sometimes recanted, amended or expanded their sworn testimony, Jean de Léry published no less than five editions of his *Histoire*. As the editions of Léry's book proliferate, it becomes virtually possible to associate the meaning of his eyewitness testimony with the linguistic act of bearing witness. Instead, the "substance" of his testimony has become the Brazilian experience it purportedly records.

If the technology of print encourages a perspective for which the referent of a discourse exists somewhere beyond any of its linguistic incarnations, it is not the only factor pushing the discourse of testimony in the direction of a discourse of abstract truth – of "science," as Léry puts it – in the sixteenth century. The nature of the substance of testimony, as well as the nature of its relationship to the signs that vehicle it, is a crux of theological debate between Catholics and Protestants in sixteenth-century France. Such questions are in fact addressed repeatedly and explicitly in tracts on martyrs. These reflections constitute an important sixteenth-centu-

---

[1] *Twilight of the Literary* 23.

ry source of approaches to first-person witnessing more generally, though their relationship to other discourses, particularly in France, has been largely unexplored.[2]

In an analysis of the writings of André Thevet, Frank Lestringant has written of what he calls a "corps-martyr," a "martyred body" that authorizes eyewitness accounts of the New World. It is a "corps souffrant, tanné par les embruns et le sel, éprouvé par la faim et la soif" ("suffering body, weathered by mist and salt, put to the test by hunger and thirst"; "Flèche" 472). However, when one of Thevet's contemporaries, the Protestant Urbain Chauveton, writes in his *Histoire de la Floride* "Qui auroit envie d'être bientôt martyr, et dépouiller sa mauvaise peau pour entrer en gloire, qu'il ne falloit qu'aller là [en Floride]" (Atkinson 288; "Whoever wants to find a quick route to martyrdom, and rid himself of his lowly flesh in order to enter into Paradise, he need only go to Florida") he does not mean simply that travel to the New World is physically rigorous. Chauveton was referring to the fate of his Protestant coreligionaries at Fort Caroline, killed by Spanish Catholics. To invoke a "corps-martyr" in the context of sixteenth-century French travel writing is thus to implicate much more than a generalized notion of physical suffering; it is to conjure the passionate currents of religious polemic that traversed a society torn apart by civil war. In France, Jean Crespin's *Histoire des martyrs* offered an ever-expanding catalogue of the words and deeds of those who had not merely suffered, but died for the Protestant cause. Moreover, Jean de Léry himself had published the quasi-martyrological *Histoire memorable de la ville de Sancerre* in 1573, thus playing the role of a specifically Protestant witness a few years before he published his eyewitness history of Brazil. Given that the question of martyrdom was at the center of French society throughout most of the sixteenth century, it is worth attempting to define with somewhat more precision how the figure of the martyr might inform testimony about the New World and the overall evolution of the early modern witness.

The letter that precedes the 1545 account of Jacques Cartier's *Second Voyage* foregrounds the physical risks that the true eye-

---

[2] The importance of the witness to martyrdom in Protestant discourse has produced a number of studies on the question of spectatorship in the English context. One of the best and most comprehensive of these is Huston Diehl's *Staging Reform, Reforming the Stage*.

witness assumes in contrast to the "philosophers" who "se contentoient seulement sans avanturer n'y mectre leurs personnes es dangiers, esquelz ilz eussent peu ancheoir a chercher l'experience de leur dire. . . . Les simples mariniers de present non ayans eu tant de craincte d'eulz mectre a l'advanture d'iceulx perilz & dangiers qu'ilz ont eu . . . ont cogneu le contraire d'icelle opinion des philosophes par vraye experience" ("having contented themselves with this view without venturing forth nor personally facing the dangers they would have encountered by putting their words to the test of experience. . . . Today's simple sailors, not fearing as they did the risk of peril and danger . . . have contradicted this opinion of the philosophers by first-hand experience"; 3). Here, the witness's body, particularly insofar as it is exposed to danger, marks his experience as authentic and plays an explicit role in authorizing his testimony over that of witnesses who have not been similarly imperiled. André Thevet's 1558 *Singularitez de la France Antarctique* is prefaced with a long-winded statement of the same principle, describing the author's "longue experience des choses . . . abandonné à la discretion et mercy d'un des elemens le plus inconstant, moins pitoyable, et asseuré qui soit entre les autres, avec petits vaisseaux de bois, fragiles et caduques (dont bien souvent lon peut plus esperer la mort que la vie) pour naviguer vers le pole Antarctique, lequel n'a iamais esté decouvert ne congneu par les Anciens" ("long experience of things . . . abandoned to the whim and mercy of one of the most inconstant, least merciful and least secure of the elements, in fragile, rickety little wooden boats (from which one can frequently expect more death than life) headed towards the South Pole, which was never discovered or known by the Ancients"; LV). In the *Historia verdadera*, Bernal Díaz del Castillo writes of the risk of death and injury he underwent in his travels to Mexico ("riesgos de muerte y heridas y mil cuentos de miserias"; 29), dangers that distinguish his experience of the New World from that of historians like Francisco López de Gómara. Clearly, the eyewitness experience here is not constituted simply by a moment of psychologically "subjective" vision; rather, it specifically implicates the body through its predication on physical suffering and, ultimately, on a brush with death. The wounded body, marked by the experience of the New World, testifies to the authenticity of the eyewitness narrative in the absence of a socially mediated ethical relation between the witness and those to whom he testifies.

Lest we assume that the *corps-martyr* described by Lestringant is a prominent feature of all firsthand accounts that make a polemical claim to experience, however, let us recall that Cartier, Thevet and Castillo were all Catholics; indeed, in their writings on the New World, both Cartier and Thevet engaged in po-lemic against the "Lutheran heresy" (and we may imagine that Casti-llo the Spaniard simply didn't find this necessary). The Catholic discourse of martyrdom brings with it a distinct view of the nature of testimonial representation. The best witness to the faith of the Catholic martyr is his own dead body. On this view, testimony is inherently sacrificial; the first-person witness must be destroyed in order for his testimony to be authoritative. Catholic New World testimony will thus depend heavily on autobiographical accounts that attempt to record the experiences of the body in pain.

By inscribing the sacrificial structure of Christ's narrative onto his testimony, the Catholic eyewitness of the New World attempts to lend it an eminently authoritative framework. The body of the Catholic martyr is resolutely nonlinguistic. It does not suffice to talk about it or read about it or hear about it; one must view it, touch it, embrace it. Consequently, unless it manages to put its collective hands on the corporeal relics that ultimately constitute this type of testimony, the European audience remains unable to receive its substance. One could say that in this sense, the Catholic martyr belongs to the regime of orality, of the face-to-face encounter in a circumscribed community. And like the strategy of staging an oral encounter to authorize a written text, the mode of testimony borrowed from Catholic martyrological doctrine suffers from an irresolvable internal tension when it is appropriated in print: if a body, be it dead or alive, is ultimately what authorizes a text, that text will necessarily remain in a secondary or derivative position with respect to the body that grounds it. As Lestringant himself notes, Thevet's repeated references to concrete artifacts of the New World which are physically inaccessible to the reader generate "un texte dont la fonction première n'est nullement d'établir une communication, mais d'imposer autoritairement, et, pourrait-on dire, par sa propre masse, la vérité d'un dire" (485; "a text whose primary function is not to establish communication, but to autocratically impose, by virtue of its own mass, the truth of a discourse"). Rather than communicate to his readers the "substance" of the New World, Thevet asserts his own physical proximity to it.

Lestringant's argument recalls Michel de Certeau's analysis of Montaigne's "Des cannibales" in *Heterologies*, in which Certeau writes, "Only an appeal to the senses . . . and a link to the body . . . seem capable of bringing closer . . . the real that was lost by language. Proximity is thus necessary; for Montaigne, it takes the double form of the traveller and the private collection, both of which are his and in his home" (74). Certeau goes on to observe that by appealing to these bodies and these artifacts, Montaigne "displaces that which founds authority" (74). But what both Montaigne and Thevet in fact do here is import a venerable reliquary tradition into the writing of geography and history. The American artifacts they claim to possess function very much like Catholic religious relics whose testimony can only be received via the physical senses. Their purported encounters with such artifacts could reasonably have been expected to lend the two writers a considerable authority to speak to an audience accustomed to venerating physical objects singled out for their former "proximity" to holy figures.

The testimony of the bare physical relic is, by contrast, not considered authoritative by the Protestant. French Protestant martyrologies explicitly reject the Catholic veneration of the martyr's dead body in favor of a written account of what his death was supposed to signify. In a liminary poem that precedes his *Histoire des martyrs* (first published in 1554), Jean Crespin indicates that hearing and seeing a martyrdom, whether in person or via the written record, does not suffice; one must contemplate that to which the martyr's testimony *refers*:

> Et qui se vient en ce lieu addresser,
> Pour voir, ouïr, & non pour y penser,
> Voyant, oyant, il ne void, & n'oid goutte

(Whoever comes here/to see, hear, and not to think/Seeing, hearing, he sees and hears nothing)

What is to be "thought" about here are religious truths that are absolutely distinct from the signs that mediate them. This is why Crespin feels at liberty to amend the court records he has gathered for his catalogue of persecuted martyrs. As he explains, in an aside that evinces the same critical attitude toward the means of gathering witness testimony we have seen in the writings of the jurists, he has modified the testimony of some of his witnesses in order better to capture its substance, since some of it was written in "assez mauvais langage . . . que j'ay fait traduire & redresser le plus fidelement que faire se pouvoit. . . . De leurs interrogatoires & responses qui ont esté quelquefois tirees des Greffes, tout y est coustumierement si confus & couché à l'appetit des Greffiers ou ignorans ou malins, que besoin a esté d'en donner extrait sommaire, en gardant une mesme substance des Demandes & Responses" ("rather bad language . . . that I had translated and corrected as faithfully as possible. . . . In the interrogatories and responses that have sometimes been taken from the legal registers, everything is customarily recorded in such a confused manner, at the whim of clerks who are either ignorant or devious, that it was necessary to give a summary excerpt while maintaining the same basic substance of the questions and answers"; XLV).

In his treatise on relics, first published in 1543, Jean Calvin warns of the danger that the corporeal relic, which is supposed to point beyond itself to a spiritual referent, ultimately ends up being venerated for its own sake. Calvin allows, however, that such idolatrous "misreading" of relics is largely the result of hermeneutical missteps on the part of those who interpret them. In other words, Calvin has nothing against bodies *per se*; he does not even deny that they may carry meaning. What he refuses to accept, however, is the idea that the reliquary body could be intelligible in and of itself, in the absence of any act of interpretation. Jean Crespin is more explicit. In the preface to the *Histoire des martyrs*, he says bluntly that ashes and bones are "dead things" ("choses mortes"). Coreligionaries should rather contemplate martyrs through the medium of their testimonies to the faith, through which they continue to live ("vivans en leurs responses, lettres & disputes, & es memoires de leur constance, afin d'en estre edifiez comme il apartient"; XLI). These testimonies – both oral and written, both verbal and physical – must be examined for their true meaning, which lies beyond their material surface.

The necessity for interpretation becomes even clearer in Calvin's treatise when he abandons the question of the potential idolization of the relic in order to focus on the problem of its authenticity. He tallies up with a triumphant relish the multiple bodies of a number of saints that supposedly reside in churches across Europe, remarking, for example, that "Lazare . . . n'a que trois corps, que je sache; l'un est à Marseille, l'autre est à Autun, le troisième à Avalon" ("Lazarus . . . as far as I know, has only three bodies: one in Marseille, another in Autun, and the third in Avalon"; 82) or "de saint Etienne, ils ont tellement parti le corps, qu'il est entier à Rome en son église, le chef à Arles, et des os en plus de deux cents lieux" ("as for St. Stephen, they've divided him up to the point where he's got one entire body in Rome, a head in Arles, and bones in over two hundred other locations"; 85). He gives us the sense that more would-be relics are turning up every day when, after having duly noted the purported existence of two foreskins of Christ, he claims that "même cependant qu'on imprimoit ce livret, on m'a averti d'un troisième prépuce de notre Seigneur, qui se montre à Hildesheim" ("even as this booklet is being printed, I got news of a third foreskin of Christ, on display at Hildesheim"; 95).

Like the multiple versions of a printed text, the multiplicity of martyrological bodies here explicitly foregrounds those bodies *as* signs, as distinct from referents. Prior to accepting the testimony of any of them, you have to find a way to determine the relationship *between* sign and referent. Calvin implies that this is simply impossible without recourse to language – in the event, of course, the Bible: "L'Evangéliste saint Luc récite bien que notre Seigneur Jésus a été circoncis; mais que la peau a été serrée, pour la réserver en relique, il n'en fait point de mention. Toutes les histoires anciennes n'en disent mot. Et par l'espace de cinq cents ans il n'en a jamais été parlé en l'Eglise chrétienne" (47; "The Evangelist Saint Luke certainly reports that our Lord Jesus was circumcised; but he doesn't say anything about the foreskin being tucked away somewhere to be kept as a relic. No ancient history says a word about it. And for a space of over five hundred years, the Christian church never spoke about it"). Calvin suggests that the potential meaning *of* the body is not legible *on* the body itself. Again, it is not a question of denying the significance of the body per se; rather, it is a question of developing a *hermeneutics* of the body. For Calvin, the reliquary body is not a natural sign infallibly linked to a single unambiguous referent. As Calvin puts it in the prefatory epistle to a 1551 edition of Marot and Bèze's psalm translations, "si on pouvoit estre edifié des choses qu'on voit, sans cognoistre ce qu'elles signifient, sainct Paul ne defendroit pas si rigoureusement de parler en langue incognue" ("if one could be edified by the things one sees, without knowing what they signify, saint Paul would not so rigorously prohibit speaking in tongues"). Writing about the sacraments in the same epistle, he observes that "c'est une coustume perverse de les celebrer en telle sorte, que le peuple n'en ait sinon la veuë" ("it is a perverse custom to celebrate them in such a way that the people get to see them and nothing more").

Both Calvin and Crespin thus devalue the act of mere seeing as superficial, and the veneration of the body as idolatrous. They promote a view of martyrological testimony in which a hermeneutic gesture is essential. It does not suffice to give a bare, factual account of physical reality; nor does it suffice to grasp a fragment of that physical reality with one's own hands. Rather, faced with a testimony, one is required to interpret. As we shall see, the distinct presuppositions about reading martyrological testimony held by Catholics and Huguenots work their way into sixteenth-century French accounts of the New World.

Sign Language I: The Talking Body

In a 1493 letter from the New World to officials in Seville, the Spanish physician Diego Chanca recounts how a wounded Caribbean *cacique* expressed his wish to see the admiral Christopher Columbus: "Dijo. . . . Guacamari por señas e como mejor pudo, que porque él estaba ansí herido que dijesen al Almirante que quisiese venir á verlo" (57; "Guacamari said by signs, as best he could, that since he was thus wounded they should tell the Admiral to be so kind as to come and see him"; 56). One attempts to imagine just what these signs consisted in; the wound itself would be easy enough to designate, but the signs Guacamari may have used to indicate the wound's status as the cause of a desire to see Columbus, and that desire itself, are rather more obscure.

Stephen Greenblatt has observed that "most of the early voyagers seem at least fitfully to share Augustine's conviction that there is a kind of universal language, consisting of expressions of the face and eyes, gestures and tones of voice, which can show whether a person means to ask for something and get it, or refuse it and have nothing to do with it." But the language of signs appears to have allowed the early voyagers and their American interlocutors to carry on elaborate conversations that went far beyond crude expressions of desire and refusal. Columbus, of course, is notorious for reporting detailed information about where to find gold even as he acknowledges that it was all communicated to him exclusively by gestures.

The following passage from the account of Jacques Cartier's first voyage, detailing an exchange that takes place after the French have planted a cross in Huron-Iroquois territory, offers a striking (if unexceptional) instance of communication by signs ("par signes"): "En apres leur donna-t-on à entendre par signes, que ceste Croix estoit là plantee, pour donner quelque marque et connoissance pour pouvoir entrer en ce port, et que nous y voulions retourner en bref, et qu'apporterions des ferremens et autres choses, et que desirions mener avec nous deux de ses fils, et qu'en apres nous retournerions en ce port . . . [ils] tenoient plusieurs paroles que nous n'entendions point, faisans signe qu'ils n'osteroient point ceste croix" ("We then gave them to understand by signs that that cross was planted there to leave a recognizable mark that would allow us to return to this port, which we wanted to do shortly, and that we would bring irons and other things, and that we wished to take two of his sons with us, and that we would afterwards return to this port . . . they uttered several words that we did not at all understand, making signs that they would not remove that cross").[3] In a paratactic rush of communication that brings to mind the image of a modern-day third-base coach, the French explain why they plant the cross, what European objects they plan to bring upon their imminent return, that they wished to take two young natives with them, and so on – all through the language of gesture. The French not only assume that their own meaning is clear; they confidently offer French translations of native gesticulations as well ("making signs that they would not remove that cross"). Of course, the third-base coach has a distinct advantage over the French here, since he uses gestures whose meaning has been verbally agreed upon in advance by the parties involved. By contrast, the French narrator makes clear here that speech contributes virtually nothing to the interpretation of the exchange ("they uttered several words that we

---

[3] Cartier's first voyage took place in 1534; the earliest published account of it appeared in Ramusio in 1556; the earliest surviving French version was published at Rouen in 1598. I quote here from the *Relation originale du voyage de Jacques Cartier,* which gives the 1598 French text.

did not understand at all"). The gestures of Cartier and his men thus consist of nothing but bodies – their own, those of the natives, the cross, the earth itself.

Of course, one could argue that the French have no choice here. Since they do not share a common language with their interlocutors, they are forced to take recourse to gesture. It is important to note, however, that the language of signs is not characterized in this scene as a primitive tool of last resort – the narrator never suggests that the exchange he reports, nor his report itself, are compromised by the non-verbal medium of the original communication. While Cartier (or his scribe) would presumably agree that speech is in general a more efficient mode of communication, the utter confidence with which he translates improvised gestures into French suggests that neither he nor his audience considered gestures to be woefully inadequate substitute for speech, but rather a satisfactory means of human communication.

Clearly, the New World eyewitness occults the role his own acts of interpretation must have played in such exchanges. The possibility that these New World bodies signify differently from European bodies is simply never entertained, despite the acknowledged gulf between the linguistic systems of the parties in question. Moreover, there is never any reported dispute among exploring party members as to what specific gestures mean. The language of signs thus appears to transcend the boundaries between both cultures and individuals. From our historical vantage point, the assurance with which Columbus, Cartier and others used and interpreted physical gestures looks like a product of arrogance and wishful thinking. But the presuppositions that implicitly ground that arrogance and those wishes are worth interrogating.

The language of gestures, unlike speech, appears in this scene as natural and universal. All human bodies apparently speak the same language. The ability to deny interpretive agency in the reading of body language depends upon a conception of the body as an absolutely transparent medium of communication. The body simply says what it means, and what it means is immediately understood. That no hermeneutical method is required to understand such a communication implies that there is no distance between the bodily signifier and its unambiguous referent. There is simply no need – indeed no room – for interpretation here, since signifier and referent virtually collapse into one another in the unfailingly efficacious gestures of Cartier and the Iroquois.

This faith in the efficacy of the body as a direct means of communication also underlay the orthodox Catholic attitude toward martyrdom. The English Catholic Reginald Pole made the most extreme version of such a view explicit: "[the persecuted apostles and disciples] were living books in which . . . the entire human race could read what the will of God and the way to happiness were . . . Even though what was written on paper was dictated by the same spirit . . . nevertheless, as the original always has more authority than the other books copied from it, so books written out in the blood of the martyrs are to be preferred above all others. . . . Through perverse human reasoning and interpretation [the written books] can be distorted and fashioned in many forms, whereas those that are written in the blood of martyrs cannot be corrupted."[4] For Pole, the body not only communicates without any linguistic support, it is also infinitely more reliable than any verbal artifact. The martyr's body figures here as an "original," while talk about it (whether it is written or oral seems irrelevant to him) constitutes an attempt to refer to that original, an attempt that necessarily produces something not only less authoritative, but also more prone to misinterpretation. Thus the Catholic martyr's body, like those of the gesticulating Frenchmen in Canada, communicates directly and unambiguously, whereas linguistic exchange opens up the Pandora's box of hermeneutics.

As does the orthodox Catholic view, Calvin's understanding of the semiotic function of the relic has implications both for the language of gesture and for the discourses of witnessing and testimony. Like Cartier, Jean Ribaut, the Huguenot leader of the French expeditions to Florida, describes exchanges with Americans that take place without the benefit of a common language. There are one or two places in his *Whole and true discoverye* in which he sounds a bit like Cartier: "As we demaunded of them for a certen towne called Sevola . . . they shewed us by signes which we understode well enough, that they might go thither with there boates by rivers in

---

[4] This passage is from Reginald Pole's Latin defense of the unity of the Roman church, addressed to Henry VIII (Rome, 1538), cited and translated in Gregory, *Salvation* 267.

XXtie days" (74-75).[5] But he describes some of the gestural exchanges between his party and the Indians in a way that resists imputing some natural "face value" to the language of signs. Here is what Ribaut reports happened after he and his men kneeled down to pray in front of a group of Timicua: "And as I made a sygne unto there king, lifting up myne arme and streching owt one finger, only to make them loke up to heavenward, he likewise lifting up his arme towardes heven, put fourth two fyngers wherby it semed that he would make us tunderstand that thay wordshipped the sonne and mone for gides, as afterward we understode yt so" (68). Ribaut's text helps to demonstrate the degree to which the mediating function of Cartier's body is occulted in his gestural exchange, since Ribaut actually describes the corporeal movements that he is both intending and taking as signs before proceeding to an account of the message they are understood to transmit.

Cartier, as we saw, never lets the reader "see" what kinds of signs ground the messages he reports. This translates into a more generalized brute empiricism in Cartier's account. Scrupulously faithful to Cartier's "experiences," the accounts of his voyages catalog, in chronological order, everything deemed noteworthy that happens to him and his men in an unadorned, realistic report. This prosaic proto-empiricism is one of the intellectual and rhetorical legacies of early reports about America, and its underlying assumptions (about what counts as "noteworthy," about what constitutes "culture," about the moral status of "Indians," etc.) have been critiqued right along with those of other realist discourses that refrain from reflection on the complexity of their relationship to their referents. The accounts of Cartier's voyages are perfect examples of what Clifford Geertz calls travel texts (as opposed to a proper ethnography), because they are "as such texts are by nature, one damn thing after another" (37). Ribaut's account, by

---

[5] I cite from H.P. Biggar's transcription of a sixteenth-century English manuscript, which provides a slightly more extensive and significantly more linguistically correct text than does the version printed at London in 1563 (included in the volume published by the University Press of Florida in 1964). Though rumors of a French "original" of the *Whole and True Discoverye* have circulated since the sixteenth century, none has ever been located. Lussagnet gives her own modern French translation in *Les Français en Floride*. Another early English printed version can be found in Hakluyt's 1582 *Divers voyages*. Many variant spellings of Ribaut's name exist in print, including Ribault, Ribauld and Rybaud.

contrast, offers scenes of interpretation which problematize the readability of physical reality.

In the case of Ribaut's account, we as readers are made to understand that we witness the gestures ourselves. Consequently, in the Ribaut passage, the gesticulating bodies appear as absolutely distinct from what they are subsequently said to signify – just as, for Calvin, the martyrological body is not coextensive with the significance of the martyr. Moreover, the meaning Ribaut gives to the gesture is presented here specifically as an interpretation ("it seemed to me"), an interpretation that awaits subsequent confirmation ("later we learned . . .") – a confirmation that, we learn in another account of the same expedition, was purely linguistic.

That other account was written by René de Laudonnière, another of the Huguenots in Florida in the 1560's. Laudonnière notes the poverty of the initial exchanges between his party and the Timicua: "ce pauvre Indien . . . nous discourut de plusieurs choses, dont nous recevions un maigre plaisir, pource que nous n'entendions que par signes ce qu'il pouvoit concevoir" ("this poor Indian . . . spoke to us of many things, from which we got little pleasure, since we could understand only by signs what he might want to tell us"; 90). It is striking that Laudonnière, like Ribaut, bothers to describe some of the physical gestures the two groups used to communicate with one another. When one of the Huguenots attempts to determine the familial relations among a group of natives, Laudonnière reports that an old Timicua man, "[en] frappant par deux fois sur la cuisse et mettant la main sur deux d'iceuxluy feit entendre par signes que ces deux etaient ses enfants" ("[by]hitting his thigh twice and putting his hand on two younger Indians, told him by signs that these two were his children"; 91). Here again, the translation of the physical gesture into a linguistic description of that gesture, *prior* to lending the gesture a particular significance, foregrounds a specifically Calvinist conception of the body as an opaque sign that must be interpreted, as opposed to the unproblematically transparent vehicle of communication we see in Cartier and Columbus.

Sign Language II: The Eucharist

In "Ralegh's Fugitive Gold," Mary C. Fuller argues against the notion of a "domain of things outside the order of language" as a paradigm for reading narratives of the discovery and exploration of the New World. She specifically critiques Certeau's argument about Montaigne: "Proximity – this term glides surreptitiously into the place vacated by experience, presence. And as proximity (to Indian artifacts, the simple traveler) replaces experience of the "real" in de Certeau's argument, it seems we are once again talking about interpretation, building upon objects – body, artifacts, cassava – grasped as signs or metonymic figures" (239). Though this analysis makes sense given the presuppositions of structuralism, it fails to take into account the different modes conjuring a "real presence" that may have been at issue for sixteenth-century eyewitness historians of the New World themselves. In a sense, Fuller here critiques the Catholic "reliquary mode" of eyewitness testimony without taking into consideration the alternative proposed by Protestant theology. And Protestant theology – more specifically, Calvinist theology – will prove to be a powerful influence on what has come to be considered a founding text of modern ethnography, and, as such, a paradigm for the modern eyewitness: Jean de Léry's *Histoire d'un voyage faict en la terre du Bresil*.

As we have already seen in the discussion of relics, the view that the body can communicate without the benefit of an intelligible linguistic accompaniment is central to orthodox Catholicism. This view also underpins the doctrine of transubstantiation. Though a bit of linguistic "hocus pocus" was required to effect transubstantiation (and it's worth recalling here that the Council of Trent reaffirmed the use of Latin in the Mass), once Christ's body was on the altar, it communicated Christ's testament directly to anyone and everyone who ingested it, whether he understood Latin or not.

Jean Calvin, by contrast, clearly does not subscribe to what Miri Rubin and others have called the "realist" interpretation of the Eucharist that dominated late-medieval culture, and that characterizes the doctrines of both transubstantiation and consubstantiation.[6]

---

[6] As Miri Rubin notes, "transubstantiation was a neologism which arose from the eleventh-century debate [about the nature of the Eucharist], and developed in

The realist model takes the "est" of the words of the Eucharistic institution, "hoc est corpus meum," as designating an ontological fact: after consecration, what's on the sacramental altar *is* the body of Christ. The realists have settled the question of the verb "est," and thus concern themselves primarily with the substantives "hoc" and "corpus."[7] Calvin, on the other hand, rejects the ontological premise of realist Eucharistic theology, and works to redefine the status of the "est" in terms of metaphor.[8]

As Bill Clinton might have put it, there has been a fair amount of controversy over what the meaning of "is" is in Calvin's discussions of the Eucharist, but Calvin is unequivocal about what it is not: as he writes in the *Institutes*, "Cela ne fut jamais accoutumé ni ouï en nulle langue, que ce verbe substantiel, *c'est*, fût pris en un tel sens, à savoir pour être converti en autre chose" ("The use of the term *is*, for being converted into something else, is unknown to every tongue and nation"; *IC* 4/17/20, 369).[9] Instead of positing a substantial transformation of sign into signified, Calvin's Eucharistic theology focuses on the *relation* between a sign and a signified (and Calvin consistently acknowledges his debt to Augustine in this regard), approaching the mystery of the Eucharist in terms of the manner in which the bread and wine *represent* or *refer* to Christ's body and blood.[10] Despite his insistence on the thoroughly symbol-

---

the twelfth century within a realist philosophy of the universe" (24). Transubstantiation in the Eucharist became official church doctrine at the fourth Lateran Council of 1215 under Innocent III.

[7] This view gave rise to questions like "is Christ naked or clothed in the Eucharist?" "Is he standing up or sitting down?" I take these examples from Philippe DuPlessis-Mornay's *Traité de l'Eucharistie*, where a list of them is prefaced with the comment that such worries "ne se trouvent point és premiers, mesmes 800. ans apres nostre Seigneur" (901-2).

[8] I will cite the 1560 French edition of the Institutes as *IC*, indicating book, chapter, section and page number. I give Henry Beveridge's 1845 English translation of the 1559 Latin edition of the *Institutes*, making slight alterations when necessary, based on my consultation of the 1560 French edition and the 1559 Latin edition, as well as previous Latin versions (in volumes one and two of *Ioannis Calvini opera quae supersunt omnia*, ed. Baum, Cunitz and Reuss; cited as "O.O." followed by volume number followed by column number). I have also occasionally consulted the translation of Ford Lewis Battles.

[9] Calvin analyzes scriptural uses of the verb "être" in *IC* 4/17/20 and 22, noting that nobody, not even his Catholic adversaries, takes the copula literally in all cases, thus putting the burden of explaining a literal reading of "ceci est mon corps" back onto the Catholics.

[10] Calvin is careful to insist that sacramental representation does not work in the same way as does everyday language: "Or ce serait un blasphème insupportable

ic nature of the Eucharistic sign, however, Calvin makes abundantly clear in the *Institutes* that the fact that the bread never undergoes an ontological conversion into the body of Christ does not mean that just anything could occupy the place of bread in the sacrament. Quite the contrary: Calvin's sacramental semiotics depend upon a very specific type of relationship between the sacramental sign and the divine reality that it signifies. Again borrowing from Augustine, Calvin calls this relation "similitude" or "analogie," and explicitly anticipates and defends against the charge of arbitrariness: "the name 'body' has been given to the bread, not in a bare, empty manner that aims to please the ear, but because of an especially appropriate similitude" ("Ce nom de corps a été attribué au pain, non pas nuement, comme les mots chantent, mais par une similitude bien convenable"; 4/17/21; 370). Calvin elaborates on the "appropriateness" of the sacramental similitude thus:

> Quand nous voyons le pain nous être présenté pour signe et sacrement du corps de Jésus Christ, il nous faut incontinent prendre cette similitude: qu'ainsi que le pain nourrit, sustente et conserve la vie de notre corps, aussi le corps de Jésus Christ est l'aliment et la nourriture pour la conservation de notre vie spirituelle. Et quand nous voyons le vin nous être offert pour signe de son sang, il nous faut penser tout ce que fait et profite le vin au corps humain, pour estimer que le sang de Jésus Christ nous fait et profite autant spirituellement. . . . Car si nous considérons bien ce que nous a profité le fait que le corps très sacré de Jésus a été livré, et son sang répandu pour nous, nous verrons clairement que ce qu'on attribue au pain et au vin, selon cette analogie et similitude, leur convient très bien (*IC* 4/17/3; 351)

> When bread is given as a symbol of the body of Christ, we must immediately think of this similitude. As bread nourishes, sustains and protects our bodily life, so the body of Christ is the food and nourishment for our spiritual life. When we behold the wine set forth as a sign of His blood, we must think that such use as wine serves to the body, the same is spiritually bestowed by the blood of Christ. . . . For if we duly consider what profit we have gained

---

de dire, sans aucune figure, qu'un élément caduc et corruptible soit Jésus Christ . . . le pain est nommé corps à la façon des sacrements. D'où il s'ensuit que les paroles de Jésus Christ ne sont point sujettes à la règle commune, et ne doivent pas être examinées selon la grammaire" (*IC* 4/17/20; 369).

by the breaking of his sacred body, and the shedding of his blood, we shall clearly perceive that the properties attributed to bread and wine by this analogy are quite appropriate (558-59)

The idea of nourishment thus grounds the analogy between the Eucharistic sign and Christ's body; moreover, this analogy is not merely quite appropriate, it is absolutely necessary, since the analogy between the sign and the thing signified cannot be destroyed without destroying the truth of the sacrament ("On ne peut rompre la proportion qui est entre le signe et la chose signifiée, que la vérité du mystère n'aille bas" [4/17/16; 365]). Rather than view them as arbitrary, then, Calvin considered bread and wine particularly fitting sacramental signs for the spiritual food that is Christ.[11] But Calvin does not consider them a Eucharistic *sine qua non*: his concept of analogy opens the door to acceptable substitutes. Calvin's position on the Eucharistic analogy is thus that the Eucharistic bread and wine are *neither* essential *nor* arbitrary.

The Eucharist is explicitly at issue in the French colony at Guanabara described in Jean de Léry's *Histoire*, both as a point of contention between Léry's Huguenot companions and the lapsed protestant leader of the colony, Nicolas Durand de Villegagnon, and as a matter of debate among the Huguenots themselves. When, near the end of their stay, their wine supply begins to run low, the Huguenots in Brazil discuss the merits of using native substitutes for the bread and wine of the Lord's Supper:

> Quelques uns ... estoyent d'opinion que le vin deffaillant il vaudroit mieux s'abstenir du signe que de le changer. Les autres au contraire disoyent, que lors que Jesus Christ institua sa Cene, au pays de Judée, il avoit parlé du bruvage qui y estoit ordinaire, et

---

[11] The misreadings of his critics notwithstanding, Calvin's early followers continue to emphasize the concept of similitude or analogy in the Eucharist. Analogia is a key term in Théodore de Bèze's formulation of the Reformed understanding of the Eucharist, as expressed in his *Confessio Christianae Fidei* (a work originally written in French in 1556, then revised and translated into Latin in 1560). In her analysis of the *Confessio*, Jill Raitt notes that "the connection between sacrament and life in Christ, between sign and signified, is drawn close in the analogy of food and drink, the sustenance of life itself" (*Eucharistic* 29). In his 1598 *Traité de l'Eucharistie*, Philippe Du Plessis-Mornay explains the suitability of the sacramental signs in terms of a similitude based on the idea of nourishment: "le pain et le vin [sont] signes tres-convenables de la vraie & parfaite nourriture des fideles qui est en Christ; nourriture, qui ne peut estre mieux expliquee, que par celle de nos corps" (771).

que s'il eust esté en la terre des sauvages il est vraysemblable qu'il eust non seulement fait mention du bruvage dont ils usent au lieu du vin, mais aussi de leur farine de racine qu'ils mangent au lieu du pain: concluoyent que tout ainsi qu'ils ne voudroyent nullement changer les signes du pain et du vin, tant qu'ils se pourroyent trouver, qu'aussi à defaut d'iceux ne feroyent ils point de difficulté de celebrer la Cene avec les choses plus communes (tenant lieu de pain et de vin) pour la nourriture des hommes du pays où ils seroyent. Mais encores que la pluspart enclinast à ceste dernière opinion, parce que nous n'en vismes pas jusques à ceste extremité, ceste matiere demeura indecise (194-5)

Some . . . were of the opinion that when wine was lacking, it would be better to abstain from the sign than to change it. Others said, on the contrary, that when Christ instituted the Lord's Supper, being in the land of Judea, he had spoken of the ordinary drink of that region, and that if he had been in the land of the savages it is probable that he would have made mention not only of the drink they use instead of wine, but also of the root flour they eat instead of bread; they concluded that while they would not change the signs of the bread and the wine as long as they could be obtained, nonetheless if they were not to be had, there would be no obstacle to celebrating the Lord's Supper with the commonest things for human nourishment that took the place of bread and wine in the land where they were (49)

Florimond de Raemond, a most enthusiastic sixteenth-century defender of Catholicism in France, cites this passage from Léry in its entirety in his presumptuously titled *Histoire de la naissance, progrez et decadence de l'heresie en ce siecle*, in order to support his claim that Calvinists can perform the Lord's Supper with beer, cider, or the *caouin* of the Savages ("faire la Coene avec de la biere, du cidre, & du Cahom des Sauvages. Voila quelle est la théologie Calvinique"; 1358. Raemond then cites a letter written by Théodore de Bèze that indicates that Calvin did in fact explicitly approve the use of Tupinamba *caouin* in the performance of the Lord's Supper.[12]

---

[12] Raemond gives a French version of this letter (1357-8). See Alain Dufour ("Un avis de Calvin à ses disciples qui étaient chez les Topinambous") for the original Latin version of the 1568 letter from Bèze to André Dudith, a Hungarian humanist who wanted to celebrate the Supper but who couldn't stomach wine:

Rogatus piae memoriae vir D. Calvinus a fratribus, qui tum in America erant, ubi nullus est vini usus, liceretne pro vino uti in Coena Domini vel

Raemond's critical reading of Léry's Calvinism helps us home in on a dimension of Eucharistic doctrine that is central for an understanding of Léry's ethnography: the nature of the Eucharistic sign. Raemond finds it unacceptable that Calvin's theology permits the substitution of other foods and drinks for the bread and wine of the Eucharist, since he saw an essential connection between bread and Christ's body, and between wine and His blood, and thought it impossible to change anything of what he terms the sacraments' "essence or nature." He insists that Scripture limits the faithful to bread and wine for this sacrament.[13] But even Raemond doesn't go as far as Frank Lestringant, who in a recent analysis of the Eucharist in Léry's history concludes that "l'arbitraire du signe culmine dans cet avatar exotique de la Cène" (*Sainte horreur* 106). According to Lestringant, Calvin's conception of the Eucharist devalues the sign to the point that the place of the sign can be occupied by simply anything. As we have seen, a careful reading of Calvin's writings on the Eucharist suggests that Calvin steers a middle course between Raemond's essentialism on the one hand, and the arbitrariness Lestringant attributes to him on the other; moreover, this semiotic *via media* will also characterize Léry's approach to the Tupinamba.

In the few available studies of the Protestant dimension in Léry's ethnography, the element of Calvinist doctrine that tends to receive the most attention is predestination. In a chapter entitled "Calvinistes et cannibales," Frank Lestringant argues that the Calvinist doctrine of predestination leads Léry to cast the Brazilian "savage" as "une confirmation *a contrario* de sa propre rédemp-

aqua simplici qua plerunque illic utuntur, vel alio illic non inusitato potionis genere, respondit fuisse Christi in hoc instituendo sacramento consilium ut spiritualis alimoniae, id est sui ipsius χοινωνιαν nobis sub communis cibi ac potus symbolis repraesentaret, ac proinde si non fuisset in Judaea communis vini usus, proculdubio alia vulgari potione usurum fuisse, quod ex ipsius scopo ac consilio liqueat

[13] I have paraphrased these fragments out of a much longer passage without, I hope, having distorted its sense: "Comme les Sacremens sont en leur essence d'institution divine: aussi n'est il pas loisible de rien alterer & changer, je dis en ce qui est de leur essence & nature . . . [Jesus and the Apostles used bread and wine]. . . . Puis donc que le commandement est exprez de faire ce que le Sauveur a fait; & que ce commandement tombe du moins sur ce qui étoit de substantiel, & comme essentiel en l'action de Jésus Christ, comme l'est la matiere ou l'objet; & partant sur le pain & sur le vin par iceus en consacrer & en faire le sacrifice & Sacrement. Le pain & le vin nous sont limitez pour matiere de ce Sacrement en l'Ecriture" (1358).

tion" (*Expérience huguenote* 85), and that Léry's theological exclusion of the Tupinamba in turn allows him to set the Americans up as objects of aesthetic exaltation. Anthony Pagden claims that Léry wrote the Tupinamba off as "cursed," and that the Huguenot consequently thought it a waste of time to missionize to a group of people who couldn't possibly be members of God's elect (*European Encounters* 42-47). Predestination is, for better or for worse, the doctrine with which Jean Calvin has come to be identified. One cannot deny that predestination became a central, even defining feature of later Calvinisms; however, in sixteenth-century France in general, and in Léry in particular, we are dealing with a Calvinism whose doctrine of predestination has not yet produced the obsession with election that characterizes its later incarnations, especially Puritanism. This obsession is of course one of the foundations of Max Weber's classic linking of protestantism to capitalism. Weber himself acknowledges the distinction between "Calvin's theology" and subsequent "Calvinism," however, and makes clear that it is with the latter, in the form of English Puritanism, that he is principally concerned.[14]

As Basil Hall has observed, "Few realise . . . how very much more [Calvin's] writings are concerned with the Church and the sacraments than with predestination" (147). The fact that predestination was seldom a point of polemic contention between Calvin and his sixteenth-century adversaries tends to confirm Hall's reading. Long a topic of Catholic theology, as well as of humanist treatises on free will, predestination receives relatively little attention by the Council of Trent, which devotes significantly more time to the sacraments (indeed, the Council produced a separate decree on the sacraments at its seventh session in March 1547). At the majority of the Catholic-Protestant (and Protestant-Protestant) colloquies in which Calvin or his immediate successor, Théodore de Bèze, took part, the main source of disagreement was the sacraments – and even more specifically, the Eucharist. This is true, for example, of Regensburg (1541); Poissy (1561); and Montbéliard (1585). Christopher Elwood has recently shown that in the years immediately following Léry's return to France from Brazil in 1558, the number of

---

[14] It is interesting to note that when Weber mentions the characteristics of this sort of Calvinism in France at all, it is to point out its affinities to certain beliefs and practices of the Jesuits and the Jansenists.

both Catholic and Protestant treatises on the Eucharist published in French fairly exploded, reaching a high of nearly fifty works from each denomination in 1561. Elwood maintains that the Eucharist "was the focus of more theological controversy in the sixteenth century than any other item of Christian confession and practice" (3-4).

The Eucharistic controversy, like the debates about martyrs, was in many ways a conflict about the nature of testimony. In Book Four of the *Institutes*, Calvin proposes that a sacrament is *"un témoignage de la grâce de Dieu envers nous, confirmé par un signe extérieur"* (4/14/267; italics in original; "a testimony of the divine favour towards us, confirmed by an external sign"; 492).[15] Similarly, in his 1552 *Catechisme*, a dialogue between a Calvinist minister and an exemplary Calvinist "enfant," Calvin has the child define a sacrament as "an external *testimony* of God's grace, that by means of a visible sign represents spiritual things to us" (emphasis mine).[16] Nearly every discussion of the nature of the sacraments in the *Institutes* uses the vocabulary of testimony.[17] The Calvinist sacraments thus "represent" the divine by means of attestation, and not imitation. As I shall suggest here, the fact that the nature of the link between worldly signs and spiritual realities in Calvin is testimonial is precisely what makes his sacramental theology particularly appropriate as a model for Léry's ethnographic discourse.

It is clear that Léry and his companions understand the Eucharistic sign to function in the testimonial manner proposed by

---

[15] The Latin versions of this passage are: "testimonium gratiae Dei, externo symbolo nobis declaratum" [1536 edition; O.O. I/102]; "divinae in nos gratiae testimonium externo signo confirmatum" [1543; O.O. I/938-39 and 1559; O.O. II/942].

[16] My translation; the original reads "un tesmoignage exterieur de la grace de Dieu, qui par un signe visible nous represente les choses spirituelles." I read the *Catechisme* in a facsimile edition prepared by the Friends of the Rutgers University Libraries (New Brunswick, 1973), bound together with Marot and Bèze's psalm translations (published by Jean Crespin in 1551) and Calvin's 1552 *Forme des prieres Ecclesiastiques*.

[17] I give a few more examples here: "Le baptême nous rend témoignage que nous sommes purifiés et lavés, et la cène de l'eucharistie, que nous sommes rachetés.... De cela est témoin l'Esprit de Dieu, ou plutôt trois en sont témoins ensemble: l'eau, le sang et l'esprit. En l'eau et au sang nous avons le témoignage de notre purification et rédemption" (*IC* 4/14/22; 288); "Les sacrements sont vraiment nommés des témoignages de la grâce de Dieu" (*IC* 4/14/7; 272); "Or quel est le signe et le témoignage de cette purification, sinon le baptême?" (*IC* 4/15/4; 297); "le baptême atteste la rémission de nos péchés" (*IC* 4/15/1; 295).

Calvin. The determination Léry and his coreligionaries ultimately make when their wine runs out is that European bread and wine are not necessary for the performance of the Supper, that the everyday food and drink of the Tupi (those that "take the place of bread and wine" in the secular realm) could be a suitable sign for spiritual food and drink; nonetheless, they do not thereby sanction the use of just anything on hand to serve as the sacramental signs of the Eucharist. (It is unlikely, for example, that the Huguenots would have approved the use of sea water and parrots – two things that were abundant in the colony, and that they did end up consuming on their arduous journey back to France.) That the Eucharistic bread and wine, though nonessential signs, are not thereby arbitrary ones, has everything to do with the fact that we are dealing here with what it is fair to call a human universal: food. *What* humans eat is a matter of custom; *that* humans eat is not. Consequently, the things humans customarily eat can be taken as signs which partake of both the natural and the conventional. Bread and wine might be conventionally European food and drink, but they have certain natural properties that make them appropriate to meet the requirements for everyday human nourishment (as do manioc and *caouin*). These are the very properties on which Calvin's Eucharistic analogy is based. The fact that Léry understands Eucharistic semiotics in Calvin's manner has important consequences for his ethnographic treatment of the Tupinamba, since it will condition his approach to custom.

Because Protestantism produces a thoroughgoing critique of (Catholic) custom, it is an important – if certainly not the only – source of the notion of cultural relativism in sixteenth-century Europe. Calvin addresses the issue of custom directly in the Epistle to François Ier that opens the *Institutes*, when, defending himself and his followers against the charge of disrupting the social order, he asserts that "Ce serait une grande iniquité, si nous étions contraints de céder à la coutume" in matters theological (IC XXXI; "it would be a great iniquity if we were constrained to follow custom"). In a passage on the debated practice of mixing of water with the Eucharistic wine in his *Traité de l'Eucharistie,* Philippe Du Plessis-Mornay brings the notion of custom to bear directly on the sacramental signs: "this mixture does not signify the mysteries that one looks for in it, but is a function solely of custom or appearance" ("cette mixtion n'est donc point significative des mysteres qu'on y recherche; mais [procède] seulement ou de la coustume du païs ou de l'apparence"; *Traité* 277). Du Plessis-Mornay here draws a contrast between the Eucharistic mysteries, which are eternal, and the customary rituals surrounding the Eucharist, which he implies are contingent. Even the acknowledgement that Jesus himself used unleavened bread and wine does not put the traditional Eucharistic signs beyond the domain of the contingent for the Calvinists: Bèze's letter explaining Calvin's acceptance of substitutes for the bread and wine of the Eucharist (the very letter that so upset Florimond de Raemond, and whose formulations Léry echoes in the passage Raemond critiques) refers to wine as the customary drink of Judea, and suggests that if this weren't the case, Jesus would have used some other common drink.[18]

The Huguenots in Brazil are themselves not wholly indifferent to church custom, since they all apparently agree that bread and wine remain the preferred elements for the performance of the Supper. However, by casting the customary relation between the Eucharistic signs and the mysteries to which they refer as contingent, Calvin's Eucharistic analogy looses the ontological bond to the divine that the doctrine of transubstantiation sought to establish. Whereas transubstantiationist Catholics like Raemond categorically refuse the use of anything but unleavened bread and red wine in the sacrament of the Eucharist, Calvin's Eucharistic analogy makes it possible for the Huguenots at Guanabara to see their own cultural preference as just that, and not as an inviolable absolute. Thus, Léry's willingness as a Calvinist to accept Tupi *caouin* and manioc mush as potential analogues to the blood and body of Christ grants him the capacity to recognize a certain parity between European and Tupi "*usages.*" Léry's ethnography of the Tupinamba will constitute a generalized application of this relativizing perspective.

The ethnologic result of Léry's specifically Calvinist approach to (Eucharistic) custom is that, rather than simply relegating the Tupi to the realm of the pagan (construed either as non-Christian and hence inferior or as pre-Christian, along with the Greeks, and hence potentially superior), Léry puts Tupi culture on the same moral plane as that of contemporary Europeans. By contrast, whenever André Thevet juxtaposes America to Europe in his 1557 *Singularitez de la*

---

[18] See note 12. The passage I refer to here is "si non fuisset in Judaea communis vini usus, proculdubio alia vulgari potione usurum fuisse." Raemond's French has "si l'usage du vin n'eût été lors commun en la Judée, [Jésus-Christ] eut sans doute usé d'autre boisson vulgaire & commune" (1357).

France Antarctique, he refers to Europe's past, and consequently makes the Americans out to be either pathetic primitives or idealized innocents.[19] Though Léry has often enough been cast as one of the founders of the discourse of the "noble savage," his comparisons of European and Tupi culture turn to the detriment of the latter as often as to that of the former. By translating the Calvinist critique of custom into ethnographic terms, Léry puts into practice Michel de Montaigne's insights on the contingent valence of human cultural practices – something Montaigne himself was unable to do with respect to the New World, as his idealizing portraits of Americans in the essays "Des coches" and "Des cannibales" suggest.[20] That Léry does not consistently favor either culture is perhaps best illustrated by the comments he makes to his European readers at the close of his description of the process by which *caouin* – the potential substitute for wine in the Eucharistic rite – is made:

> Je ne doute point que quelques uns de ceux qui auront ouy ce que ja'y dit cy dessus, touchant la mascheure et tortilleure, tant des racines que du mil, parmi la bouche des femmes sauvages quand elle compose leur breuvage dit *Caou-in*, n'ayent eu mal au coeur, et en ayent craché: à fin que je leur oste aucunement ce desgoust, je les prie de se resouvenir de la façon qu'on tient quand on fait le vin par deça. Car s'ils considerent seulement cecy: qu'ès lieux mesmes où croissent les bons vins, les vignerons, en temps de vendanges, se mettent dans les tinnes et dans les cuves esquelles à beaux pieds, et quelques fois avec leurs soulliers, ils foulent les raisins, voire comme j'ay veu, les patrouillent encor ainsi sur les pressoirs, ils trouveront qui s'y passe beaucoup de choses, lesquelles n'ont guere meilleure grace que ceste maniere de machiller, accoustumée aux femmes Ameri-

---

[19] For a discussion of the category of the pagan as it was used by early modern Europeans to come to terms with exotic peoples, see Michael T. Ryan, "Assimilating New Worlds in the Sixteenth and Seventeenth Centuries."

[20] Léry's willingness to criticize the Tupinamba, together with his lack of missionary zeal, distinguishes the French Huguenot not only from Montaigne, but also from the most famous early European defender of the indigenous peoples of America, Bartolomé de Las Casas. Las Casas's inflammatory *Brevíssima relación de la destrucción de las Indias* (1552) casts the "indios" as utterly guileless innocents, lambs in the merciless hands of savage Spanish lions. Ironically – and more important from the point of view of modern ethnography – Las Casas's view of the Indians as in many respects closer to God than were the conquistadors was not only a defense of their humanity, but an argument for their conversion to Catholicism.

quaines. Que si on dit là dessus, Voire mais, le vin en cuvant et bouillant jette toute ceste ordure: je respons que nostre *Caou-in* se purge aussi, et partant, quant à ce poinct, qu'il y a mesme raison de l'un à l'autre (255-6)

I have no doubt that some of those who have heard what I have said concerning the chewing and twisting around of the roots and millet in the mouths of the savage women when they concoct their *caouin*, will have been nauseated, and will have spit. To allay this disgust, I entreat them to remember what we do when we make wine over here. Let them consider merely this: in the very places where the good wines grow, at the time of grape-harvest the winemakers get into tubs and vats, and with their bare feet and sometimes with their shoes, they tread the grapes; as I have seen, they crush them again the same way on the winepresses. Many things go on which are hardly more pleasing than this custom of chewing among the American women. If thereupon someone says "Yes, but as it ferments in the vats the wine expells all that filth," I reply that our *caouin* is purged the same way, and that therefore on this point the one custom is as good as the other (77)

Similarly, Léry's attitude toward Tupinamba nudity transcends the reductive alternatives of "heathen" versus "noble savage":

Ce lieu-ci requiert que je responde, tant à ceux qui ont escrit, qu'à ceux qui pensent que la frequentation entre ces sauvages tous nuds, et principalement parmi les femmes, incite à lubricité et paillardise. Sur quoy je diray en un mot, qu'encores voirement qu'en apparence il n'y ait que trop d'occasion d'estimer qu'outre la deshonnesteté de voir ces femmes nues, cela ne semble aussi servir comme d'un appast ordinaire à la convoitise: toutesfois, pour en parler selon ce qui s'en est communement apperceu pour lors, ceste nudité ainsi grossiere en telle femme est beaucoup moins attrayante qu'on ne cuideroit. Et partant, je maintien que les attifets, fards, fausses perruqes, cheveux tortillez, grands collets friasez, vertugales, robbes sur robbes, et autres infinies bagatelles dont les femmes et filles de par-deça se contrefont et n'en ont jamais assez, sont sans comparaison, cause de plus de maux que n'en est la nudité ordinaire des femmes sauvages: lesquelles cependant, quant au naturel, ne doivent rien aux autres en beauté. . . . Ce n'est pas cependant que contre ce que dit la saincte Escriture . . . je vueille en façon que ce soit approuver ceste nudité. . . . Mais ce que j'ay dit de ces sauvages est,

> pour monstrer qu'en les condamnans si austerement, de ce que sans nulle vergogne ils vont ainsi le corps entierement descouvert, nous excedans en l'autre extremité, c'est à dire en nos boubances, superfluitez et exces en habits, ne sommes gueres plus louables. Et pleust à Dieu, pour mettre fin à ce poinct, qu'un chacun de nous, plus pour l'honnesteté et nécessité, que pour gloire et mondanité, s'habillast modestement (235-6)

> I must respond to those who think that the frequenting of these naked savages, especially of the women, arouses wanton desire and lust . . . this crude nakedness in such a woman is much less alluring than one might expect. And I maintain that the elaborate attire, paint, wigs, curled hair, great ruffs, farthingales, robes upon robes, and all the infinity of trifles with which the women and girls over here [in Europe] disguise themselves and of which they never have enough, are beyond comparison the cause of more ills than the ordinary nakedness of the savage women – whose natural beauty is by no means inferior to that of the others. . . . I do not mean, however, to contradict what the Holy Scripture says . . . nor do I wish in any way that this nakedness be approved. . . . But what I have said about these savages is to show that, while we condemn them so austerely for going about shamelessly with their bodies entirely uncovered, we ourselves, going to the other extreme in the sumptuous display, superfluity, and excess of our own costume, are hardly more laudable. . . . I would to God that each of us dressed modestly (67-8)

Lestringant claims Léry here "allegorizes" the nudity of the Tupi women "qui de toute évidence, le fascine"; ultimately, according to Lestringant, "l'exaltation du nu exotique conduit à la satire misogyne des «sucrées» et coquettes de la vielle Europe" (*Sainte horreur* 108). Such a view is hard to sustain. Léry eschews appartenance to either community here, presenting both Tupi nudity and European dress in a negative light. Moreover, Léry's point is, precisely, that the nudity of the Tupi women evokes nothing beyond itself, while European dress sends all sorts of unsavory messages. (If anything appears to fascinate Léry here, it's the European feminine accoutrements that he catalogs at some length.)

Léry's espousal of a Calvinist "modesty" creates a standard of which both Europeans and Americans fall short: here, one custom is as bad as the other. The critique of extravagant European vestimentary habits is not put forward as a neat complement to an admiration for some sort of idealized simplicity ascribed to the naked Tupi, but is rather paired with a clear disapproval of their nudity. Both customs represent extremes to be avoided. Léry's double condemnation equalizes the two customs – and by extension the two cultures – on the moral plane, locating both far from the Godly ideal. In a sense, one could say that Léry's anthropology is a logical (if certainly not inevitable) product of Calvin's, since Calvin does not locate alterity in this or that culture, but rather in humanity in general (with respect to God). Léry never unequivocally consigns the Tupi to the realm of the damned, even if he believes, as he confesses in his preface, "s'il y a nation qui soit et vive sans Dieu au monde, ce sont vrayement eux" (92; "if there is a nation in the world that exists and lives without God, it is truly this one"; lx). Calvin, of course, goes so far as to say that "in regard to the true knowledge of [God], all are so degenerate, that in no part of the world can genuine godliness be found."[21] The Tupi are thus not unlike all human beings in this regard. Moreover, as Léry observes, "toutesfois en ce poinct sont-ils peut-estre moins condamnables: c'est qu'en advouant et confessant leur malheur et aveuglissment . . . ils not font semblant d'estre autres que ce qu'ils sont" (92-3; "on this point they are perhaps not utterly condemnable: in admitting and confessing somewhat their misfortune and blindness . . . they do not pretend to be other than what they are"; lx). Hypocrisy is, of course, the defining characteristic of the one person who is unequivocally condemned in the *Histoire*: Léry devotes an entire chapter to the demonstration of "the dissimulation of Villegagnon." Obviously, we still have a thoroughly European metanarrative here – a Christian God grounds Léry's anthropology – but Léry does not present his own culture (or himself) as enjoying a privileged link to this ultimate reference point.[22]

---

[21] Beveridge 46. The French version is noticeably briefer than the Latin from which Beveridge worked: "Tous s'égarent de la vraie connaissance de Dieu" (*IC* 1/4/1; 12).

[22] Michel Jeanneret makes a similar point: "Le résultat pratique de la doctrine calvinienne du péché, c'est [chez Léry] la tolérance et le sentiment d'une fondamentale égalité parmi les hommes – égalité dans la réprobation et dans l'incertitude du salut" (233). It is thus bitterly ironic that Calvinism came (and continues) to be identified with groups of people remarkable principally for their intolerance towards social and cultural deviation.

Calvin's analogy between earthly and spiritual food, which opens the way for an analogy between the ordinary comestibles of Europe and Brazil, thus culminates in a broader moral analogy between the Tupi and the French.

I have been arguing that the concept of analogy that grounds Calvin's Eucharistic semiotics constitutes the basis for Léry's relativistic view of Tupi and European customs by providing a theory of cultural practices as contingent (but not arbitrary) signs. Other recent readers of the *Histoire*, however, have commented that we witness the end of "analogical" thinking in Léry – and that this is precisely what makes his text seem more modern to us than something like his rival Thevet's unwieldy collections of cosmographical cross-references. [23] Moreover, in studies ranging from Michel Foucault's sweeping synthesis in *Les mots et les choses* to more recent, detailed analyses of early literature about the New World such as Anthony Grafton's, the tendency to perceive analogies within and among cultures is seen as an old-fashioned intellectual tradition typical of the European Renaissance, a tradition that would soon be displaced by more "modern," "scientific" approaches to knowledge – governed, precisely, by eyewitnessing. [24] On the one hand, then, we have analogy as a privileged trope in a text generally considered to be a triumph of early modern anthropological science; on the other, we have analogy associated with all that came to be considered unscientific, and thus deemed absent from that very same text.

These apparently opposed views are not irreconcilable. It is difficult to deny that the kind of analogy that Foucault found ubiquitous in the sixteenth century is largely absent from Léry's *Histoire*. We may indeed witness in Léry's ethnography the end of "analogical thinking" as it has been defined by Foucault and documented by students of Renaissance culture – but certainly not because the notion of analogy is foreign to Léry's way of thinking. Here it is imperative to understand that Calvin's concept of analogy, as elaborated in his Eucharistic theology and put into practice in Léry's account of the Tupinamba, is not simply a version of the "resem-

---

[23] Jeanneret suggests that in Léry we witness the disappearance of the "perspective analogique, fondée sur des similitudes" ("Léry et Thevet" 237). Frank Lestringant makes a similar observation in *Le Huguenot et le sauvage* (in the chapter "Calvinistes et cannibales").

[24] See chapter 2 of Foucault's *Les mots et les choses* and the whole of Grafton's *New Worlds, Ancient Texts*.

blance" Foucault proposed over thirty years ago as the master trope of Renaissance thought.

Indeed, no one emphasized the lack of resemblance between the human and heavenly realms more than did Calvin, who wrote that God is "as different from flesh as fire is from water." [25] Far from positing a direct link – much less an Aquinian "analogy of being" – between the Christian believer and his God, Calvin maintains that "we are deficient in natural powers that might enable us to rise to a pure and clear knowledge of God." [26] Calvin's unrelenting emphasis on the gulf between God and Man helps to explain the fact that, despite his explicit belief in the necessity of some sort of analogy between the sacramental signs and the spiritual realities to which they refer, he continually faced versions of Lestringant's charge of espousing a Eucharistic "arbitraire du signe." It was precisely Calvin's unyielding insistence on the *disparity* between the Eucharistic sign and that which it signified that drew attacks from both his Catholic and Lutheran contemporaries, and what has led many of his modern readers to assert that Calvin reduced the divine to a spiritual abstraction that dwells in an ungraspable other world to which humans can have no real access. [27]

It is certainly the case that the fundamental dissimilarity between the human and the divine, and thus between earthly and spiritual food, is never abolished in Calvin's sacrament of the Eucharist; his analogy of bread to body does not work to convert one into the other. Calvin's Supper is not meant to eliminate the dis-

---

[25] "cui nihilo minus est cum carne dissidium quam igni cum aqua." This passage is from Calvin's commentary on the Gospel of John, as cited and translated in Carlos M.N. Eire's *War against the Idols*, 197.

[26] Beveridge 62. "La faculté nous [défaut] de nature pour être amenés jusqu'à une pure et claire connaissance de Dieu" (IC 1/5/14; 31).

[27] Lestringant claims that Calvin's "metonymical" construction of the Eucharist is responsible for what he characterizes as a "processus de dissociation sémantique . . . [un] processus d'abstraction" in the Eucharist for Léry (*Sainte horreur* 106). Lestringant refers to an article by Bernard Cottret, who simply ignores the role played by "similitude" in Calvin's Eucharistic theology; see "Pour une sémiotique de la Réforme." Miri Rubin puts forth a similar reading of Calvin when she writes that "with Zwingli and Calvin the mass evolved into a symbolic re-enactment – no more was it properly tangible, usable" (352). In my view, the most accurate recent discussion of the semiotics that underlie Calvin's Eucharistic theology is Christopher Elwood's succinct account in Chapter Three of *The Body Broken* (see especially pages 72-74). See also Brian Gerrish, *Grace and Gratitude*. For a sense of the evolution of Calvin's doctrine of the Eucharist, see Thomas J. Davis, *The Clearest Promises of God*.

tance between the faithful and God, but rather to *span* it, and this not by positing some sort of resemblance between heaven and earth, but by *putting into communication* two realms that remain not only distinct, but also thoroughly dissimilar. What those who doubt the real presence in the Calvinist Eucharist fail to understand, then, is the *mode* in which the Calvinist God communicates – and thus communes – with Man. In Book 1, chapter 6 of the *Institutes*, Calvin claims that "God bestows the actual knowledge of himself upon us only in the Scriptures." In the following chapter, he explains how God's word gains its proper authority among men: "For as God alone can properly bear witness to his own words, so these words [Scripture] will not obtain full credit in the hearts of men, until they are sealed by the inward testimony of the Spirit." In other words, Calvin's God accommodates the limitations of fallen Man by means of a witness.

Despite its centrality to Calvin's theology, the nature of the mediation of the Holy Spirit has been consistently misread with regard to Calvin's doctrine of the Eucharist. The polemics surrounding Calvin's position on the question of "real presence" in the Eucharist are plentiful and well known: while his Catholic and Lutheran critics charged that his theory of sacramental signification effectively denied Christ's bodily presence in the Supper, Calvin himself maintained that Christ, in both his corporeal and spiritual dimensions, was indeed present to the faithful in the Eucharist.[28] As Elwood notes, "The habit of opposing the spiritual to the real was a central feature of almost all Catholic polemics against the Reformed doctrine of the Supper" (124). But for Calvin (as later for Bèze), the notion of a "spiritual" presence in the Eucharist means the *real* presence, to the believer, of Christ in both his corporal and divine

---

[28] Because his position on the Eucharist was so frequently assailed, Calvin published a good deal of material on the matter. See, besides Book Four of the *Institutes*, his *Petit traicté de la saincte Cene* (Geneva, 1540); the *Brieve resolution sur les disputes qui ont esté de nostre temps quant aux Sacrements* (Geneva, 1555; Latin original Zürich, 1555); and his response to the attacks of Tileman Heshusius, the *Dilucuda explicatio sanae doctrinae de vera participatione carnis et sanguinis in sacra coena* (Geneva, 1561). The only place where Calvin denies a substantial presence of Christ in the Eucharist is in the first edition of the *Institutes* (1539), in a passage that receives (dare I say it) substantial revisions for subsequent editions. See Elwood chapters 2-3 for an economical and to my mind accurate recent synthesis of this material.

natures *through the agency of the Holy Spirit*.[29] In the sacrament of the Lord's Supper, according to Calvin, "the Spirit is the primary witness who gives us a full assurance of this testimony [of the Eucharist]."[30] What ultimately makes Calvin's "spiritual" Eucharist capable of representing the divine is the presence of a transparent witness who testifies God efficaciously to Man.

The Holy Spirit in Calvin's theology is the paradigmatic symbol of efficacious – yet (or, from the protestant point of view, *because*) transparent – testimony of one world to another, radically different world. Calvin thus explains the nature of the (necessary) mediation between the believer and God in terms that speak directly to the discursive needs of the eyewitness ethnographer who attempts to represent one culture to another. As we shall see, Léry's appropriation of Calvin's "spiritual" mode of testimony constitutes a crucial contribution to the modern discourse of eyewitness testimony.

Just as "resemblance" cannot be said to characterize the relationship between the earthly and heavenly realms in Calvin's theology, neither does the term apply to Léry's view of the relationship between the New World and the Old. As I suggested above, Léry's Calvinism can be linked to his practice of evaluating European and Tupi customs side by side in a manner that grants a fundamental equality between European and American culture ("one custom is as good as the other"). But this equality never collapses into some version of identity; one could hardly consider Léry's account of Brazil and the Brazilians an attempt to demonstrate that, on a cultural level, "they're just like us" – or just like we used to be, or just like we wished we were. Though he does point out the occasional similarity, Léry's moral analogy between Tupi and European customs never translates into a catalogue of resemblances, potential or actual, between the two cultures.

In fact, the notion of *dissimilarity* dominates Léry's portrait of the Tupinamba. This is immediately evident in the preface to the *Histoire*, where Léry suggests that the whole concept of a "New World" springs from a perception on the part of the Europeans that nothing in America resembles anything they know: "Tout ce

---

[29] Besides Elwood, cf. Raitt 36, 39, 45; Davis 99-100; Gerrish 175.

[30] Beveridge 597. "Le Saint-Esprit, qui est le principal témoin, nous prouve avec certitude ce témoignage, nous le fait croire, entendre et reconnaître; car autrement nous ne le pourrions comprendre" (*IC* 4/14/22; 288).

qui s'y voit, soit en la façon de vivre des habitans, forme des animaux et en general en ce que la terre produit, estant dissemblable de ce que nous avons en Europe, Asie et Afrique, [l'Amérique] peut bien estre appelé monde nouveau, à nostre esgard" (95; "everything to be seen [there] – the way of life of its inhabitants, the form of the animals, what the earth produces – is so unlike ["dissemblable"] what we have in Europe, Asia and Africa that it may very well be called a 'New World' with respect to us"; lv-lvi). Here, Léry even relativizes novelty: as the term "dissemblable" suggests, the "new" aspect of the New World is not a quality inherent to America and its inhabitants for Léry, but is instead an effect of the relationship between Brazilians and the Old World. As this emphasis on difference suggests, Léry's ethnography resists assimilating the Tupi to previously-known cultures. As a result, Léry never finds a settled "place" for the Tupi in the European imaginary. They represent neither an accepted anthropological thesis nor its antithesis; they are above all simply "dissemblables." In Léry's *Histoire*, then, the ontological contrast between the human and the divine that underlies Calvin's theology is translated onto a cultural level.

As Léry himself notes, the dissimilarity between Europeans and Americans makes it difficult for him to describe the Tupi in terms intelligible to his European audience: "A cause de leur gestes et contenances du tout dissemblables des nostres, je confesse qu'il est mal-aisé de les bien representer, ni par escrit, ni mesme par peinture . . . il les faut voir et visiter en leur pays" (234; "their gestures and expressions are so completely different ["dissemblables"] from ours, that it is difficult, I confess, to represent them well by writing or by pictures"; 67). The difficulty in representing the Tupi results not from a sense that language and painting are inherently estranged from reality, but from a sense that "they" are intractably different from "us." After he deems the mimetic capacities of language and painting inadequate to the task of representing the Tupinamba to the French, Léry concludes, "it is necessary to go and see them in their country" – just what Léry himself claims to have done. While the tenacious "dissemblance" of the Tupi signals a disjunction between the New World and the Old, then, at the same time, it creates a space in which the European eyewitness, as the one who *has* seen and visited America, acquires his unique authority. Léry's way of establishing this authority, however, will not be simply another version of reliquary "proximity" under another name.[31]

Like the signs of the divine in Calvin's theology, Léry's ethnography acquires its authority not through the implicit claim that signs can make their referents present, but through the presence of a witness who remains invisible. Rather than argue for a relationship of resemblance between his experience in Brazil and his verbal report of it, Léry emphasizes his very status as a witness – a witness whose ghostly agency grounds communication between the Old World and the New. Léry's distinctive rhetoric of transparency can best be observed in the way the notion of "experience" functions in his history. Léry doesn't really participate in the polemic against traditional cosmography (certainly not a moribund one even as late as 1580, as Montaigne's ostentatious rejection of "cosmographes" in favor of eyewitnesses in his essay "Des cannibales" indicates). More importantly, though, the explicit appeal to corporeal sense experience, so prominent in the work of his eyewitness contemporaries, rarely functions as a source of authority in Léry's account. There are a number of key passages in which Léry positions his testimony as especially authoritative in a manner that elides physical experience altogether.

As the prologue to the *Histoire* makes explicit, Léry offers his testimony first and foremost as a corrective to another eyewitness account of Brazil, that of André Thevet in his *Cosmographie universelle*. Rather than recount his own adventures and juxtapose

---

[31] In his classic analysis of the *Histoire d'un voyage* in *The Writing of History*, Michel de Certeau also made the dissimilarity between Europe and America the founding principle of Léry's ethnography: "The narrative plays on the relation between the structure which establishes the separation and the operation which overcomes it, creating effects of meaning in this fashion. The break is what is taken for granted everywhere by the text itself, itself a labor of suturing" (218). Certeau analyzes Léry's testimony from the point of view of a "hermeneutics of the Other," suggesting that "the break between over here and over there [that is, between Brazil and Europe, Brazilians and Europeans] is transformed into a rift between nature [which for Certeau includes esthetics and religiosity – the "estheticized Other" – and the aural] and culture [labor, science, ethics, and the visual]" (220). In a deconstructive reading of the *Histoire* that explicitly rejects Certeau's thesis, Irma Majer uses the Brazilian parrots Léry tried but failed to bring back to France as an emblem for the *Histoire* itself, casting Léry as yet another unwitting victim of the inexorable complexities of *itérabilité*: "Le perroquet est l'emblème du traducteur, mais aussi l'incarnation de son échec. L'imitation offerte par le perroquet est l'antithèse de la traduction. C'est un langage à sens unique qu'il est impossible de transférer" ("La fin des voyages" 81).

them to Thevet's claims, Léry uses two other strategies in his prologue, neither of which positions the Huguenot's Brazilian experience as an authoritative reference point. First, he points out a series of internal consistencies in Thevet's account ("I have shown by his own testimony . . ."; "[confronting] him with arguments so firm, citing his own writings as evidence, that you will not have to go as far as America to judge their worth"); and second, he anticipates refutations he will make in the body of his text ("as I will show in this history"; "I will cite it against him in the sixth chapter of this history"; "as will be seen as this story unfolds"; "What is true, as you will see in due time . . ."; "it will not be found that . . ."; "as I shall show elsewhere"). One might reasonably expect the latter use of prolepsis in a prologue, but a curious thing happens when we reach the passage in the *Histoire* (it turns out to be just one) in which Léry supposedly "proves" Thevet's unfitness as a witness: we are sent straight back to the prologue. We have already seen this passage, since it is the place where Léry dramatically cuts off the dialogue between himself and Thevet: "[je prie] derechef les lecteurs de noter icy en passant, que comme je n'ay fait, ny ne feray aucune mention de luy [Thevet] en tout le discours present, touchant les disputes que Villegagnon et Cointa eurent contre nous au fort de Colligny en la terre du Bresil, qu'aussi n'y a-il jamais veu les ministres dont il parle, ny eux semblablement luy . . . comme j'ay prouvé en la preface de ce livre . . . ce bon Catholique Thevet n'y [estoit] pas de nostre temps" (186). "I beg the reader to note here in passing that, since I have not made, nor will I make any mention of [Thevet] in connection with the disputes that Villegagnon and Cointa had with us at Fort Colligny in the land of Brazil, so did he never see the ministers of whom he speaks, nor they, him . . . as I have proved in the preface of this book . . . this good Catholic Thevet was not there in our time" (45). Instead of casting Thevet's absence as an *experience* ("I didn't see Thevet in Brazil"), Léry's demonstration of the unreliability of Thevet's testimony consists simply in signalling the fact that Thevet is never mentioned in Léry's own account ("since I have not made, nor will I make any mention of [Thevet]"), and in referring back to his prefatory anticipation of his refutation of Thevet's claims ("as I have proved in the preface"). The experience that one might expect Léry to put forth as the "primary witness who gives us a full assurance of [his] testimony" is here displaced by the discourse of the testimony itself, which has taken over for Brazil as the "place" one will search in vain for Thevet.

Léry repeatedly calls upon his own testimony, and not his experience, to demonstrate the authority of his account. Since the validity of my claim ultimately depends on the fact that these displacements are not just occasional occurrences in the *Histoire*, but rather its characteristic mode of "representing" Brazil, I supply some statistics here. In chapter nine (entitled "Des grosses racines et gros mil dont les sauvages font farine qu'ils mangent au lieu de pain; et de leur breuvage qu'ils nomment caou-in"), "je vis" or some variant (such as "je vis par experience"), which clearly refers to Léry as the subject of vision, occurs only eight times, and one of these is in fact a reference to Europe; by contrast, "je dis" and other references to speaking, telling, or writing conjugated in the first person singular (such as "comme j'ai touché ailleurs"; "comme vous avez entendu au chapitre précédent") appear twenty-seven times. Such expressions occur most frequently in the very chapters (9-19) that deal most extensively with the Tupinamba, and that thus may be considered specifically ethnographic.

Perhaps the best way to evaluate the claim that physical experience does not act as the primary guarantor of Léry's testimony is to test it against a story that nearly frames the narrative of the *Histoire d'un voyage*, and that has been read as an example of the kind of "authorization-via-bodily-risk" strategy we saw described in Cartier's account. Lestringant argues for the importance of this episode in the construction of Léry's identity as a specifically protestant witness, and convincingly shows that Léry exaggerates his central role here, borrowing material from the protestant martyrologist Jean Crespin in order to establish his privileged position as a witness (*Le Huguenot et le sauvage* 61-66). In this story, Léry relates the fate of three Protestants who were killed at the hands of Villegagnon, the lapsed-Protestant leader of the colony at Guanabara. Léry gives himself a prominent place in this episode by suggesting that he would have been among the dead had he not impulsively chosen to leave one boat and get on another at a crucial moment. The dramatic claim to near-martyrdom and miraculous escape could thus be seen to attest to the physical risks of having been in Brazil, and consequently as the authoritative ground for Léry's testimony. But this story is not quite the transcendental reference point it may first appear to be, since, as we shall see, the experience it evokes never actually "takes place" in the narrative.

Léry mentions the martyrs in three places in the *Histoire*. Their fate, and Léry's divine deliverance, is first anticipated in the prologue: "Vray est, *ainsi qu'il sera aussi veu en son lieu*, que de cinq de nostre troupe qui . . . s'en retournerent dans une barque a la terre des sauvages. [Villegagnon] en fit voirement, cruellement et inhumainement precipiter trois en mer" (75-6; my emphasis; "What is true, *as it will be seen in its place*, is that five men of our band . . . returned in a boat to the land of the savages. [Villegagnon] did, indeed, cruelly and inhumanely, have three of these five thrown out to sea"; liii). Léry reminds us of what's to come as his departure from Brazil approaches: "Quittant une partie de mes besognes, que je lassay dans la barque, remontant en grande haste au navire, *je fus par ce moyen preservé du danger que vous orrez ci-apres* . . . cinq autres . . . s'en retournerent en la terre du Bresil: en laquelle *(comme je diray à la fin de ceste histoire)* . . . [Villegagnon] fit mourir les trois premiers" (511; my emphases; "leaving some of my belongings behind me in a boat, and hastily climbing back into the ship, I was thus preserved from *the danger that you will hear about here later* . . . five others . . . returned to Brazil, where, *as I shall recount at the end of this history* . . . [Villegagnon] had the first three put to death"; 200). Near the end of the *Histoire*, as promised, the "five others" reappear:

> Ne reste plus pour mettre fin à la presente histoire, sinon sçavoir que devindrent les cinq de nostre compagnie: lesquels, *comme il a esté dit ci-dessus*, apres le premier naufrage que nous cuidasmes faire, s'en retournerent en la terre de Bresil: et voici par quel moyen il a esté sceu. Certains personnages dignes de foy . . . avoyent esté spectateurs quand Villegagnon à cause de l'Evangile en fit noyer trois . . . mais aussi outre cela, ayans apporté par escrit tant leur confession de foy que toute la procédure que Villegagnon tint contre eux . . . [et] je la recouvray aussi bien tost apres. Tellement qu'ayant veu par là . . . [comment] ces fideles serviteurs de Jesus-Christ enduroyent les tourmens, voire la mort cruelle que Villegagnon leur fit souffrir, en me ressouvenant que moy seul de nostre compagnie (*ainsi qu'il a esté veu en son lieu*) estois ressorti de la barque, dans laquelle je fus tout pres de m'en retourner avec eux (548)

> To bring this present history to a close, nothing remains to be told except what became of the five men of our company; those

who, *as it was stated above*, after our first near-shipwreck, returned to Brazil; and here is how it came to be known. Certain trustworthy persons . . . had been spectators when Villegagnon had three of the five drowned . . . because of their adherence to the Gospel. . . . Moreover, these same persons brought back the written confession of those three, as well as the whole indictment that Villegagnon brought against them . . . [and] I obtained it soon after. Thus I saw how . . . these faithful servants of Jesus Christ were enduring the torments, indeed the cruel death that Villegagnon made them suffer; and I remembered that I alone of our company, *(as has been seen in its place)* got out of that boat, in which I was all ready to return with the others (218)

As we might expect from a Huguenot witness, the bodies of the three martyrs are never described here, with the rhetoric of the "corps-martyr"; rather, Léry assures us that he has seen their written confessions of faith. This, rather than a claim to having been there at the moment of their death, is what allows him to bear witness to their martyrdom. What is more striking, however, is the fact that this account of martyrdom and witnessing isn't really "in" Léry's *Histoire* either, but is instead, as the passages I have italicized indicate, repeatedly *cited* there. Its place seems constantly to shift, since Léry's account of it propels us forward, then sends us back, then directs us to the end of the *Histoire*, then back to some enigmatic *lieu* we can never quite pinpoint. None of the passages about the protestant martyrs anchors itself in Léry's extra-textual experience; none functions as the "original" episode that the others cite. Rather than attempt to represent his experience mimetically, Léry makes it the ineffable center of a network of references within his text. In other words, Léry's discourse itself displaces his body as the mediating link between the signifiers that make up the *Histoire* and their Brazilian referents. No body is needed to link "the danger that you will hear about here later" with "[what] was stated above."

Léry will make the act of cross-referencing and collating depositions – a habit that began with the increased use of writing in juridical proceedings and that ultimately destroyed the credibility of the ethical witness – work to his advantage by creating a complex network of references within his book that mutually reinforce one another. The book compresses the several moments of the written composition of witness testimony – those moments that, for Philibert Boyer, inevitably produce discrepancies that would prove a witness's *perfidie* – into a single textual deposition whose component parts are in self-consciously corroborative dialogue with one another. We have already seen this "monologic dialogue" at work in Léry's prologue: as a result of the roundabout history of its composition – a history Léry takes the trouble to relate at great length – every passage of the *Histoire* explicitly becomes a self-citation. These self-citations create a discourse in which the business of mediating between sign and referent is an enterprise performed by Léry's language itself: By citing his own discourse, Léry positions it as a ghostly witness to the experiences described therein, the incorporeal guarantor of a testimony which thus seems magically to mediate itself.

This dynamic of self-citation has two important effects. One is that of corroboration. Like Thevet's citations of sources ancient and modern in his cosmographical accounts, Léry's citations of his own text function as authoritative witnesses to the fiability of his report. Léry's method has the advantage of maintaining his position as privileged mediator between the Old World and the New: unique and singular, his testimony can be related only to itself. A corollary to this is the fact that, because Léry does not embed his observations of the Tupi in material from other texts specific to his own culture, the *Histoire* is not only capable of standing alone, but also of circulating well beyond the historical nexus in which Thevet's heavily annotated cosmographies are hopelessly entangled.

The second effect of Léry's tendency to cite his account rather than to describe his experiences is that his testimony thereby acquires a certain atemporal quality. The spatio-temporal limitations of the physical experience that authorizes eyewitness testimonies like those attributed to Cartier naturally circumscribe the referent of such testimony. By contrast, Léry's appeal to his own discourse locates both the authority and the referent of his testimony in the eternal present of his text, thereby allowing his ethnography to transcend the limitations of his particular experience. In other words, one consequence of Léry's appeal via self-citation to his own testimony is that the authority of Léry's testimony is not circumscribed by the experiential source of his information; it is limited only by what Léry can point to in the *Histoire* itself. Whereas the typical eyewitness account of the New World directs the reader's attention to physical experiences outside of the text, in the realm of the witness's physical body, Léry's self-citations continually send the reader back and forth *inside* of his account (conceived of as the *Histoire* together with its manuscript antecedents). Léry's turn away from physical experience and towards his own ethnographic testimony about that experience as a source of ethnographic authority allows his portrait of the Tupinamba to transcend the historical moment of his encounter with them and rise to the level of generality that is missing from travel accounts like Cartier's, but that is fundamental to the scientific pretensions of subsequent European ethnography and to the knowledge claims of the modern eyewitness.

Despite the illusion of transparency his account creates, what Léry's act of testimonial communication ultimately demonstrates is what medieval folklaw had taken as its basis; namely, that there can be no testimony without a witness – or more precisely, without *witnesses* in the plural. Even God requires a witness in order that his presence may be attested. The semiotics of Calvin's Eucharist, unlike those of the Catholics (or of Luther), do not confound signs with bodies, or posit a stable link between them. For Calvin, as for Léry, the link between signs and their referents – between language and the real – must be continually reattested through the mechanism of testimony. Léry himself thus turns to the very language of his book as his own witness (as his "second," so to speak). He also turns, ultimately, to the reader.

As Léry himself suggests, he has not found a way to "represent" the Tupi in words and pictures. Rather, he has found a way to make his eyewitness account of them credible to his European readers. Léry sensed that the credibility of his account depended in some important way on the role his addressees would play in the construction of his testimony. Thus, he sets them to cross-checking and cross-referencing in such a way as to make the credibility of his account the *end product* of their act of reading, and not an attribute of his testimony that precedes that act of reception. Here again, we can see Calvin's Eucharistic theology at work. As Calvin's opponents in the Eucharistic controversy understood, Calvin's theology reconceived the notion of "presence" as it had been consolidated at the Fourth Lateran Council in 1215 when transubstantiation was officially adopted as Catholic doctrine. Calvin, for his part, is unwavering in his position that the faithful truly receive Christ's body in the Eucharist; but he put an important condition on that presence: "Mais je nie que [la chair du Christ] se puisse manger sans quelque goût de foi" (*IC* 4/17/33, 385-6; "but I deny that it can be eaten without the taste of faith"). Christ is indeed present in the testimony of the Calvinist Eucharist, but the efficacy of Calvinist testimonial representation requires faith on the part of those who receive that testimony.

Calvin's version of Christ's presence suggests that a leap of faith on the part of the recipient (the reader, the addressee) is in the end necessary if the mechanism of representation is to function successfully. Though God's presence in Calvin's Eucharist is certainly meant to be taken as real, it is not posited as objective in the positivist sense, for it depends upon the faith of the recipient. Thus, while the Eucharist is a form of testimonial communication for Calvin, we must not assume the simple model of communication that posits a sender, a message and a receiver in that order of priority. What is communicated in the Calvinist Eucharist depends as much upon the orientation of the communicant as it does on the thing communicated. The Calvinist communicant is thus in the position of a dialogic addressee rather than that of a passive recipient who either comprehends or misreads a preconstituted message.

Léry himself ably sets out the Calvinist position on the Eucharist in the course of his chapter on the theological disputes between the Huguenots and Villegagnon: "Le pain et le vin n'estoyent point reellement changez au corps et au sang du Seigneur, lequel n'estoit pas enclos dans iceux, ains que Jesus Christ est au ciel, d'où, par la vertu de son sainct Esprit, il se communique en nourriture spirituelle à ceux qui reçoivent les signes en foy" (175; "the bread and wine were not really changed into the Body and Blood of the Lord, which also was not contained within them; rather Jesus Christ is in heaven, whence, by virtue of his Holy Spirit, he communicates himself in spiritual nourishment to those who receive the signs in faith"; 40-41). For Calvin and Léry, all testimony, even Eucharistic testimony, requires a "faithful" interlocutor in order to become meaningful. The presence of a witness thus always implies the presence of another witness, even if that witness is a (holy) ghost. Set into the context of the legal models, technological constraints, and theological debates that shaped it, Jean de Léry's *Histoire* suggests that modern testimony is indeed haunted – by none other than the specter of the witness.

Epilogue

A RETURN TO DIALOGUE

CALVIN'S version of Eucharistic presence makes the good faith of the communicant a necessary prerequisite to communication. By contrast, the very concept of a faithful addressee is superfluous in the context of the doctrine of transubstantiation. The ontology of the transubstantiated Eucharist precedes its communication; therefore, neither what it means nor what it is (a non-distinction in this case) depends upon who or what receives it. Based on one of the most fundamental paradigms of communication in the Christian West – that of communion between the human and the divine – the Catholic Eucharist thus erects a model of communication as monologic, according to which meaning emanates from a unified source and is subsequently transmitted to a passive recipient. This is of course the very model of signs that will be elaborated in the *Logique* of Port Royal, which explicitly posits what Louis Marin called "a perfect adequation" between the logic of transubstantiation and an all-encompassing semiotic theory.[1]

As Marin has shown, the ideology of transubstantiation continues to inform contemporary semiology, particularly insofar as it posits an "acte de parole qui donne à un déictique ["ceci" or "hoc"], par une affirmation ontologique ["est"], un prédicat qui n'est autre que l'être même du sujet de l'énonciation ["mon corps" or "corpus meum"]" (*Critique* 33; "a speech act that, by an ontologic affirmation, bestows upon a deictic a predicate that is none

---

[1] See his *Critique du discours* and *La Parole mangée*; the citation is from Mette Hjort's English translation of the latter, entitled *Food for Thought*, 25.

other than the very being of the speaking subject"). With the advent of structuralism and poststructuralism, however, this model of representation – of presence in language – has come to command considerably less belief than it once did. As we saw in chapter one, this model makes of the second-person witness a first-person judge, an autonomous subject whose testimony is equated with philosophical judgments about the world. In Holocaust studies in particular, the figure of the witness-as-judge has been found to be inadequate.

In chapter one, I passed over in silence the fact that Derrida's discussion of witnessing takes a specific historical event – the genocide of the Jews under Hitler – as the quintessential object of testimony. The epistemic model of the witness has always been especially problematic in this context, and as the number of survivors dwindles, it will eventually cease to function altogether. It is perhaps for this reason that recent work on (and of) Holocaust testimony has begun to abandon the epistemic model and to articulate modes of witnessing that restore to prominence the ethically-based testimony characteristic of medieval folklaw (and dismissively termed "irrational" in most histories of legal procedure). By initiating an exploration of the possibilities for a discourse of testimony that is not predicated on knowledge, such interventions revive pre- and early modern perspectives on witnessing.

In *Testimony: Crises of Witnessing in Literature, Psychoanalysis and History*, Shoshana Felman examines the silence of witnesses to the historical catastrophe of the Holocaust. Rather than characterize this silence as the absence of testimony, Felman suggests that we can in fact hear it in what she calls the "cryptic forms of modern narrative and modern art" (201) and that has "the power of a call" to which the reader (as "Other") must respond (203) by bearing witness in turn to "the impossibility of bearing witness to the Holocaust." Citing Jean-François Lyotard, Felman writes that the witness to Auschwitz must learn to "lend his ear to what is not presentable under the rules of knowledge" (202).

By contrast, Lyotard's own version of the differend does not call out to the reader or listener, demanding an ethical response; rather, it leaves him or her open-mouthed yet speechless, unable to phrase his experience. Speechlessness here thus stands for a more generalized ethical muteness, an inability to respond to one's fellow man. The rhetoric of unspeakability has in fact been criticized for what amounts to a silencing of the silences Felman explicitly characterizes in terms of a "call," and for choosing a distancing aesthetics over an engaging ethics, as if the aesthetic could redeem the immoral (see Mandel). Moreover, Lyotard's critique of totalizing understanding sweeps away the possibility of partial, fragmentary, provisional understanding in its wake. As Allen Dunn points out, even if the language of traditional systems of adjudication "will probably not provide a complete account of the wrongs to be redressed . . . what it includes may be at least as important as what it leaves out" (205). Similarly, though Felman's discussion is full of apparently paradoxical statements about bearing witness to the impossibility of bearing witness, it becomes clear that the impossibility she means to evoke here, like the impossibility that is ultimately the horizon of Lyotard's differend, is the impossibility of knowledge construed as *synthesis*. In Claude Lanzmann's film *Shoah*, observes Felman, "the gathering of testimonial incommensurates does not amount to either a generalizable theoretical statement or to a narrative monologic sum" (223). In other words, it is not *scientia*. In Lanzmann's film and in Felman's analysis, testimony and *scientia* are distinguished, as they were for the medieval glossaters.

In *Remnants of Auschwitz*, Giorgio Agamben proposes that we might profitably seek a middle ground between a pretension to "explain everything" (the equivalent, I would suggest, of *scientia*) and the "mystifying" pole of the "unspeakable" (32). In a passage that echoes Felman's discussion of impossible testimony, Agamben writes that

> testimony is the disjunction between two impossibilities of bearing witness; it means that language, in order to bear witness, must give way to a non-language in order to show the impossibility of bearing witness. The language of testimony is a language that no longer signifies and that, in not signifying, advances into that which is without language, to the point of taking on a different insignificance – that of the complete witness, that of he who by definition cannot bear witness. To bear witness, it is therefore not enough to bring language to its own non-sense. It is necessary that this senseless sound be, in turn, the voice of something or someone that, for entirely other reasons cannot bear witness (39).

Agamben goes beyond Felman here to evoke not simply a fragmentary lack of synthesis within testimony, but an absolute alterity, akin to the figure of the Other in the work of Emmanuel Lévinas. Agamben describes testimony in terms that recall Lévinas's Saying – as a language that cannot be understood in terms of signification (the Said).

For Lévinas, as for Agamben, the testimonial aspect of existence is deeply bound up with the figure of the Other. Thomas Trezise notes in a recent essay, "If, as Lévinas contends, we discover our responsibility when, as second persons, we are interpellated by an other not like us, and only become first persons in responding to that interpellation, then responsibility is not entailed by agency but rather produces it" (61). It is in Lévinas's work that one can perceive the most persistent echoes of the ethics of medieval folklaw, particularly with respect to the witness. As we have seen, the folklaw witness only comes into existence via the call of an other (not as a result of having some privileged experience), and only in order to risk his life for that other (to second his or her oath or to fight a duel). In order to function as a witness – and thus, as a member of an ethical community – the folklaw witness must understand that he owes his very existence to others. This debt extends both backwards and forwards: the other who calls upon the witness to testify on his behalf is both the origin and the end of the witness and his testimony, which are thus in effect one and the same.

What Lévinas calls "the one-for-the-other of subjectivity" (102) takes root in the social realm (though it cannot be reduced to a specific set of social relations). Moreover, as Philippe Nemo paraphrases it in a conversation with Lévinas, "there is an infinity in this ethical demand" (101) that this one-for-the-other entails. The debt to the Other is never paid in full, but persists as an infinite obligation. The (infinite) ethical responsibility that Lévinas describes is not so far from the kinds of ethical relations we see through the lens of pre-modern folklaw. Of course, there can really be no specific "examples" of the Lévinasian ethical relation, since Lévinas strove precisely to divorce the concept of the ethical from any particular content by making it prior to any given ethical system (or to any system at all). Yet Lévinas's effort to transcend thematization, it seems to me, brings us even closer to the pre-modern juridical context in which, as I have emphasized here, testimony is not a proposition but an *act*. Folklaw testimony does not provide knowledge or understanding of an event; rather, it enacts an ethical relation of solidarity with a person. That solidarity is not, moreover, the "theme" of folklaw testimony, but rather the very stuff of which the testimony is made. Though he obviously has no interest in recuperating a specific historical practice, Lévinas's philosophy proposes a kind of testimony that resonates with the past.

In the work of Felman, Agamben and especially Lévinas, testimony becomes an act that is not predicated on the knowledge of facts. It is an engagement of the self that presupposes neither the self nor self knowledge, much less comprehensive knowledge of any particular event. For his part, Agamben even suggests that the relationship between being and language is inherently testimonial, and that the subject as such is in the position of a witness: "[the] impossibility of conjoining the living being with language – far from authorizing the infinite deferral of signification – is what allows for testimony" (130). He concludes that "to be a subject and to bear witness are in the final analysis one and the same" (158). Such formulations bring us back to the pre-modern context in which testimony was conceived first and foremost as an act, devoid of any representational content, and in which the witness *qua* witness only came into being in the act of testifying, as a second-person subject.

In the wake of such reflections, recent critical work in Holocaust studies, following the lead of Holocaust survivors like Primo Levi and Jorge Semprún, has begun to emphasize the importance of the *audience* for testimony. As Thomas Trezise notes, citing Jorge Semprún, "the listener or reader is essential to the survivor's speech, and this because speech and the representational or interpretive and normative frameworks it implicitly articulates are all essentially social or intersubjective" (59n40). Tresize himself observes: "To say "I" was, no doubt, to risk "misrepresenting" the depersonalization and silencing of those who did not survive. But it was also to respond to them, to break the silence imposed on their silencing and in so doing to reaffirm the very relation on which the destructive force of Nazism was concentrated. And in this, again, it is not only a question of what can or cannot be said, of what should or should not be said, of how it can or cannot, may or may not be said – but of the saying itself" (52). What counts here, then, is not the mimetic virtuosity of the language or the claim of the speaker to absolute knowledge, but rather the ethical relation of trying to speak.

Taking this model to its logical extreme, Michael Donal-Williams has used a dialogic conception of testimony to address the question of "fiction" with which we began in chapter one. In 1995, Binjamin Wilkomirski published *Fragments*, which purported to be the memoirs of a Holocaust survivor. The name turned out to be a pseudonym, and subsequent research demonstrated that "the events depicted in *Fragments* and the events of the author's life as found in the historical record do not coincide" ("Beyond" 1303). Donal-Williams maintains, however, that although it is a "false testimony," *Fragments* "can still produce an effect on readers that induces them to witness" (1303). Ultimately, he concludes, "testimony's status as evidence depends in part on its effect" (1311) – a conclusion that foregrounds the ways in which testimony may be understood as the product of a dialogue between a witness and his or her addressees, who in turn become witnesses themselves.

Donal-Williams's discussion of *Fragments* brings to the fore the central questions posed by the reemergence of the dialogic model of witnessing, and that Lévinas's reflections leave entirely open (as shall mine): If testimony is a dialogue, who are its participants? Now that we have questioned the priority of the witness, what are we to make of his or her addressees? What kinds of rules govern the dialogic exchange between witness and audience? How are ethical relationships, much less ethical communities, defined and formed in places where human beings spend large amounts of time alone, regularly travel great distances and communicate electronically? Can a single person belong to several ethical communities? Are all ethical communities – and thus all testimonial dialogues – morally equivalent? How, in the end, are we to evaluate the "effects" of the testimony described by Donal-Williams?

At the same time that there is a growing belief in the importance of dialogue, there is also an increasingly powerful sense of the existence of multiple and conflicting dialogues, and of multiple ethical communities. It was in part due to the writings studied in this book – firsthand accounts of America – that Europeans were forced to confront the existence of a multiplicity of ethical communities. The old distinction between "Christian" and "pagan" was found to be inadequate in the context of the cultural complexities of the colonial experience. Thus, early modern eyewitness accounts both register the persistence of ethical modes of witnessing and record the circumstances of their decay. Though one can perceive the rediscovery of some pre-modern assumptions about testimony in contemporary debates, then, one must acknowledge the degree to which that sociopolitical conditions have changed since the days of feudalism. Nonetheless, recent attention to the role of social intercourse in the production of testimony is an index of potential philosophical affinities between pre- and postmodern worldviews. Both perspectives serve to relativize some of the most tenacious presuppositions of the modern era in the West: namely, that human beings are to be understood primarily as individuals; and that questions of knowledge, of being, and of morality are thus to be approached in terms of the relationship between the first-person subject and an objective world. This book's focus on the witness emerged in part out of a desire to move away from the subjective first person, and its complement, the objective third person, as the privileged objects of cultural analysis. Given that the figure of the autonomous judge has lost a considerable amount of its authority over the last half century, rather than taking this "objective subject" – or its deconstruction – as the point of departure for an analysis of testimony, we might consider taking the pre-modern witness as a powerful resource for thinking the post-modern subject. We will have to adapt the figure to our own needs and circumstances, of course, and reinvent the eyewitness anew.

BIBLIOGRAPHY

Acosta, José de. *Historia natural y moral de las Indias* (1590). Ed. José Alcina Franch. Madrid, 1986.
Adorno, Rolena. "History, law and the eyewitness. Protocols of authority in Bernal Díaz del Castillo's *Historia verdadera de la conquista de la Nueva España.*" *The Project of Prose in Early Modern Europe and the New World.* Eds. Elizabeth Fowler and Roland Greene. Cambridge and London: Cambridge UP, 1997. 154-175.
Agamben, Giorgio. *Remnants of Auschwitz: The Witness and the Archive.* Tr. Daniel Heller-Roazen. New York: Zone Books, 2000.
Allard, Albéric. *Histoire de la justice criminelle au XVIe siècle.* Aalen: Scientia Verlag, 1970.
Allen, Michael J.B., Robert Louis Benson, and Fredi Chiappelli, eds. *First Images of America: The Impact of the New World on the Old.* Berkeley: U of California P, 1976.
Anderson, Benedict. *Imagined Communities: Reflections on the Origin and Spread of Nationalism.* London; New York: Verso, 1991.
Atkinson, Geoffroy. *La Littérature géographique française de la renaissance, répertoire bibliographique.* Paris: Picard, 1927.
——, *Les nouveaux horizons de la renaissance française.* Paris: E. Droz, 1935.
Aubert, Félix. *Histoire du parlement de Paris de l'origine à François 1er 1250-1515.* Paris: Picard, 1894.
Auerbach, Erich. *Mimesis.* Tr. Willard Trask. Princeton: Princeton UP, 1953.
Ayrault, Pierre. *De l'ordre et instruction judiciaire, dont les anciens Grecs et Romains ont usé en accusations publiques. Conféré à l'usage de nostre France.* Paris: Jacques du Puys, 1576.
Barthes, Roland. *Le Bruissement de la langue.* Paris: Seuil, 1984.
Beaumanoir, Philippe de Remi. *Coutumes de Beauvaisis.* Ed. Amédée Salmon. Paris: Picard, 1899.
Benedetto, Luigi Foscolo. *La Tradizione Manoscritta del "Milione" di Marco Polo.* Torino: Bottega d'Erasmo, 1962.
Benveniste, Emile. *Problèmes de linguistique générale.* Paris: Gallimard, 1997.
Benzoni, Girolamo. *Histoire nouvelle du nouveau monde.* Tr. Urbain Chauveton. Lyon: E. Vignon, 1579.
Biggar, Henry Percival. *A Collection of Documents Relating to Jacques Cartier and the Sieur De Roberval.* Ottawa: Public Archives of Canada, 1930.
Bloch, R. Howard. *Etymologies and Genealogies.* Chicago: U of Chicago P, 1983.

Bloch, R. Howard. *Medieval French Literature and Law.* Berkeley: U of California P, 1977.
Boiceau, Jean. *Traité de la preuve par témoins en matière civile.* Paris: Guillaume Cavalier, 1697.
Boyer, Philibert. *Le Stile de la cour de Parlement.* Paris, 1610.
Buffet, Henri-François. "L'Amirauté." *Guide des recherches dans les fonds judiciaires de l'ancien régime.* Ed. Michel Antoine et al. Paris: Imprimerie nationale, 1958. 257-282.
Cabeza de Vaca, Alvar Núñez. *Naufragios y comentarios.* Ed. Enrique de Vedia. México: Editorial Porrúa, 1988.
Calvin, Jean. *Ioannis Calvini Opera Quae Supersunt Omnia.* eds. G. Baum, A. Cunitz et al. Brunsvigae: C.A. Schwetschke, 1863.
―――, *Institution de la religion chrétienne.* Geneva: Labor et Fides, 1955.
―――, *Institutes of the Christian Religion.* Tr. Henry Beveridge. Grand Rapids: Eerdman's, 1997 (1845).
―――, *Institutes of the Christian Religion.* Tr. Ford Lewis Battles. Philadelphia: Westminster, 1960.
―――, *Catechisme.* Friends of the Rutgers U Libraries: New Brunswick, 1973.
―――, *Petit traicté de la saincte Cene.* Geneva, 1540.
―――, *Brieve resolution sur les disputes qui ont esté de nostre temps quant aux Sacrements.* Geneva, 1555.
―――, *Dilucuda explicatio sanae doctrinae de vera participatione carnis et sanguinis in sacra coena.* Geneva, 1561.
―――, *Tracts Containing Treatises on the Sacraments.* Tr. Henry Beveridge. Edinburgh: Calvin Translation Society, 1849.
Campbell, Mary B. *Wonder & Science: Imagining Worlds in Early Modern Europe.* Ithaca: Cornell UP, 1999.
―――, *The Witness and the Other World: Exotic European Travel Writing, 400-1600.* Ithaca: Cornell UP, 1988.
Cartier, Jacques. *Relation originale du voyage de Jacques Cartier.* Ed. H. Michelant and A. Ramé. Paris: Tross, 1867.
―――, *Voyage de Jacques Cartier au Canada en 1534.* Ed. H. Michelant and A. Ramé. Paris: Tross, 1865.
―――, *Bref et succinte narration de la navigation faite en 1535 et 1536 par le capitaine Jacques Cartier aux iles de Canada* (1545). Ed. M. d'Avezac. Paris: Tross, 1863.
―――, *Voyages de découverte au Canada entre les années 1534 et 1542, par Jacques Cartier etc.* Quebec: Literary and Historical Society of Quebec, 1843.
Cave, Terence. "Travelers and Others: Cultural Connections in the Works of Rabelais." *François Rabelais: Critical Assessments.* Ed. Jean-Claude Carron. Baltimore: Johns Hopkins UP, 1995. 39-56.
―――, *The Cornucopian Text.* Oxford: Clarendon, 1979.
Certeau, Michel de. *Heterologies: Discourse on the Other.* Tr. Brian Massumi. Minneapolis: U of Minnesota P, 1986.
―――, *L'Ecriture de l'histoire.* Paris: Gallimard, 1975. English tr. Tom Conley. New York: Columbia UP, 1988.
Chartier, Roger. *L'ordre des livres.* Paris: Alinea, 1992.
Chinard, Gilbert. *L'Exotisme américain dans la littérature française au XVIe siècle.* Geneva: Slatkine Reprints, 1970.
Chroniques gargantuines. Ed. Christiane Lauvergnat-Gagnière and Guy Demerson. Paris: Nizet, 1988.
[Cicero.] *Ad Herennium.* Tr. Harry Caplan. Cambridge, MA: Harvard UP [1954], 1989.

Cicero, Marcus Tullius. *Pro Caelio; De Provinciis Consularibus; Pro Balbo.* Tr. R. Gardner. Cambridge, MA: Harvard UP, 1958.
———, *De Partitione Oratoria.* Tr. H. Rackham. Cambridge, MA: Harvard UP, 1942.
———, *Orator.* Tr. H. M. Hubbell. Cambridge, MA: Harvard UP, 1997 [1939].
Clanchy, M.T. *From Memory to Written Record, England, 1066-1307.* London: Edward Arnold, 1979.
Clifford, James and George E. Marcus, eds. *Writing Culture: The Poetics and Politics of Ethnography.* Berkeley: U of California P, 1986.
Coady, C.A.J. *Testimony: A Philosophical Study.* Oxford: Clarendon, 1992.
Cochran, Terry. *Twilight of the Literary: Figures of Thought in the Age of Print.* Cambridge, MA: Harvard UP, 2001.
Columbus, Christopher. *The Four Voyages of Columbus.* (Bilingual edition.) Ed. and tr. Cecil Jane. London: Argonaut, 1930.
Cotgrave, Randle. *Dictionarie of the French and English Tongues* (1611). London: Islip, 1632.
Cottret, Bernard. "Pour une sémiotique de la Réforme." *Annales ESC* 2 (1984): 265-85.
Crespin, Jean. *Histoire des martyrs* (1619). Ed. Matthieu Lelièvre. Toulouse: Société des livres religieux, 1885.
Critchley, John. *Marco Polo's Book.* Aldershot: Variorum, 1992.
Damhoudere, Josse (Joost Damhouder). *Practique judiciaire ès causes criminelles.* Anvers: I. Bellère, 1564.
Danty, Jean. *Traité de la preuve par témoins en matière civile.* Paris: Guillaume Cavalier, 1697.
Davis, Thomas J. *The Clearest Promises of God.* New York: AMS Press, 1995.
Dear, Peter. *Revolutionizing the Sciences.* Princeton, NJ: Princeton UP, 2001.
Defaux, Gérard. "Un cannibale en haut de chausses : Montaigne, la différence et la logique de l'identité". *MLN* 97.4 (May 1982): 918-957.
Derrida, Jacques. *Demeure: Fiction and Testimony.* Tr. Elizabeth Rottenberg. Stanford: Stanford UP, 2000.
———, "'A Self-Unsealing Poetic Text': Poetics and Politics of Witnessing." Tr. Rachel Bowlby. In *Revenge of the Aesthetic*, ed. Michael P. Clark. Berkeley and Los Angeles: U of California P, 2000. 180-207.
———, *Politics of Friendship.* Tr. George Collins. London; New York: Verso, 1997.
———, "Signature Event Context." *Margins of Philosophy.* Tr. Alan Bass. Chicago: U of Chicago P, 1982. 307-330.
Descartes, René. *Meditationes de prima philosophia* [1641] in *Oeuvres et lettres.* Ed. André Bridoux. Paris: Gallimard, 1953.
Diehl, Huston. *Staging Reform, Reforming the Stage: Protestantism and Popular Theater in Early Modern England.* Ithaca: Cornell UP, 1997.
Donal-Williams, Michael. "Beyond the Question of Authenticity: Witness and Testimony in the *Fragments* Controversy." *PMLA* 166.5 (2001): 1302-1315.
Dufour, Alain. "Un avis de Calvin à ses disciples qui étaient chez les Topinambous." *BHR* 39 (1977): 151-52.
Dunn, Allen. "A Tyranny of Justice: The Ethics of Lyotard's Differend." *boundary 2* 20.1 (1993): 193-220.
Du Plessis-Mornay, Philippe. *Traité de l'eucharistie.* La Rochelle: H. Haultin, 1598.
Duval, Edwin. *The Design of Rabelais's Pantagruel.* New Haven and London: Yale UP, 1991.
———, "Rabelais and Textual Architecture" in *A New History of French Literature.* Eds. Denis Hollier and R. Howard Bloch. Cambridge, MA: Harvard UP, 1989. 154-159.

Eire, Carlos M.N. *War against the Idols: The Reformation of Worship from Erasmus to Calvin.* Cambridge and New York: Cambridge UP, 1986.
Eisenstein, Elizabeth L. *The Printing Revolution in Early Modern Europe.* Cambridge and New York: Cambridge UP, 1983.
Elliott, John Huxtable. *The Old World and the New 1492-1650.* Cambridge and New York: Cambridge UP, 1970.
Elwood, Christopher. *The Body Broken: The Calvinist Doctrine of the Eucharist and the Symbolization of Power in Sixteenth-Century France.* New York: Oxford UP, 1999.
Esmein, Aldhémar. *Histoire de la procédure criminelle en France.* Paris: Larose et Forcel, 1882. English trans. William Ephraim Mikell. South Hackensack, NJ: Rothman Reprints, 1968.
Estienne. Robert. *Dictionnaire Français-Latin.* Paris: R. Estienne, 1549.
Fabian, Johannes. *Time and the Other: How Anthropology Makes Its Object.* New York: Columbia UP, 1983.
Febvre, Lucien and Henri-Jean Martin. *The Coming of the Book: The Impact of Printing 1450-1800.* London: Verso, 1997.
Felman, Shoshana and Dori Lamb. *Testimony: Crises of Witnessing in Literature, Psychoanalysis and History.* New York and London: Routledge, 1992.
Foucault, Michel. "Qu'est-ce qu'un auteur?" *Bulletin de la Société française de philosophie* 44 (1969): 73-104
———, *Les mots et les choses.* Paris: Gallimard, 1966. English trans. *The Order of Things: An Archaeology of the Human Sciences.* New York: Vintage, 1994 (1970).
Frisch, Andrea. "In a Sacramental Mode: Jean de Léry's Calvinist Ethnography," *Representations* 77 (Winter 2002): 86-112.
———, "*Quod vidimus testamur*: Testimony, Narrative Agency and the World in Pantagruel's Mouth." *French Forum* 24 (September 1999): 261-283.
Fuller, Mary C. *Voyages in Print: English Travel to America, 1576-1624.* New York: Cambridge UP, 1995.
———, "Ralegh's Fugitive Gold" in Greenblatt, Stephen, ed. *New World Encounters.* Berkeley and Los Angeles: U of California P, 1992. 218-240.
Gaffarel, Paul. *Histoire du Brésil français au seizième siècle.* Paris: Maisonneuve, 1878.
Geertz, Clifford. *Works and Lives: The Anthropologist as Author.* Stanford: Stanford UP, 1988.
Gerrish, B.A. *Grace and Gratitude: The Eucharistic Theology of John Calvin.* Minneapolis: Fortress, 1993.
Ginzburg, Carlo. *The Cheese and the Worms.* Tr. John and Anne Tedeschi. New York: Penguin Books, 1982.
Glare, P.G.W. *Oxford Latin Dictionary.* New York: Oxford UP, 1982.
Gonneville, Paulmier de. *Relation authentique du voyage de Gonneville.* Ed. M. D'Avezac. Paris: Challamel, 1869.
Gorphe, François. *La critique du témoignage.* Paris: Dalloz, 1927.
Grafton, Anthony, April Shelford, and Nancy G. Siraisi. *New Worlds, Ancient Texts.* Cambridge, MA: Belknap, 1992.
Gray, Floyd. "Rabelais's First Readers." *Rabelais's Incomparable Book*, ed. Raymond LaCharité. Lexington, KY: French Forum, 1986. 15-29.
Green, Richard Firth. *A Crisis of Truth: Literature and Law in Ricardian England.* Philadelphia: U of Pennsylvania P, 1999.
Greenblatt, Stephen. *Marvelous Possessions: The Wonder of the New World.* Chicago: U of Chicago P, 1992.
Gregory, Brad S. *Salvation at Stake: Christian Martyrdom in Early Modern Europe.* Cambridge, MA: Harvard UP, 1999.

Guenois, Pierre, ed. *Practique judiciaire*. Paris: Nicolas Buon, 1609.
Guilhiermoz, Paul Emilien. "De la persistance du caractère orale dans la procédure civile française." *Revue historique de droit français et étranger* 3:13 (Jan-Feb 1889): 21-65.
———, *Enquêtes et procès*. Paris: Picard, 1892.
Habermas, Jürgen. *The Structural Transformation of the Public Sphere* (1962). Tr. Thomas Burger. Cambridge, MA: MIT Press, 1992.
Hacking, Ian. *The Emergence of Probability*. New York: Cambridge UP, 1975.
Hakluyt, Richard. *Divers voyages touching the discoverie of America*. London: Thomas Dawson, 1582.
Hall, Basil. *Humanists and Protestants, 1500-1900*. Edinburgh: T. & T. Clark, 1990.
Hampton, Timothy. *Literature and Nation in the Sixteenth Century: Inventing Renaissance France*. Ithaca: Cornell UP, 2001.
Hanke, Lewis. "Las Casas historiador." Pref. to Bartolomé de Las Casas, *Historia de las Indias*. México: Porrúa, 1951.
Hartog, François. *Le Miroir d'Hérodote*. Paris: Gallimard, 1991.
———, "Herodotus and the Historiographical Operation." *Diacritics* 22.2 (1992): 47-56.
Helmholz, R.H. "Crime, Punishment and the Courts of the Medieval Church." *Law and History Review* I (1983): 1-26.
Higgins, Iain Macleod. *Writing East: The "Travels" of Sir John Mandeville*. Philadelphia: U of Pennsylvania P, 1997.
Hoffman, George. *Montaigne's Career*. New York and London: Oxford UP, 1998.
Hollier, Denis, and R. Howard Bloch, eds. *A New History of French Literature*. Cambridge, MA: Harvard UP, 1989.
Imbert, Jean. *Institutes de praticque en matiere civile et criminelle*. Lyon: Benoist Rigaud, 1566.
———, *Practique judiciaire*. Paris: Enguilbert de Marnef, 1563. [French trans.; Latin orig. 1543.]
———, *Practique judiciaire*. Edition augmentée par Pierre Guenois. Paris: Nicolas Buon, 1609.
Isambert, François-André, ed. *Recueil général des anciennes lois françaises, depuis l'an 420 jusqu'à la révolution de 1789*. Ridgewood, NJ: Gregg, 1964.
Jaudin, Guillaume. *Traité des tesmoings et des enquestes*. Paris, 1564.
Jeanneret, Michel. "Léry et Thevet: Comment parler d'un monde nouveau?" *Mélanges à la mémoire de Franco Simone*. Geneva: Slatkine, 1983. 227-245.
———, "Antarctic France." *A New History of French Literature*, eds. Denis Hollier and R. Howard Bloch. Cambridge, MA and London: Harvard UP, 1989. 240-242.
Julien, Charles André, ed. *Les voyages de découverte et les premiers établissements*. Paris: Presses Universitaires de France, 1948.
———, *Les Francais en Amérique pendant la première moitié du XVIe siècle*. Paris: Presses Universitaires de France, 1946. Modernized edition: Paris: La Découverte, 1992.
Kelley, Donald R. *Foundations of Modern Historical Scholarship: Language, Law, and History in the French Renaissance*. New York: Columbia UP, 1970.
Kittel, Gerhard, Gerhard Friedrich, and Geoffrey William Bromiley, eds. *Theological Dictionary of the New Testament*. Grand Rapids, MI: Eerdmans, 1985.
Langbein, John H. *Torture and the Law of Proof: Europe and England in the Ancien Régime*. Chicago: U of Chicago P, 1977.
———, *Prosecuting Crime in the Renaissance*. Cambridge, MA: Harvard University Press, 1974.

Larner, John. *Marco Polo and the Discovery of the World.* New Haven: Yale UP, 1999.
Las Casas, Bartolomé. *Brevíssima relación de la destrucción de las Indias.* Sevilla: Sebastian Trugillo, 1552.
———, *Historia de las Indias.* Ed. André Saint-Lu. Caracas: Biblioteca Ayacucho, 1986.
———, *Apologética historia sumaria.* Ed. Edmundo O'Gorman. México, 1967.
Le Blant, Robert. "Les Ecrits attribués à Jacques Cartier." *Revue d'histoire de l'Amérique française* 15.1 (1961): 90-103.
Léry, Jean de. *Histoire mémorable de la ville de Sancerre.* Marseille: Lafitte, 1980.
———, *Histoire d'un voyage faict en la terre du Bresil* (1580). Ed. Frank Lestringant. Paris: Livre de Poche, 1994. English trans. Janet Whatley. Berkeley: U of California P, 1990.
Lescarbot, Marc. *Histoire de la nouvelle France.* Paris: Jean Milot, 1609.
Lestringant, Frank. *André Thevet: cosmographe des derniers Valois.* Geneva: Droz, 1991.
———, *Jean de Léry, ou, L'invention du sauvage.* Geneva: Champion, 1999.
———, *L'Atelier du cosmographe.* Paris: Albin Michel, 1991.
———, *L'Expérience huguenote au nouveau monde.* Geneva: Droz, 1996.
———, *Le Huguenot et le sauvage.* Paris: Klincksieck, 1990.
———, *Une Sainte horreur, ou, le voyage en eucharistie.* Paris: Presses Universitaires de France, 1996.
———, "La flèche du Patagon ou la preuve des lointains: sur un chapitre d'André Thevet." *Voyager à la Renaissance.* Eds. Jean Céard et J-C. Margolin. Paris: Maisonneuve et Larose, 1987.
Lévinas, Emmanuel and Philippe Nemo. *Ethique et infini: dialogues avec Philippe Nemo.* Paris: Fayard, 1982.
Lévi-Strauss, Claude. *Tristes tropiques.* Paris: Plon, 1955.
Lévy, Jean-Philippe. *La Hiérarchie des preuves dans le droit savant du moyen âge.* Paris: Sirey, 1939.
Loftus, Elizabeth and Katherine Ketcham. *Witness for the Defense.* New York: St. Martin's Press, 1991.
Loftus, Elizabeth and Gary L. Wells, eds. *Eyewitness Testimony: Psychological Perspectives.* Cambridge; New York: Cambridge UP, 1984.
Loftus, Elizabeth. *Eyewitness Testimony.* Cambridge, MA: Harvard UP, 1979.
López de Gómara, Francisco. *Historia general de las Indias y vida de Hernán Cortés.* Ed. Jorge Lacroix. Caracas: Biblioteca Ayacucho, 1979.
Lussagnet, Suzanne, ed. *Les Français en Floride.* Paris: Presses Universitaires de France, 1958.
———, *Le Brésil et les Brésiliens.* Paris: Presses Universitaires de France, 1953.
Lyotard, Jean-François. *Le Différend.* Paris: Editions de Minuit, 1986. English tr. Georges van den Abbeele. Minneapolis: U of Minnesota P, 1988.
Maclean, Ian. *Interpretation and Meaning in the Renaissance: The Case of Law.* Cambridge and New York: Cambridge UP, 1992.
Majer, Irma. "La fin des voyages: écriture et souvenirs chez Jean de Léry." *Revue des Sciences Humaines* 90.214 (1981): 71-83.
Mandel, Naomi. "Rethinking "After Auschwitz": Against a Rhetoric of the Unspeakable in Holocaust Writing." *boundary 2* 28.2 (2001): 203-228.
Mandeville, Jean. *Le Livre des merveilles du monde.* Ed. Christiane Deluz. Paris: CNRS, 2000.
———, *Mandeville's Travels; Texts and Translations.* Ed. and tr. Malcolm Letts. London: Hakluyt Society, 1953.

Marin, Louis. *La Parole mangée*. Paris: Méridiens Klincksieck, 1986. English trans. Mette Hjort. *Food for Thought*. Baltimore: Johns Hopkins UP, 1989.

——, *La Critique du discours*. Paris: Editions de Minuit, 1975.

McLuhan, Marshall. *The Medium is the Massage*. With Quentin Fiore. New York: Simon and Schuster, 1989.

Montaigne, Michel de. *Les Essais*. Ed. Pierre Villey and Verdun L. Saulnier. 3 vols. Paris: Presses Universitaires de France, 1965. English tr. Donald Frame. Stanford: Stanford UP, 1958.

Nemo, Philippe. See Lévinas.

Ogilvie, Brian. "Travel and Natural History in the Sixteenth Century." *Sammeln in der Frühen Neuzeit*. Eds. Brian Ogilvie, Anke te Heesen, and Martin Gierl. Berlin: Max Planck Institut für Wissenschaftsgeschichte, 1996. 3-28.

Olivier-Martin, François. *Histoire du droit français des origines à la révolution*. Paris: CNRS, 1984.

Ong, Walter J. *Orality and Literacy: The Technologizing of the Word*. London and New York: Routledge, 1991.

Pagden, Anthony. *European Encounters with the New World: From Renaissance to Romanticism*. New Haven: Yale UP, 1992.

Pasquier, Etienne. *Les recherches de la France*. Ed. Marie-Luce Demonet. Paris: H. Champion, 1996.

——, *L'Interprétation des Institutes de Justinien*. Ed. Etienne-Denis Pasquier. Paris: A. Durand, 1847.

Picot, Georges. *Histoire des états généraux...de 1355 à 1614*. Paris: Hachette, 1872.

Polo, Marco. *Le devisement du monde*. Ed. Marie-Luce Chênerie, Michèle Guéret-Laferté, and Philippe Ménard. Geneva: Droz, 2001.

——, *Le Livre De Marco Polo*. Ed. Jean Pierre Guillaume Pauthier. Paris: Firmin Didot, 1865.

——, *Travels*. Ed. Henry Yule and Henri Cordier. New York: Dover, 1993 [1903].

Pratt, Mary Louise. *Imperial Eyes*. London: Routledge, 1992.

Quint, David. *Montaigne and the Quality of Mercy*. Princeton, NJ: Princeton UP, 1998.

——, *Origin and Originality in Renaissance Literature: Versions of the Source*. New Haven: Yale UP, 1983.

Rabelais, François. *Oeuvres complètes*. Ed. Mireille Huchon. Paris: Gallimard, 1994.

Raemond, Florimond de. *Histoire de la naissance, progrez et decadence de l'heresie de ce siecle*. 2 vols. Cambray: Jean de la Riviere, 1611.

Raitt, Jill. *The Colloquy of Montbéliard: Religion and Politics in the Sixteenth Century*. New York: Oxford UP, 1993.

——, *The Eucharistic Theology of Theodore Beza*. Chambersburg, PA: American Academy of Religion, 1972.

Ramusio, Giovanni Battista. *Navigazioni e viaggi*. Ed. Marica Milanesi. Torino: Einaudi, 1978.

Reiss, Timothy J. *Mirages of the Selfe*. Stanford: Stanford UP, 2003.

——, *The Discourse of Modernism*. Ithaca: Cornell UP, 1982.

Ribaut, Jean. *The Whole and True Discoverye of Terra Florida*. Gainesville: UP of Florida, 1964.

Ricoeur, Paul. *Figuring the Sacred*. Ed. and tr. Mark I. Wallace. Minneapolis: Fortress, 1995.

Rubin, Miri. *Corpus Christi: The Eucharist in Late Medieval Culture*. Cambridge and New York: Cambridge UP, 1991.

Ruidíaz y Caravia, Eugenio. *La Florida, su conquista y colonización por Pedro Menéndez de Avilés*. 2 vols. Madrid: J.A. García, 1893-4.
Ryan, Michael T. "Assimilating New Worlds in the Sixteenth and Seventeenth Centuries." *Comparative Studies in Society and History* 23 (1984): 519-538.
Schnapper, Bernard. "Testes inhabiles: Les témoins reprochables dans l'ancien droit pénal." *Revue de droit français et étranger* 52 (1974): 252-84.
Sébillot, Paul. *Gargantua dans les traditions populaires*. Paris: Maisonneuve et Cie., 1883.
Shapin, Steven. *A Social History of Truth*. Chicago: U of Chicago P, 1994.
Shapiro, Barbara J. *A Culture of Fact: England, 1550-1720*. Ithaca: Cornell UP, 2000.
——, *Probability and Certainty in Seventeenth-Century England*. Princeton: Princeton UP, 1983.
Silving, Helen. "The Oath." *The Yale Law Journal* 68.7 (June 1959): 1329-1390.
Smith, Pamela H. "Artists as Scientists: Nature and Realism in Early Modern Europe." *Endeavour* 24.1 (2000): 13-21.
Suplee, Dennis R. and Diana S. Donaldson. "Dealing With the Difficult Opponent. Judicial approaches to deposition dynamics." *Pennsylvania Law Weekly* 26.16 (April 21, 2003): 6.
Thevet, André. *Les Singularités De La France Antarctique* (1558). Paris: Le Temps, 1982.
——, *André Thevet's North America: A Sixteenth-Century View*. Ed. and tr. Arthur Phillips Stabler and Roger Schlesinger. Kingston, Ont.: McGill-Queen's UP, 1986.
Thevet, André. *Le Brésil et les Brésiliens*. Ed. Suzanne Lussagnet. Paris: Presses Universitaires de France, 1953.
Tournon, André. "L'Essai: un témoignage en suspens." *Carrefour Montaigne*. Ed. J. Brody et al. Geneva: Slatkine, 1994. 117-145.
——, *La Glose et l'essai*. Lyon: Presses Universitaires de Lyon, 1983.
Trezise, Thomas. "Unspeakable." *Yale Journal of Criticism* 14.1 (2001): 39-66.
Villey, Pierre. *Les Sources et l'évolution des Essais de Montaigne*. New York: B. Franklin, 1968.
Warden, Rob. "How Mistaken and Perjured Eyewitness Identification Testimony Put 46 Innocent Americans on Death Row." Date**Online. Available at http://www.law.northwestern.edu/depts/clinic/wrongful/exonerations/Research/eyewitnessstudy1.htm
Weber, Max. *The Protestant Ethic and the Spirit of Capitalism*. Ed. and tr. Talcott Parsons and R. H. Tawney. London: G. Allen & Unwin Ltd., 1930.
Weimann, Robert, and David Hillman. *Authority and Representation in Early Modern Discourse*. Baltimore: Johns Hopkins UP, 1996.
Weinberg, Bernard. "Montaigne's Readings for 'Des Cannibales.'" *Renaissance and other Studies in Honor of William Leon Wiley*. Ed. George B. Daniel, Jr. Chapel Hill: U of North Carolina P, 1968. 261-279.
Whatley, Janet. "Impression and Initiation: Jean de Léry's Brazil Voyage." *Modern Language Studies* 19.3 (Summer 1989): 15-25.
——, "Une révérence réciproque: Huguenot Writing on the New World." *University of Toronto Quarterly* 57 (1987-8): 270-89.
Wisse, Jakob. *Ethos and Pathos from Aristotle to Cicero*. Amsterdam: A.M. Hakkert, 1989.
Zumthor, Paul. *Merlin le prophète*. Lausanne: Payot, 1943.

NORTH CAROLINA STUDIES IN THE ROMANCE LANGUAGES AND LITERATURES
I.S.B.N. Prefix 0-8078-

Recent Titles

GALDÓS'S *SEGUNDA MANERA*: RHETORICAL STRATEGIES AND AFFECTIVE RESPONSE, by Linda M. Willem. 1998. (No. 260). *-9264-5*.
A MEDIEVAL PILGRIM'S COMPANION. REASSESSING *EL LIBRO DE LOS HUÉSPEDES* (ESCORIAL MS. h.I.13), by Thomas D. Spaccarelli. 1998. (No. 261). *-9265-3*.
'PUEBLOS ENFERMOS': THE DISCOURSE OF ILLNESS IN THE TURN-OF-THE-CENTURY SPANISH AND LATIN AMERICAN ESSAY, by Michael Aronna. 1999. (No. 262). *-9266-1*.
RESONANT THEMES. LITERATURE, HISTORY, AND THE ARTS IN NINETEENTH- AND TWENTIETH-CENTURY EUROPE. ESSAYS IN HONOR OF VICTOR BROMBERT, by Stirling Haig. 1999. (No. 263). *-9267-X*.
RAZA, GÉNERO E HIBRIDEZ EN *EL LAZARILLO DE CIEGOS CAMINANTES*, por Mariselle Meléndez. 1999. (No. 264). *-9268-8*.
DEL ESCENARIO A LA PANTALLA: LA ADAPTACIÓN CINEMATOGRÁFICA DEL TEATRO ESPAÑOL, por María Asunción Gómez. 2000. (No. 265). *-9269-6*.
THE LEPER IN BLUE: COERCIVE PERFORMANCE AND THE CONTEMPORARY LATIN AMERICAN THEATER, by Amalia Gladhart. 2000. (No. 266). *-9270-X*.
THE CHARM OF CATASTROPHE: A STUDY OF RABELAIS'S *QUART LIVRE*, by Alice Fiola Berry. 2000. (No. 267). *-9271-8*.
PUERTO RICAN CULTURAL IDENTITY AND THE WORK OF LUIS RAFAEL SÁNCHEZ, by John Dimitri Perivolaris. 2000. (No. 268). *-9272-6*.
MANNERISM AND BAROQUE IN SEVENTEENTH-CENTURY FRENCH POETRY: THE EXAMPLE OF TRISTAN L'HERMITE, by James Crenshaw Shepard. 2001. (No. 269). *-9273-4*.
RECLAIMING THE BODY: MARÍA DE ZAYA'S EARLY MODERN FEMINISM, by Lisa Vollendorf. 2001. (No. 270). *-9274-2*.
FORGED GENEALOGIES: SAINT-JOHN PERSE'S CONVERSATIONS WITH CULTURE, by Carol Rigolot. 2001. (No. 271). *-9275-0*.
VISIONES DE ESTEREOSCOPIO (PARADIGMA DE HIBRIDACIÓN EN EL ARTE Y LA NARRATIVA DE LA VANGUARDIA ESPAÑOLA), por María Soledad Fernández Utrera. 2001. (No. 272). *-9276-9*.
TRANSPOSING ART INTO TEXTS IN FRENCH ROMANTIC LITERATURE, by Henry F. Majewski. 2002. (No. 273). *-9277-7*.
IMAGES IN MIND: LOVESICKNESS, SPANISH SENTIMENTAL FICTION AND *DON QUIJOTE*, by Robert Folger. 2002. (No. 274). *-9278-5*.
INDISCERNIBLE COUNTERPARTS: THE INVENTION OF THE TEXT IN FRENCH CLASSICAL DRAMA, by Christopher Braider. 2002. (No. 275). *-9279-3*.
SAVAGE SIGHT/CONSTRUCTED NOISE. POETIC ADAPTATIONS OF PAINTERLY TECHNIQUES IN THE FRENCH AND AMERICAN AVANT-GARDES, by David LeHardy Sweet. 2003. (No. 276). *-9281-5*.
AN EARLY BOURGEOIS LITERATURE IN GOLDEN AGE SPAIN. *LAZARILLO DE TORMES, GUZMÁN DE ALFARACHE* AND BALTASAR GRACIÁN, by Francisco J. Sánchez. 2003. (No. 277). *-9280-7*.
METAFACT: ESSAYISTIC SCIENCE IN EIGHTEENTH-CENTURY FRANCE, by Lars O. Erickson. 2004. (No. 278). *-9282-3*.
THE INVENTION OF THE EYEWITNESS: WITNESSING AND TESTIMONY IN EARLY MODERN FRANCE, by Andrea Frisch. 2004. (No. 279). *-9283-1*.

When ordering please cite the ISBN *Prefix* plus the last four digits for each title.

Send orders to: University of North Carolina Press
P.O. Box 2288
Chapel Hill, NC 27515-2288
U.S.A.
www.uncpress.unc.edu
FAX: 919 966-3829

www.ingramcontent.com/pod-product-compliance
Lightning Source LLC
Chambersburg PA
CBHW020738230426
43665CB00009B/479